BEDE

A HISTORY OF THE ENGLISH CHURCH AND PEOPLE

Translated and with an Introduction by
Leo Sherley-Price
Revised by R. E. Latham

PENGUIN BOOKS

Penguin Books Ltd, Harmondsworth, Middlesex, England
Penguin Books Inc., 7110 Ambassador Road, Baltimore, Maryland 21207, U.S.A.
Penguin Books Australia Ltd, Ringwood, Victoria, Australia

—

This translation first published 1955
Reprinted 1956, 1960, 1962, 1964
Reprinted with revisions 1965
Revised edition 1968
Copyright © Leo Sherley-Price, 1955, 1968

—

Made and printed in Great Britain by
Cox and Wyman Ltd, London, Reading, and Fakenham
Set in Monotype Bembo

CONTENTS

5

Contents

Contents

BOOK TWO

7

Contents

Contents

BOOK THREE

Contents

Contents

BOOK FOUR

Contents

Contents

BOOK FIVE

Contents

INTRODUCTION

THE LIFE OF BEDE

BEDE (Baeda) was probably born in the year of the Council of Hertford (A.D. 673) on lands that were shortly afterwards granted by King Egfrid of Northumbria to S. Benedict Biscop's new monastery of Saint Peter at Wearmouth. He himself tells us (v. 24) that when he reached the age of seven, his parents – of whom we know nothing – placed him under the care of Abbot Benedict for his education and upbringing. But when the monastery of Saint Paul was established as a joint-foundation at Jarrow in the year 682, Bede seems to have been transferred to the care of its first abbot, Ceolfrid, and to have remained a monk there for the remainder of his life.

To have served under abbots of such learning and ability as Benedict and such holiness as Ceolfrid (whose biographies Bede was to write in his *Lives of the Abbots*) can have had no small influence on Bede's own life and activities, and his own inborn love of learning and devotion to the spiritual life must have received constant stimulation and encouragement. A touching incident which almost certainly refers to Bede's boyhood is preserved in the anonymous *Life of Abbot Ceolfrid*, which tells how the plague of 686 attacked Ceolfrid's monastery and swept away all the choir monks capable of maintaining the regular services of the Church 'with the exception of the Abbot himself and one boy reared and educated by him, who is now a priest of the same monastery and commends the Abbot's admirable doings both verbally and in writing to all who desire to learn them. Greatly distressed by this catastrophe, the Abbot decided to discontinue their usual practice, and to recite and sing all the psalms without antiphons except at Vespers and Matins. But when they had done this for a week with great sorrow and regret, he could bear it no longer and directed that the psalms and their antiphons were to be restored in their appointed course. So with the help of all [survivors], he and the aforesaid boy carried his decision with no little trouble until such time as he could either train or procure from elsewhere sufficient numbers to assist at the Divine Office.' Only a boy as naturally scholarly and devout as Bede would have been capable of performing the duties of a choir-monk in this way, and the story almost certainly refers to him. This early training endowed Bede with a deep and lasting love for the Church's regular Hours of worship, and in a letter written by Alcuin to the Wearmouth community, he says in reference to Bede's latter years: 'It is told how blessed Bede, our master and your patron, said "I know that the angels are present at the canonical Hours, and what if they do not find me among the brethren when they assemble? Will they not say, Where is Bede? Why does he not attend the appointed devotions with his brethren?"'

Benedict Biscop, who founded and ruled both Wearmouth and Jarrow, was of noble birth, and a man of wide learning and culture. He had been trained at Lérins, and had accompanied Archbishop Theodore and Abbot Hadrian from Rome in 669, when the former had been consecrated to the Archbishopric of Canterbury. His learning and artistic knowledge was to influence all England, and greatly enriched both Church and national life. Not only was he a Greek and Latin scholar, and taught theology, astronomy, art, and music, but he also made many visits to the Continent and Rome, from which he brought back treasures for the English churches – books, altar-vessels, paintings, and vestments – which had no small influence on native standards. He also brought stone-masons and glaziers from Gaul to build and furnish the churches, and in order that they might teach their crafts to the English, who had hitherto built almost exclusively in timber. Further, with the approval of Pope Agatho, he brought John, the Arch-cantor of Saint Peter's, to teach his monks the liturgical chant *sicut ad sanctum Petrum Romae agebatur* (IV. 18), a visit that had widespread influence on the development of English church music, since many monasteries sent monks to Wearmouth to receive instruction from him, while others invited him to visit them for the purpose.

Bede tells us that he was made deacon at the age of nineteen by Bishop John of Hexham (later known as Saint John of Beverley). And since canon law laid down the age of twenty-five as the norm for admission to the diaconate, Bede's scholarship and devotion

16

must have been recognized as exceptional for him to have been presented by Abbot Ceolfrid six years early. He was advanced to the priesthood by Bishop John eleven years later, and tells us that 'from the time of my receiving the priesthood until my fifty-ninth year, I have worked, both for my own profit and that of my brethren, to compile extracts from the works of the venerable Fathers on holy scripture, and to make commentaries on their meaning and interpretation.' During all these years, Bede was doubtless gathering material for his *History*, which he completed in 731.

Both in his *History* and in his *Lives of the Abbots* Bede gives us much valuable information about the daily life of a monastery in Saxon times, as well as many illuminating character-sketches. From abbot to lay-brother, all took an active share in the well-ordered day of work and prayer, and Bede tells how Abbot Eosterwin, a former King's Thane, 'remained so humble that he loved to thresh and winnow, milk the cows and ewes, and occupied himself obediently in the bakery, garden, kitchen, and all the work of the monastery'. At the same time, this humble and democratic abbot 'corrected offenders with regular discipline' and exercised unquestioned authority. Apart from any specialized work that monks were directed to undertake in accordance with their knowledge and capabilities, whether writing, copying and illuminating manuscripts, cooking or care of the infirm, the life of the whole community centred around its church, with the offering of Mass and the maintenance of the regular Hours of prayer, beginning with Matins and Lauds in the early hours of the morning, and closing with Compline as darkness ended the activities of the day. A post of considerable importance under the Abbot and Prior (*Praepositus*) was that of Guestmaster, for there was a constant coming and going between monasteries, while persons of all walks of life from king to peasant were assured of simple hospitality in a monastery when on their travels. Among visitors of interest Bede certainly met Adamnan, abbot of the Celtic monastery of Iona (v. 15) who came to visit King Alfrid and to 'observe the rites of the Church canonically performed'; which visit resulted in his adoption of the Roman usages. Thanks to the artistic tastes of Abbot Benedict and his journeys to the Continent and Rome, the church in Bede's own monastery was built of stone, and well furnished with service-books, vestments, relics, and pictures. Bede describes these latter in his *Lives of the Abbots* as 'vividly portraying the relationship of the Old and New Testaments, such as Isaac carrying the wood for his own sacrifice, and our Lord carrying the cross on which He was to suffer.'

Bede's life centred on his own monastery of Jarrow, and it does not seem likely that he left it very frequently, although he paid visits to other monastic houses from time to time. He is known to have visited Lindisfarne, and he stayed for a short while with his friend Egbert, Archbishop of York. He also probably visited King Ceolwulf of Northumbria, a ruler of considerable learning, who resigned his crown three years after Bede's death and became a monk at Lindisfarne. The story that Bede visited Rome at the invitation of Pope Sergius is very unlikely, and rests on a statement by William of Malmesbury which has never been satisfactorily explained.

In the year 735 Bede fell ill, and the day drew near that he had so often described in his account of others as their 'heavenly birthday'. We are fortunate in possessing a touching eyewitness account of his last days in a letter written by Cuthbert, one of Bede's scholars and later Abbot of Wearmouth and Jarrow, to his friend and contemporary Cuthwin. I have no hesitation in quoting this moving account in full.

'To his fellow teacher Cuthwin, most beloved in Christ, from his school-friend Cuthbert. Health for ever in God.

'I was delighted to receive your little gift, and was pleased to read your devout and learned letter in which I learned that, as I had greatly hoped, you are diligently offering Masses and holy prayers for our father and master Bede, whom God loved so well. Out of love for him rather than any confidence in my ability to do so, I am glad to give you a short account of his passing from this world, since I understand that you wish and request this.

'For nearly a fortnight before the Feast of our Lord's Resurrection he was troubled by weakness and breathed with great difficulty, although he suffered little pain. Thenceforward until Ascension Day he remained cheerful and happy, giving thanks to God each hour day and night. He gave daily lessons to us his students, and spent the rest of the day in singing the psalms so far as his strength allowed. He passed the whole night in joyful prayer and thanksgiving to God, except when slumber overcame him; but directly he awoke, he continued to meditate on scriptural themes, and never failed to thank God with hands outstretched. I can truthfully affirm that I have

18

never seen or heard of anyone who gave thanks so unceasingly to the living God as he. O truly blessed man! He used to repeat the saying of the holy Apostle Paul, *It is a fearful thing to fall into the hands of the living God*, and many other sayings from holy scripture, and in this manner he used to arouse our souls by the consideration of our last hour. Being well-versed in our native songs, he described to us the dread departure of the soul from the body by a verse in our own tongue, which translated means: "Before setting forth on that inevitable journey, none is wiser than the man who considers – before his soul departs hence – what good or evil he has done, and what judgement his soul will receive after its passing." To comfort both us and himself, he also used to sing antiphons, one of which is, "O King of glory, Lord of might, Who on this day ascended in triumph above all heavens, do not leave us orphaned, but send to us the Spirit of truth, the promise of the Father. Alleluia." And when he reached the words "do not leave us orphaned", he broke into tears and wept much. An hour later he began to repeat what he had begun and so continued all day, so that we who heard him sorrowed and wept with him. In such grace we passed the days of Lent until the above day, and he remained full of joy, thanking God that he had deserved this weakness. He often quoted, "God scourgeth every son that He receiveth", and Saint Ambrose's saying, "I have not lived so that I am ashamed to live among you, and I do not fear to die for God is gracious."[1]

'During these days, in addition to the daily instruction that he gave us and his recitation of the psalter, he was working to complete two books worthy of mention. For he translated the Gospel of Saint John into our own language for the benefit of the Church of God as far as the words *but what are these among so many*. He also made some extracts from the works of Bishop Isidore (of Seville), saying "I do not wish my sons to read anything untrue, or to labour unprofitably after my death." But on the Tuesday before our Lord's Ascension his breathing became increasingly laboured, and his feet began to swell. Despite this he continued cheerfully to teach and dictate all day, saying from time to time, "Learn quickly. I do not know how long I can continue, for my Lord may call me in a short while." It seemed to us that he might well be aware of the time of his departure, and he spent that night without sleeping, giving thanks to God.

1. Paulinus' *Life of Saint Ambrose*, chap. 45.

When dawn broke on Wednesday, he told us to write diligently what we had begun, and we did this until Terce. After Terce we walked in procession with the relics of the Saints as the customs of the day required, but one of us remained with him, who said, "There is still one chapter missing in the book that you have been dictating; but it seems hard that I should trouble you any further." "It is no trouble," he answered: "Take your pen and sharpen it, and write quickly." And he did so. But at None he said to me, "I have a few articles of value in my casket, such as pepper, linen and incense. Run quickly and fetch the priests of the monastery, so that I may distribute among them the gifts that God has given me." In great distress I did as he bid me. And when they arrived, he spoke to each of them in turn, requesting and reminding them diligently to offer Masses and prayers for him. They readily promised to do so, and all were sad and wept, grieving above all else at his statement that they must not expect to see his face much longer in this world. But they were heartened when he said, "If it be the will of my Maker, the time has come when I shall be freed from the body and return to Him Who created me out of nothing when I had no being. I have had a long life, and the merciful Judge has ordered it graciously. The time of my departure is at hand, and my soul longs to see Christ my King in His beauty." He also told us many other edifying things, and passed his last day happily until evening. Then the same lad, named Wilbert, said again: "Dear master, there is one sentence still unfinished." "Very well," he replied: "write it down." After a short while the lad said, "Now it is finished." "You have spoken truly," he replied: "It is well finished. Now raise my head in your hands, for it would give me great joy to sit facing the holy place where I used to pray, so that I may sit and call on my Father." And thus, on the floor of his cell, he chanted "Glory be to the Father, and to the Son, and to the Holy Spirit" to its ending, and breathed his last.

'We may confidently believe that as he had devoted himself with such ardour to the praises of God here on earth, his soul was borne by the angels to the longed-for joys of Heaven. And all who saw and heard of the death of our father Bede declared that they had never known anyone end his days in such deep devotion and peace. For as you have learned, as long as his soul remained in his body, he said "Glory be to the Father" and other chants to the glory of God, offering unceasing thanks to God with hands outstretched. And although my lack of eloquence renders this present account brief, you should know that many other things could be related of him. However, in due course I hope with God's help to describe all that I have seen and heard more fully.'

Bede passed away on the evening of May the twenty-fifth, 735, after First Vespers of the Feast of the Ascension. He is commemorated in the Church's Calendar on May the twenty-seventh.

Bede's body was first laid to rest in the south porch of his monastery church, but was later translated to a place of honour near the altar. About the year 1020, a Durham monk named Aelred stole his relics and brought them secretly to Durham, where they were placed in the tomb of Saint Cuthbert and became a cherished possession of that church. During the episcopate of Bishop Hugh Puiset they were enshrined in a silver and gold reliquary set on a marble base supported by five pillars in the Galilee, and were carried in procession at great festivals. During the spoliation of the monasteries by Henry VIII the reliquary was seized, but the bones are said to have been secreted in a tomb in the Galilee, where certain remains were discovered when the tomb was examined in 1831. But the principal and lasting memorial of the first of English historians, whom Saint Boniface described as *Candela ecclesiae quam illuxit Spiritus Sanctus* is the inspiration of his holy life and the value of the great work that he bequeathed to posterity.

BEDE AS AN HISTORIAN

The centuries on which Bede concentrates are a crucial and formative period in our island history, during which the future shape and pattern of the English Church and nation were beginning to emerge. Once the shield of Roman protection was withdrawn, the Celtic peoples of Britain were steadily forced to yield ground before the ever increasing pressure of the incoming Angles, Saxons, and Jutes, and were driven westward into the remote and inaccessible regions along the storm-swept Atlantic coast. Even here they enjoyed little security, and were harried by raiding parties of Irish pirates, as Saint Patrick, himself a victim, describes in his *Confessions*. Here in Devon and Cornwall, Wales, Cumberland, and south-west Scotland the Romano-Britons clung desperately to the shreds of their native independence and customs. Many were sustained by the Christian faith, brought to this island centuries before Augustine (A.D. 597) in the more peaceful days when Britain enjoyed the protection and administration of Rome as an integral *Provincia* of the Empire. Rallied by such contrasting leaders as Ambrosius, 'last of the Romans' (I. 16), Saint Germanus (I. 20) and the semi-legendary King Arthur, the Britons won sufficient successes against the Saxons to maintain a constantly menaced independence, but were isolated from the remainder of Christendom by their heathen enemies, for whom they felt nothing but bitterness and contempt. Meanwhile the Picts and Scots in their northern fastnesses remained as hostile to Briton and Saxon as they had to the legions of Rome. Bede traces the gradual conversion of all these mutually antipathetic peoples to the religion of Christ, and illustrates the enriching influence of the Catholic Church, which brought them into contact with the rest of Christendom, and, in so doing, brought to these semi-barbaric peoples the wisdom, art, and civilization of Christian Rome. During these vital centuries we see Columba and Aidan bring the Gospel to the north; Ninian to the Picts; Patrick to the Irish; David and his contemporaries to the Celts of Wales and Cornwall; and Augustine to the newly established Saxon peoples.

In Bede's pages we trace the gradual decay of the Celtic tribal and monastic systems, and their supersession by the highly developed and centralized system of the Roman Church. As Dom Louis Gougaud shows in his *Christianity in Celtic Lands,* the principal difference between the Celtic and Roman system of church administration was that the former was monastic, while the latter was diocesan. In the Celtic churches the highest administrative officer was the Abbot, who might or might not be in episcopal orders, and who, as in the case of the Abbot of Iona, ruled the churches over a considerable *provincia*. A striking example of this is Saint Columba, who never received episcopal consecration, but who exercised a wide and unquestioned authority. The Celtic bishop, as a member of a monastic community, was subject to his abbot, and exercised his spiritual functions at the latter's request and direction (see III. 4). It was the abbot who chose and presented candidates for ordination or consecration to the bishop (IV. 24), and appointed members of the community to their various tasks inside or outside the monastery. The duties of the Celtic bishop, therefore, were wholly spiritual, in contrast to those of the Roman prelate, who gradually acquired or had thrust upon him onerous administrative responsibilities, not only in ecclesiastical but in national and provincial affairs. This Celtic emphasis on the spiritual and apostolic nature of the episcopal office might well be borne in mind in these days when bishops are overburdened by countless financial and administrative details, and their true function obscured. However, although one can readily appreciate that the free-lance methods of the learned and saintly Celtic missionaries were supremely effective in breaking new ground and winning converts for Christ, they were not such as would develop and administer a growing Christian community of nation-wide extent. None will deny the holiness of the wandering Celtic saints or their appeal to the imagination, but they were bound to give place to the more regular, stable, and disciplined ways of life introduced and practised by the monks of Saint Benedict. And while much was lost as Celtic Christianity and culture declined, even more was gained. For although the leaders of the British Church rejected Augustine's claim to jurisdiction and refused their cooperation in evangelizing the pagan Saxons, contacts between the Roman and Celtic Churches increased as time went on. Mutual appreciation began to heal the wounds of suspicion and controversy, and a common belief in Christ gradually drew together the peoples of Britain into the English nation.

A decisive step towards this national and spiritual unity was taken in A.D. 664 at the Council of Whitby (IV. 25), described by R. H. Hodgkin in his *History of the Anglo-Saxons* as 'one of the great turning-points in the history of the race. ... The Synod turned the scales, and decided that the English should take their religion and their civilization from the Roman world rather than from what Wilfrid called "one remote corner of the most remote island".' From that day the Celtic cause was doomed to gradual extinction. These bonds of national unity were to be greatly tempered and strengthened in the fiery trials of the Danish invasions that began sixty years after Bede's death, when under the devoted leadership of Alfred, noblest of England's kings, one may fairly say that the spirit of England was born. This unification of many races into one people is the imperishable memorial of this great king, who said: 'I have always striven to live worthily, and at my death to leave to those who follow me a worthy memorial of my deeds.' And in Bede we see how Christian leaders and scholars such as Aidan, Cuthbert, and

Augustine became the pastors and counsellors of king and peasant alike, laying the foundations of that close alliance between the power spiritual and the power temporal which was to bring such strength and stability to the English nation in centuries to come.

It is almost certain that the first (partial) translation of Bede's *History* from Latin into the vernacular was made by King Alfred himself, who, despite his countless pressing problems and responsibilities, made time for this task in order to inform and inspire his English subjects. This high tribute is evidence that the *History* quickly established itself as a unique and authoritative record of our national history. Even during his lifetime Bede's reputation for learning extended far into Europe, and for generations after his death his *Commentaries*, *Martyrology*, and other works were recognized as standard works of reference in the West. That a new translation of his *History* is published in the Penguin Classics today testifies that the work which he compiled with such skill and labour over twelve centuries ago still retains its value and freshness for readers of this age.

There should be few in these islands to whom the name of Bede is unknown, but there are perhaps many who do not realize the greatness of our debt to him. Nevertheless, were it not for the rich fund of information that he gathered and sifted with such care, our knowledge of the vital and stirring centuries that he describes would be scanty, while a treasury of tales loved by every English child would have been lost for ever. So any readers who take up this book for the first time can rest assured that they will not find it a dreary chronicle of events and dates; on the contrary, a rich living tapestry will unfold before them, and they will discover a source of interest and enjoyment that may well be lifelong, and stimulate them to learn more about the storied past on which our present and future is built. Such is the interest of the subject-matter and the vividness of Bede's characteristic style that the scenes and folk of long ago live again. We are transported back into the fens and forests, highlands and islands of Celtic Britain and Saxon England, and we feel strangely 'at home'. These are our own people and our own land, and with a little imagination and historical sense we have little difficulty in picturing the contemporary scene, or in appreciating the viewpoint, plans, and problems of the kings, saints, and lesser folk whom Bede describes so well. We can understand Augustine's sense of inadequacy when summoned from his quiet Roman cloister and directed to the tremendous task of converting the heathen Saxons about whom he had heard such grim rumours (I. 23). We can visualize the tense scene as the heathen high-priest Coifi rides out before King Edwin and his thanes to defy his gods and defile their temple (II. 13). We can stand beside the gallant King Oswald at Heavenfield as he sets up a great oaken cross with his own hands, and summons his army to prayer before engaging the heathen hordes in desperate battle (III. 2). Above all, we cannot but be impressed and deeply moved by the selfless Christ-like lives of the northern Celtic saints – Columba, Cuthbert, and Aidan – and their disciples. Men of great personal gifts and radiant faith, they fearlessly carried the Gospel alone among alien peoples, gladly accepting lifelong 'exile for Christ' as his apostles. Redoubtable travellers by sea and land, able scholars, scribes, and craftsmen, the loveliness of their hard and holy lives has won the admiration and captured the imagination of all succeeding centuries. When we read Bede's account of such men and their doings, we realize ever more clearly that the past is not dead and done with, but a force to be reckoned with, silently moulding the present and the future.

As already mentioned, Bede's *History* belongs to his latter years, when he had already won a wide reputation by his many other works, a list of which he appends to the closing chapter of the *History*. But it is by the latter that he is best known today, and by which he has richly earned the title of 'Father of English History'. For Bede was not content to compile a bare chronicle of events and dates, or to restrict himself to hagiography as his predecessors had done. He set himself to examine all available records, to secure verbal or written accounts from reliable living authorities, to record local traditions and stories, to interpret significant events, and, in short, to compile as complete and continuous a history of the English Church and people as lay within his power. He was the first to conceive or attempt such a formidable project, and posterity acknowledges his pioneer work as a remarkably successful achievement.

In order to accomplish his purpose, Bede sets out his *History* in five convenient periods or 'books'. In the first Book, after a preliminary geographical survey of Britain drawn entirely from earlier authorities such as Pliny, Orosius, and Gildas, and a brief account of the Roman occupation, Bede proceeds to tell the story of Christianity in Britain up to the period immediately preceding the death of its great apostle Gregory the Great. The second Book continues the story from his death up to the death of King Edwin and the overthrow of the Northumbrian kingdom by the pagan chieftain Penda. The third Book recounts the Church's struggle against heathenism in the North, and the planting of the Faith among the Mercians and East Saxons. The fourth Book records the appointment of Theodore the Greek to the Archbishopric of Canterbury and his reform and reorganization of the English Church; the lives of Cuthbert and Wilfrid; and the progress of the Church in the south-eastern provinces. The fifth Book carries on the story from the time of Bishop John of Beverley up to the date of the work's completion in A.D. 731.

BEDE'S TREATMENT OF MATERIAL

As he mentions in his Preface, Bede was encouraged to undertake the writing of a history by 'the learned and reverend Abbot Albinus', who succeeded Archbishop Theodore's colleague Hadrian as abbot of the monastery of Saint Peter and Saint Paul at Canterbury in the year A.D. 709. Abbot Albinus was a close and valued friend of Bede, who addresses him elsewhere as his 'best and most beloved father in Christ', and who received great assistance from the latter's researches into the history of the Church in Kent and the adjoining provinces. Bede's Preface affords concise information on his sources, and testifies to his careful treatment of all material, whether written or verbal. He tells how Nothelm, 'a devout priest of the Church in London' (later Archbishop of Canterbury, A.D. 735–40), had made a journey to Rome and obtained permission from Pope Gregory II to examine the papal archives, and to make copies of all letters relevant to the mission of Augustine and the subsequent progress of the Church in England. Doubtless a considerable number of documents were also available at Canterbury. Bede also mentions that he had sought and obtained assistance from various provincial bishops. He mentions in particular Bishop Daniel of the West Saxons, who had provided information about that province and the Isle of Wight; Abbot Esius, who gave facts about East Anglia; and the monks of Lastingham, who did the same for Mercia. And while Bede is naturally best acquainted with events in his own Northumbria, he is careful to supplement and check his facts by recourse to 'innumerable witnesses', such as his friend Bishop Acca and the monks of Lindisfarne, to whom he submitted the draft of his *Life of Saint Cuthbert* for their comment and approval.

Bede's industry and scholarship are generally acknowledged, but his most significant achievement lies in his inspired ability to select and integrate the vast mass of facts and traditions that he had gathered into a single framework. He doubtless rejected much material as unreliable or irrelevant, but all that he retained he welded together into a coherent and eminently readable unity. Even a modern historian, with the advantage of greatly superior facilities and assisted by the researches of many generations of experts, faces a formidable task when compiling a history covering several centuries. And when we consider Bede's limited facilities and resources, it is clear that his achievement is unique. For although Bede's monastery at Jarrow possessed a library, it would seem insignificant by modern standards, and while it contained theological works of the Greek and Latin Fathers, there was little material useful for Bede's purpose except Gildas' *History* and a number of individual *Lives*, such as Constantius' *Life of Saint Germanus* and Possidius' *Life of Saint Augustine*. Furthermore, in addition to the slowness and uncertainty of communications, the physical conditions under which the writers of that day had to work were extremely inconvenient and austere during the long northern winters. Writing to Lullus, Archbishop of Mainz, not long after Bede's death, Abbot Cuthbert of Wearmouth apologizes for the delay in sending copies of Bede's works for which the Archbishop had asked, and explains that the hands of the scribes had been so numbed by the bitter winter weather that they had been forced to discontinue their work for considerable periods. And it is easy to visualize the ageing Bede himself, wrapped in a sheepskin cloak, busily working away under such conditions with a pile of documents on his desk, and rising from time to time to beat his frozen limbs into restored circulation. But it is noteworthy that despite the many difficulties under which it was written, Bede's *History* contains relatively few errors, and modern research has confirmed the accuracy of most of his statements. In his Preface Bede himself concedes that there may be unintentional inaccuracies in his pages, and begs the reader not to blame him too severely since, 'as the laws of history demand, I have laboured honestly to transmit whatever I could learn from common report for the instruction of posterity.' And although he is remarkably accurate and well informed on events in his own north country where he is able to check facts and interrogate responsible persons, he is naturally on less sure ground when dealing with happenings in far distant provinces. Nevertheless he makes every attempt to verify facts and present them in an orderly sequence, and to give us an accurate insight into the beliefs, customs, and everyday life of the times.

Like all writers, Bede is influenced by the circumstances and outlook of his own day, and some of his personal convictions are clearly indicated in his interpretations of events. The modern reader may find it difficult to envisage the intensity of feeling aroused by such matters as the paschal controversy, or he may consider Bede unduly prejudiced when he describes the Britons as *perfida gens* – a faithless race – because of their refusal to admit Augustine's jurisdiction (II. 2). In such matters Bede reflects the viewpoint of his race and generation as we of our own, but he is free from all pettiness and personal rancour, and never stoops to misrepresent the actions of those whose convictions he cannot share. For instance, although a convinced upholder of Roman customs as against Celtic, he records the lives and holiness of the Celtic saints with unstinted admiration, and writes of the Roman and Celtic leaders with equal justice and appreciation. An eloquent tribute to these noble qualities in Bede was paid by Bishop Hensley Henson of Durham in 1935 on the twelve hundredth anniversary of the former's death: 'The more closely Bede's career is studied, the more amazing it appears. In him two streams of spiritual influence seemed to meet and blend – the evangelistic passion of the Celtic missionaries, and the disciplined devotion of the Benedictine monks. He was near enough to the original conversion to have personal links with those who had companied with the missionaries from Iona, and to feel the thrill of their triumphant enthusiasm: and yet he was remote enough to have grown up in another atmosphere, and to have been shaped by the system which disallowed and replaced theirs. He was too near not to know their merits; too generous not to recognize them; too religious not to revere their sanctity; too wise not to perceive their defects. So he stood at the point of a new departure – a Benedictine monk in the yet living tradition of Celtic piety, an English student in the rich treasury of Celtic learning, a disciple of Rome inspired by the intellectual passion of Ireland.'

Introduction

THE MIRACULOUS ELEMENT IN BEDE'S HISTORY

The age of Bede was an age of faith. Almighty God was acknowledged as the Source of all life; the world was God's world, and Christians were God's people. The workings of God were recognized in everyday life, and any unusual or striking events, whether storms and comets, victories and recoveries of health, were regarded as signs of his direct intervention in human affairs. God heard and answered prayer, and the holiness of his saints enabled them to draw upon the hidden powers of the spiritual world in order to work wonders and miracles in his Name. The veil separating the seen from the unseen world was not impenetrable, and mortal man might at times have converse with angels and with saints departed. It would therefore be very strange if we found no miracles and wonders among the events and traditions recorded by Bede. But while the modern reader will subject these stories to closer scrutiny than Bede's earlier readers, there is no need to question his sincerity or to assume that he uncritically accepted them all as of equal accuracy. It should be remembered that Bede not only records historical events, but also preserves the stories and legends current in his day. In this way he gives us some account of what people thought and believed, which is a most valuable contribution to our knowledge of the times. He records nothing that he has not subjected to careful consideration, whether it be a description of events or the telling of a popular tale. At the same time, he has a deep respect for tradition and long-established beliefs, and he reproduces current tales and legends of wonder-working relics if he thinks them interesting or edifying to his readers. In this respect Bede is more careful and less credulous than many later medieval writers.

Lest the inclusion of miracles may cause any reader to jump to the unjustified conclusion that all Bede's statements are suspect, let us see briefly how he deals with his sources in this respect. Firstly, these sources are of greatly varying historical value. Some material – such as the legend of Saint Alban – Bede has taken direct from an early manuscript of unknown authorship. Other miracle-stories are based on current traditional stories. Others were reported to Bede by those who claimed to have personal acquaintance either with the saint performing the miracle or with the persons benefiting from it.

Secondly, Bede does not write as an eyewitness of everything that he records, but simply gives an account of what is reliably said to have happened, whether miraculous or otherwise. And it is note-worthy that when describing events or persons of which he had direct personal knowledge, as in his *Lives of the Abbots*, Bede does not record any miracles, although in the preface to his poem on Saint Cuthbert he claims to have been healed by that Saint, saying: 'Fresh miracles occur daily through his relics . . . one of which took place in my own case, when I was cured [of an impediment?] in my tongue while I was writing in praise of his miracles.' On the other hand, when recording the miracles of such saints as Oswald and Chad, he mentions the source of his information, while in the pro-logue to his *Life of Saint Cuthbert* he expressly states that he has made a careful investigation into the events described and submitted his draft to the monks of Lindisfarne for their comment and approval. So Bede can be acquitted of carelessness or undue credulity.

When we examine the miracles themselves, we find that some may be discounted as plagiarisms of Gospel miracles, and originally introduced in order to emphasize the similarity between the life of Christ and that of his saintly follower. Others are clearly pious for-geries woven into the life of an historic person such as Saint Alban (I. 7) to impress the pagans with the superiority of the Christian saints over the old heathen gods. Others may spring from perfervid imagination or from coincidence. Others, again, may be due to causes that would not be regarded as miraculous today. But even when ruthless pruning has greatly reduced their number, there re-mains an indissoluble core that cannot be explained by any known natural means, and attributable solely to the supernatural power of God displayed in and through His saints. And this is as it should be. For a true miracle (and who may doubt that such occur?) is not due to the supersession or inversion of the natural laws of the universe ordained by the Creator, but to the operation of cosmic laws as yet unrealized by man, activated by non-material forces whose potency is amply demonstrated in the Gospels.

In his valuable work *Psychology, Religion, and Healing*, Dr Leslie Weatherhead defines a miracle as 'a law-abiding event by which God accomplishes His redemptive purposes through the release of energies which belong to a plane of being higher than any with which we are normally familiar'. And what we term a miracle, whether occurring in the second century or the twentieth, may take place as a result of the interaction of many forces and factors such as faith in God, the influence of mind over matter, and the power of suggestion. In a miracle a combination of spiritual and mental forces acts upon the material, and modern medicine and psychology are only beginning to recognize the potency of those forces today. God is not bound or restricted in the means by which he manifests his power or answers *the prayer of faith*, and the well-attested miracles that occur today should be a salutary reminder to our materialistic generation that greater things are effected by prayer and faith than we can ever know or comprehend. It is an indication of the temper of the age in which we live that some who profess and call themselves Christians have so little faith in the reality of God's power and mercy that they regard an unmistakable answer to prayer as something unlooked for and extraordinary, almost indecent. It was otherwise among the Christians of Bede's day.

THE PRESENT TRANSLATION

I have been moved to undertake this task by the realization that increasing numbers of people in all walks of life are finding interest and pleasure in historical matters. This is evident in the widespread reading of historical works, biographies, novels, and articles, and in the popular appeal of historical pageants and films, as well as in the interest taken in historical buildings and sites both of regional and national significance. This is largely due to the fortunate circumstance that England has several contemporary historians of the first rank, whose work has shown that historical studies can be of absorbing interest and significance not only to the expert, but to ordinary folk as well. But the foundation of all modern English historical writing was well laid long ago by the Father of English History, and the reading of his unique work will prove a valuable groundwork and prelude to anyone who wishes to read and appreciate history today.

The present translation is based on the annotated Latin text of Bede's works prepared by Charles Plummer, and first published by the Clarendon Press. My purpose is to offer an accurate and readable version in modern English, and with this in mind I have restricted notes to the minimum. Where these are necessary to elucidate a statement, the word or passage is marked by an asterisk, and the note can be found under its page number at the end of the book. Place names are normally left in their original form, but where the ancient name is not readily recognizable, its modern form is placed as a foot-note. In conclusion, I would like to acknowledge my indebtedness to Dr E. V. Rieu, C.B.E., Editor of the Penguin Classics, for much patience and wise guidance during the preparation of this work.

LEO SHERLEY-PRICE

PREFACE

¶ *To the Most Glorious King Ceolwulf* *
Bede the Priest and Servant
of Christ

SOME while ago, at Your Majesty's request, I gladly sent you the history of the English Church and People which I had recently completed, in order that you might read it and give it your approval. I now send it once again to be transcribed, so that Your Majesty may consider it at greater leisure. I warmly welcome the diligent zeal and sincerity with which you study the words of Holy Scripture and your eager desire to know something of the doings and sayings of men of the past, and of famous men of our own nation in particular. For if history records good things of good men, the thoughtful hearer is encouraged to imitate what is good: or if it records evil of wicked men, the devout, religious listener or reader is encouraged to avoid all that is sinful and perverse and to follow what he knows to be good and pleasing to God. Your Majesty is well aware of this; and since you feel so deeply responsible for the general good of those over whom divine Providence has set you, you wish that this history may be made better known both to yourself and to your people.

But in order to avoid any doubts in the mind of yourself, or of any who may listen to or read this history, as to the accuracy of what I have written, allow me briefly to state the authorities upon whom I chiefly depend.

My principal authority and adviser in this work has been the most reverend Abbot Albinus,* an eminent scholar educated in the church of Canterbury by Archbishop Theodore and Abbot Hadrian, both of them respected and learned men. He carefully transmitted to me verbally or in writing through Nothelm, a priest of the church of London, anything he considered worthy of mention that had been done by disciples of the blessed Pope Gregory in the province of Kent or the surrounding regions. Such facts he ascertained either from records or from the recollection of older men. Nothelm himself later visited Rome, and obtained permission from the present Pope Gregory (II) to examine the archives of the holy Roman Church. He found there letters of Pope Gregory (I) and other Popes, and when he returned, the reverend father Albinus advised him to bring them to me for inclusion in this history. So from the period at which this volume begins until the time when the English nation received the Faith of Christ, I have drawn extensively on the works of earlier writers gathered from various sources. But from that time until the present, I owe much of my information about what was done in the Church of Canterbury by the disciples of Pope Gregory and their successors, and under what kings events occurred, to the industry of the said Abbot Albinus made known to me through Nothelm. They also provided some of my information about the bishops from whom the provinces of the East and West Saxons, the East Angles and the Northumbrians received the grace of the Gospel, and the kings who were then reigning. Indeed, it was mainly owing to the persuasion of Albinus that I was encouraged to begin this work. Also the most reverend Bishop Daniel of the West Saxons, who is still alive, sent to me in writing certain facts about the history of the Church in his province, in the adjoining province of the South Saxons, and in the Isle of Wight. I have learnt by careful enquiry from the brethren of Lastingham monastery how by the ministration of the holy priests Cedd and Chad, their founders, the faith of Christ came to the province of the Mercians, which had never known it, and returned to that of the East Saxons, which had let it die out, and how these holy fathers lived and died. In addition, I have traced the progress of the Church in the province of the East Angles, partly from writings or old traditions and writings, and partly from the account given by the most reverend Abbot Esi. The growth of the Christian Faith and succession of bishops in the province of Lindsey I have learned either from the letters of the most reverend Bishop Cynibert, or by word of mouth from other reliable persons. With regard to events in the various districts of the province of the Northumbrians, from the time that it received the Faith of Christ up to the present day, I am not dependent on any one author, but on countless faithful witnesses who either know or remember the facts, apart from what I know myself. In this connexion, it should be noted that whatever I have written concerning our most holy father and Bishop Cuthbert, whether in this book or in my separate account of his life and doings, I have in part taken and accurately copied from a Life already compiled by the brethren of the Church of Lindisfarne; and I have carefully added to this whatever I could learn from the reliable accounts of those who knew him. Should the reader discover any inaccuracies in what I have written, I humbly beg that he will not impute them to me, because, as the laws of history require, I have laboured honestly to transmit whatever I could ascertain from common report for the instruction of posterity.

I earnestly request all who may hear or read this history of our nation to ask God's mercy on my many failings of mind and body. And in return for the diligent toil that I have bestowed on the recording of memorable events in the various provinces and places of greater note, I beg that their inhabitants may grant me the favour of frequent mention in their devout prayers.

The
BRITISH ISLES
at the time of
BEDE

BOOK ONE

CHAPTER 1 : *The situation of Britain and Ireland: their earliest inhabitants*★

BRITAIN, formerly known as Albion, is an island in the ocean, lying towards the north west at a considerable distance from the coasts of Germany, Gaul, and Spain, which together form the greater part of Europe. It extends 800 miles northwards, and is 200 in breadth, except where a number of promontories stretch further, so that the total coastline extends to 3600 miles. To the south lies Belgic Gaul, to whose coast the shortest crossing is from the city known as Rutubi Portus, which the English have corrupted to Reptacaestir.[1] The distance from there across the sea to Gessoriacum,[2] the nearest coast of the Morini, is fifty miles, or, as some have written, 450 furlongs. On the opposite side of Britain, which lies open to the boundless ocean, lie the isles of the Orcades.[3] Britain is rich in grain and timber; it has good pasturage for cattle and draught animals, and vines are cultivated in various localities. There are many land and sea birds of various species, and it is well known for its plentiful springs and rivers abounding in fish. Salmon and eels are especially plentiful, while seals, dolphins, and sometimes whales are caught. There are also many varieties of shell-fish, such as mussels, in which are often found excellent pearls of several colours, red, purple, violet, and green, but mainly white. Whelks are abundant, and a beautiful scarlet dye is extracted from them which remains unfaded by sunshine or rain; indeed, the older the cloth, the more beautiful its colour. The country has both

1. Richborough.　2. Boulogne.　3. The Orkneys.

salt springs and hot springs, and the waters flowing from them provide hot baths, in which the people bathe separately according to age and sex. As Saint Basil says: 'Water receives heat when it flows across certain metals, and becomes hot, and even scalding.' The land has rich veins of many metals, including copper, iron, lead, and silver. There is also much jet of fine quality, a black jewel which can be set on fire and, when burned, drives away snakes and, like amber, when it is warmed by friction, it holds fast whatever is applied to it. In old times, the country had twenty-eight noble cities, besides innumerable strongholds, which also were guarded by walls, towers, and barred gates.

Since Britain lies far north toward the pole, the nights are short in summer, and at midnight it is hard to tell whether the evening twilight still lingers or whether dawn is approaching, since the sun at night passes not far below the earth in its journey round the north back to the east. Consequently the days are long in summer, as are the nights in winter when the sun withdraws into African regions, as long in fact as eighteen hours, whereas the summer nights and winter days are very short, and last only six hours. In Armenia, Macedonia, and Italy, and other countries of that latitude, the longest day or night lasts only fifteen hours and the shortest nine.

At the present time there are in Britain, in harmony with the five books of the divine law, five languages and four nations – English, British, Scots,★ and Picts. Each of these have their own language; but all are united in their study of God's truth by the fifth – Latin – which has become a common medium through the study of the scriptures. At first the only inhabitants of the island were the Britons, from whom it takes its name, and who, according to tradition, crossed into Britain from Armorica,[1] and occupied the southern parts. When they had spread northwards and possessed the greater part of the island, it is said that some Picts from Scythia[2] put to sea in a few longships, and were driven by storms around

1. Brittany.   2. Here probably Scandinavia.

the coasts of Britain, arriving at length on the north coast of
Ireland. Here they found the nation of the Scots, from whom
they asked permission to settle; but their request was refused.
Ireland is the largest island after Britain, and lies to the west of
it. It is shorter than Britain to the north, but extends far
beyond it to the south towards the northern coasts of Spain,
although a wide sea separates them. These Pictish seafarers, as
I have said, asked for a grant of land so that they too could
make a settlement. The Scots replied that there was not room
for them both, but said: 'We can give you good advice. We
know that there is another island not far to the east, which
we often see in the distance on clear days. If you choose to go
there, you can make it fit to live in; should you meet resistance, we will come to your help.' So the Picts crossed into
Britain, and began to settle in the north of the island, since
the Britons were in possession of the south. Having no women
with them, these Picts asked wives of the Scots, who consented on condition that, when any dispute arose, they should
choose a king from the female royal line rather than the male.
This custom continues among the Picts to this day. As time
went on, Britain received a third nation, that of the Scots,
who migrated from Ireland under their chieftain Reuda and
by a combination of force and treaty, obtained from the Picts
the settlements that they still hold. From the name of this
chieftain, they are still known as Dalreudians, for in their
tongue *dal* means a division.

Ireland is far more favoured than Britain by latitude, and by
its mild and healthy climate. Snow rarely lies longer than
three days, so that there is no need to store hay in summer for
winter use or to build stables for beasts. There are no reptiles,
and no snake can exist there; for although often brought over
from Britain, as soon as the ship nears land, they breathe the
scent of its air, and die. In fact, almost everything in this isle
confers immunity to poison, and I have seen that folk suffering
from snake-bite have drunk water in which scrapings from
the leaves of books from Ireland had been steeped, and that

this remedy checked the spreading poison and reduced the swelling. The island abounds in milk and honey, and there is no lack of vines, fish, and birds, while red deer and roe are widely hunted. It is the original home of the Scots, who, as already mentioned, later migrated and added a third nation to the Britons and Picts in Britain.

There is a very extensive arm of the sea,[1] which originally formed the boundary between the Britons and the Picts. This runs inland from the west for a great distance, where there stands to this day the strongly fortified British city of Alcluith.[2] It was to the northern shores of this firth that the Scots came and established their new homeland.

CHAPTER 2: *On Gaius Julius Caesar, the first Roman to reach Britain*

BRITAIN remained unknown and unvisited by the Romans until the time of Gaius Julius Caesar, who became Consul with Lucius Bibulus 693 years after the founding of Rome, and sixty years before the birth of our Lord. During a campaign against the Germans and Gauls, whose common boundary was the Rhine, he entered the province of the Morini, from which is the nearest and quickest crossing into Britain. Here he assembled about eighty transports and galleys, and crossed into Britain, where his forces suffered in a fierce battle. Next, encountering a violent gale, he lost most of his fleet and many troops, including almost all his cavalry. So he returned to Gaul, dispersed his legions to winter quarters, and gave orders for the construction of 600 vessels of both types. With these he made a second attempt on Britain in the spring; but while he was advancing against the enemy with large forces, the fleet lying at anchor was struck by a storm, and the ships were either dashed against each other, or driven on the sands and destroyed. Forty ships were wrecked, and the remainder were

1. Firth of Clyde.   2. Dumbarton.

only repaired with great difficulty. At the first encounter, Caesar's cavalry suffered a defeat at the hands of the Britons, and the tribune Labienus was killed. In a second battle, which involved considerable risk, he put the Britons to flight. His next objective was the Thames, where a vast host of the enemy under Cassobellaunus was holding the far bank, and had constructed a defence system of sharpened stakes which ran along the bank, and under water across the ford. Traces of these stakes can still be seen; cased in lead and thick as a man's thigh, they were fixed immovably in the river-bed. But they were noticed and avoided by the Romans, and the barbarians, unable to resist the charge of the legions, hid themselves in the forests and harassed the Romans by frequent fierce sorties. Meanwhile the strongest city of the Trinovantes and its commander Androgius surrendered to Caesar and gave him forty hostages. Following its example, several other cities came to terms with the Romans and, acting on their information, Caesar, after a severe struggle, captured the stronghold of Cassobellaunus, which was sited between two swamps, flanked by forests and well provisioned. After this, Caesar left Britain for Gaul; but no sooner had he sent his legions into winter quarters than he was suddenly troubled and distracted by sudden wars and revolts on all sides.

CHAPTER 3: *Claudius, the second Roman to reach Britain, annexes the Isles of Orkney to the Roman Empire: under his direction Vespasian subdues the Isle of Wight*

IN the 798th year after the founding of Rome, Claudius, fourth emperor in the succession beginning with Augustus, wishing to prove himself a benefactor to the State, applied himself to war and conquest on a grand scale, and undertook an expedition against Britain which had been roused to revolt by the Roman refusal to give up certain deserters. Before Claudius no Roman, either before or since Julius Caesar, had dared to land on the island; yet, within a few days, without battle or bloodshed, he received the surrender of the greater part of the island. He also annexed to the Empire the Isles of Orkney,* which lie in the ocean beyond Britain; and returning to Rome only six months after his departure, he granted his son the title of Britannicus. He brought this campaign to a close in the fourth year of his reign, and in the forty-sixth year after the birth of our Lord. This was the year in which a very serious famine occurred in Syria, which is mentioned in the Acts of the Apostles as having been foretold by the prophet Agabus. Vespasian, who was to succeed Nero as Emperor, was sent by the same Claudius, and brought the Isle of Wight under Roman rule. This island lies off the south coast of Britain and is about thirty miles in length from east to west, and twelve from north to south. Six miles of sea separate it from the mainland at its eastern end, but only three at the west. When Nero succeeded Claudius as Emperor, he attempted no military expeditions, and in consequence, apart from countless other injuries to the Roman State, he nearly lost Britain, for during his reign two most noble towns there were taken and destroyed.

CHAPTER 4: *Lucius, a British king, writes to Pope Eleutherus and asks to be made a Christian*

IN the year of our Lord's Incarnation 156, Marcus Antoninus Verus, fourteenth from Augustus, became Emperor jointly with his brother Aurelius Commodus. During their reign, and while the holy Eleutherus ruled the Roman Church, Lucius, a British king, sent him a letter, asking to be made a Christian by his direction. This pious request was quickly granted, and the Britons received the Faith and held it peacefully in all its purity and fullness until the time of the Emperor Diocletian.

CHAPTER 5: *Severus divides Roman Britain from the rest by an earthwork*

IN the year of our Lord 189, Severus, an African born at Leptis in the province of Tripolitania, became seventeenth Emperor from Augustus and ruled seventeen years. Harsh by nature, he was engaged in almost constant warfare, and ruled the State with courage, but with great difficulty. He was victorious in the grave civil wars that troubled his reign. He was compelled to come to Britain by the desertion of nearly all the tribes allied to Rome, and after many critical and hard-fought battles he decided to separate that portion of the island under his control from the remaining unconquered peoples. He did this not with a wall, as some imagine, but with an earthwork. For a wall is built of stone, but an earthwork, such as protects a camp from enemy attack, is constructed with sods cut from the earth and raised high above ground level, fronted by the ditch from which the sods were cut, and surmounted by a strong palisade of logs. Severus built a rampart and ditch of this type from sea to sea and fortified it by a series of towers. After this he was taken ill and died in Eboracum,[1] leaving two sons, Bassianus and Geta. The latter was subsequently condemned to death as an enemy of the State, but Bassianus became Emperor with the cognomen of Antoninus.

CHAPTER 6: *The reign of Diocletian: his persecution of the Christian Church*

IN the year of our Lord 286, Diocletian, a nominee of the army, became thirty-third in the succession of Augustus. He ruled twenty years, and chose Maximian, known as Herculius, as his co-Emperor. During their reign, Carausius, a man

1. York

43

of humble birth but a capable and energetic soldier, was appointed to protect the sea-coasts, which were then being ravaged by Franks and Saxons. But he put his own interests before those of the Republic, and suspicion arose that he was deliberately permitting the enemy to raid the frontiers: any loot that he recovered from the pirates was not restored to its rightful owners, but retained for his own advantage. Maximian ordered his execution, but Carausius assumed the imperial purple and seized Britain, which he won and held for seven years with great daring. He lost his life through the betrayal of his colleague Allectus, who then held the island for three years, after which he was defeated by Asclepiodotus, Prefect of the Praetorian Guard, who thus restored Britain to the Empire after ten years.

Meanwhile Diocletian in the East and Herculius in the West ordered all churches to be destroyed and all Christians to be hunted out and killed. This was the tenth persecution since Nero, and was more protracted and horrible than all that had preceded it. It was carried out without any respite for ten years, with the burning of churches, the outlawing of innocent people, and the slaughter of martyrs. But at length the glory of these martyrs' devoted loyalty to God was to light even Britain.

CHAPTER 7: *The martyrdom of Saint Alban and his companions, who shed their life-blood for Christ at this time* [A.D. 301]

IN this country occurred the suffering of Saint Alban, of whom the priest Fortunatus in his *Praise of Virgins*, in which he mentions all the blessed martyrs who came to God from every part of the world, says:

> In fertile Britain's land
> Was noble Alban born.

When these unbelieving Emperors were issuing savage edicts against all Christians, Alban, as yet a pagan, gave shelter to a Christian priest fleeing from his pursuers. And when he observed this man's unbroken activity of prayer and vigil, he was suddenly touched by the grace of God and began to follow the priest's example of faith and devotion. Gradually instructed by his teaching of salvation, Alban renounced the darkness of idolatry, and sincerely accepted Christ. But when the priest had lived in his house some days, word came to the ears of the evil ruler that Christ's confessor, whose place of martyrdom had not yet been appointed, lay hidden in Alban's house. Accordingly he gave orders to his soldiers to make a thorough search, and when they arrived at the martyr's house, holy Alban, wearing the priest's long cloak, at once surrendered himself in the place of his guest and teacher, and was led bound before the judge.

When Alban was brought in, the judge happened to be standing before an altar, offering sacrifice to devils. Seeing Alban, he was furious that he had presumed to put himself in such hazard by surrendering himself to the soldiers in place of his guest, and ordered him to be dragged before the idols where he stood. 'Since you have chosen to conceal a sacrilegious rebel,' he said, 'rather than surrender him to my soldiers to pay the well-deserved penalty for his blasphemy against our gods you shall undergo all the tortures due to him if you dare to abandon the practice of our religion.' But Saint Alban, who had freely confessed himself a Christian to the enemies of the Faith, was unmoved by these threats, and armed with spiritual strength, openly refused to obey this order. 'What is your family and race?' demanded the judge. 'How does my family concern you?' replied Alban; 'if you wish to know the truth about my religion, know that I am a Christian, and carry out Christian rites.' 'I demand to know your name,' insisted the judge, 'tell me at once.' 'My parents named me Alban,' he answered, 'and I worship and adore the living and true God, who created all things.' The judge was very angry, and said: 'If you want to enjoy eternal life, sacrifice at once to the great gods.' Alban replied: 'You are offering these sacrifices to devils, who cannot help their suppliants, nor answer their prayers and vows. On the contrary, whosoever offers sacrifice to idols is doomed to the pains of hell.'

Incensed at this reply, the judge ordered God's holy confessor Alban to be flogged by the executioners, declaring that he would shake his constancy of heart by wounds, since words had no effect. But, for Christ's sake, he bore the most horrible torments patiently and even gladly, and when the judge saw that no torture could break him or make him renounce the worship of Christ, he ordered his immediate decapitation. Led out to execution, the saint came to a river which flowed swiftly between the wall of the town and the arena where he was to die. There he saw a great crowd of men and women of all ages and conditions, who were doubtless moved by God's will to attend the death of his blessed confessor and martyr. This crowd had collected in such numbers and so blocked the bridge that he could hardly have crossed that evening, and so many people had come out from the city that the judge was left unattended. Saint Alban, who ardently desired a speedy martyrdom, approached the river, and as he raised his eyes to heaven in prayer, the river ran dry in its bed and left him a way to cross. When among others the appointed executioner himself saw this, he was so moved in spirit that he hurried to meet Alban at the place of execution, and throwing down his drawn sword, fell at his feet, begging that he might be thought worthy to die with the martyr if he could not die in his place.

While this man changed from a persecutor to a companion in the true Faith, and other executioners hesitated to pick up his sword from the ground, the most reverend confessor of God ascended a hill about five hundred paces from the arena, accompanied by the crowd. This hill, a lovely spot as befitted the occasion, was clad in a gay mantle of many kinds of flowers. Here was neither cliff nor crag, but a gently rising slope made smooth by nature, its beauty providing a worthy place to be hallowed by a martyr's blood. As he reached the summit, holy Alban asked God to give him water, and at once a perennial spring bubbled up at his feet – a sign to all present that it was at the martyr's prayer that the river also had dried in its course. For it was not likely that the martyr who had dried up the waters of the river should lack water on a hill-top unless he willed it so. But the river, having performed its due service, gave proof of its obedience, and returned to its natural course. Here, then, the gallant martyr met his death, and received the crown of life which God has promised to those who love him. But the man whose impious hands struck off that pious head was not permitted to boast of his deed, for as the martyr's head fell, the executioner's eyes dropped out on the ground.

The soldier who had been moved by divine intuition to refuse to slay God's confessor was beheaded at the same time as Alban. And although he had not received the purification of Baptism, there was no doubt that he was cleansed by the shedding of his own blood, and rendered fit to enter the kingdom of heaven. Astonished by these many strange miracles, the judge called a halt to the persecution, and whereas he had formerly fought to crush devotion to Christ, he now began to honour the death of his saints.

Saint Alban suffered on the twenty-second day of June near the city of Verulamium, which the English now call Verlamacaestir or Vaeclingacaestir. Here, when the peace of Christian times was restored, a beautiful church worthy of his martyrdom was built, where sick folk are healed and frequent miracles take place to this day.

In the same persecution suffered Aaron and Julius, citizens of the City of Legions,[1] and many others of both sexes throughout the land. After they had endured many horrible physical tortures, death brought an end to the struggle, and their souls entered the joys of the heavenly City.

1. Possibly Caerleon-on-Usk.

CHAPTER 8: *The Church in Britain enjoys peace from the end of this persecution until the time of the Arian heresy*

WHEN this storm of persecution came to an end, faithful Christians, who during the time of danger had taken refuge in woods, deserted places, and hidden caves, came into the open, and rebuilt the ruined churches. Shrines of the martyrs were founded and completed and openly displayed everywhere as tokens of victory. The festivals of the Church were observed, and its rites performed reverently and sincerely. The Christian churches in Britain continued to enjoy this peace until the time of the Arian heresy.* This poisonous error after corrupting the whole world, at length crossed the sea and infected even this remote island; and, once the doorway had been opened, every sort of pestilential heresy at once poured into this island, whose people are ready to listen to anything novel, and never hold firmly to anything.

At this time, Constantius, a man of exceptional kindness and courtesy, who had governed Gaul and Spain during the lifetime of Diocletian, died in Britain. His son Constantine, the child of Helena his concubine, succeeded him as ruler of Gaul. Eutropius writes that Constantine, proclaimed Emperor in Britain, succeeded to his father's domains. In his time, the Arian heresy sprang up, and although it was exposed and condemned at the Council of Nicaea, the deadly poison of its false teaching nevertheless infected, as we have said, not only the continental churches, but even those of these islands.

CHAPTER 9: *During the reign of Gratian, Maximus is created Emperor in Britain, and returns to Gaul with a large army*

IN the year of our Lord 377, Gratian, fortieth in line from Augustus, ruled as Emperor for six years from the death of Valens; he had already reigned as co-Emperor with his uncle

Valens and his brother Valentinian. Finding the affairs of the
State in grave disorder and approaching disaster, he chose the
Spaniard Theodosius to restore the Empire in its need, invest-
ing him with the royal purple at Sirmium, and creating him
Emperor of Thrace and the East.

At this juncture, however, Maximus, an able and energetic
man, well fitted to be Emperor had not ambition led him to
break his oath of allegiance, was elected Emperor by the army
in Britain almost against his will, and he crossed into Gaul at
its head. Here he treacherously killed the Emperor Gratian
who had been dumbfounded at his sudden attack, and was
attempting to escape into Italy. His brother the Emperor
Valentinian was driven out of Italy, and took refuge in the
east, where Theodosius received him with fatherly affection.
Within a short time, however, he regained the Empire, and
trapping the despot Maximus in Aquileia, he captured him
and put him to death.

CHAPTER 10: *During the reign of Arcadius, the Briton
Pelagius presumptuously belittles the grace of God*

IN the year of our Lord 394, Arcadius, son of Theodosius,
forty-third in line from Augustus, became joint-Emperor
with his brother Honorius, and ruled for thirteen years. In his
time, the Briton Pelagius* spread far and wide his noxious and
abominable teaching that man had no need of God's grace,
and in this he was supported by Julian of Campania, a deposed
bishop eager to recover his bishopric. Saint Augustine and
other orthodox fathers quoted many thousand Catholic
authorities against them, but they refused to abandon their
folly; on the contrary, their obstinacy was hardened by con-
tradiction, and they refused to return to the true faith. Prosper
the rhetorician has aptly expressed this in heroic verse:

> Against the great Augustine see him crawl,
> This wretched scribbler with his pen of gall!

In what black caverns was this snakeling bred
That from the dirt presumes to rear its head?
Its food is grain that wave-washed Britain yields,
Or the rank pasture of Campanian fields.

CHAPTER 11: *During the reign of Honorius, Gratian and Constantine set up as despots in Britain: the former is killed shortly afterwards in Britain, and the latter in Gaul*

IN the year 407, Honorius, the younger son of Theodosius, was Emperor, and the forty-fourth in line from Augustus. This was two years before the invasion of Rome by Alaric, King of the Goths, on which occasion the nations of the Alani, Suevi, Vandals, and many others defeated the Franks, crossed the Rhine, and devastated all Gaul. At this juncture, Gratian, a citizen of the island, set himself up as a despot and was killed. In his place Constantine, a common trooper of no merit, was chosen Emperor solely on account of his auspicious name. Once he had obtained power, he crossed into Gaul, where he was hoodwinked into many worthless treaties by the barbarians and caused great harm to the commonwealth. Before long, at the orders of Honorius, Count Constantius entered Gaul with an army, besieged Constantine in the city of Arles, captured him, and put him to death. His son Constans, a monk whom he had created Caesar, was also put to death by Count Gerontius in Vienne.

Rome fell to the Goths in the 1164th year after its foundation. At the same time Roman rule came to an end in Britain, almost 470 years after the landing of Gaius Julius Caesar. The Romans had occupied the country south of the earthwork which, as I have said, Severus built across the island, as cities, forts,[1] bridges, and paved roads bear witness to this day: they also held nominal jurisdiction over the more remote parts of Britain and the islands beyond it.

1. Or 'lighthouses'.

CHAPTER 12: *The Britons, harassed by the Scots and Picts, seek help from the Romans, who come and build a second wall across the island. Notwithstanding, these enemies again break in and reduce the Britons to worse straits*

HENCEFORWARD, the part of Britain inhabited by the Britons which had been hurriedly stripped of all troops and military equipment and robbed of the flower of its young men, who had been led away by ambitious despots and were never to return, lay wholly exposed to attack, since its people were untrained in the science of war. Consequently for many years this region suffered attacks from two savage extraneous races, Scots from the northwest, and Picts from the north. I term these races extraneous, not because they came from outside Britain, but because their lands were sundered from that of the Britons: for two sea estuaries lay between, one of which runs broad and deep into the country from the sea to the east and the other from the west, although they do not actually meet. In the middle of the eastern estuary stands the city of Giudi,[1] while on the right bank of the western stands the city of Alcluith,[2] which in their language means 'the rock of Cluith', as it stands near a river of that name.

When these tribes invaded them, the Britons sent messengers to Rome with moving appeals for help, promising perpetual submission if only the Romans would drive out their enemies. An armed Legion was quickly dispatched to the island, where it engaged the enemy, inflicted heavy losses on them, and drove the survivors out of the territory of Rome's allies. Having thus freed the Britons for a time from dire oppression, the Romans advised them to construct a protective wall across the island from sea to sea in order to keep their foes at bay. The victorious Legion then returned home. The islanders built this wall as they had been instructed, but having no engineers capable of so great an undertaking, they built it of turf and not of stone, so that it was of small value.

1. The island of Inchkeith.   2. Dumbarton.

However, they built it for many miles between the two above-mentioned estuaries or inlets, hoping that where the sea provided no protection, they might use the rampart to preserve their borders from hostile attack. Clear traces of this wide and lofty earthwork can be seen to this day. It begins about two miles west of the monastery of Aebbercurnig[1] at a place which the Picts call Peanfahel and the English Penneltun,[2] and runs westward to the vicinity of the city of Alcluith. But as soon as the old enemies of the Britons saw that the Roman forces had left, they made a seaborne invasion, breaking in and destroying wholesale, slaughtering right and left as men cut ripe corn. The Britons therefore sent more envoys to Rome with pitiful appeals for help, without which their unhappy land would be utterly ravaged and the name of a once illustrious Roman province be brought into disgrace and obliterated by barbarous tribes, who year by year were carrying off their plunder unchecked. Once more a Legion was dispatched, which arrived unexpectedly in autumn and inflicted heavy casualties on the invaders, forcing all who survived to escape by sea.

The Romans, however, now informed the Britons that they could no longer undertake such troublesome expeditions for their defence, and urged them to take up arms for their own part and cultivate the will to fight, pointing out that it was solely their lack of spirit which gave their enemies an advantage over them. In addition, in order to assist these allies whom they were forced to abandon, they built a strong wall of stone directly from sea to sea in a straight line between the towns that had been built as strong-points, where Severus had built his earthwork. This famous and still conspicuous wall was built from public and private resources, with the Britons lending assistance. It is eight feet in breadth, and twelve in height; and, as can be clearly seen to this day, ran straight from east to west. When the wall was completed, the Romans gave firm advice to the dispirited Britons, together with

1. Abercorn.   2. Old Kilpatrick.

instructions on the manufacture of weapons. In addition, they built towers at intervals overlooking the south coast where their ships lay, because there was a danger of barbarian raids even from this quarter. Then they bade farewell to their allies, with no intention of ever returning.

On the departure of the Romans, the Picts and Scots, learning that they did not mean to return, were quick to return themselves, and becoming bolder than ever, occupied all the northern and outer part of the island up to the wall, as if it belonged to them. Here a dispirited British garrison stationed on the fortifications pined in terror night and day, while from beyond the wall the enemy constantly harassed them with hooked weapons, dragging the cowardly defenders down from their wall and dashing them to the ground. At length the Britons abandoned their cities and wall and fled in disorder, pursued by their foes. The slaughter was more ghastly than ever before, and the wretched citizens were torn in pieces by their enemies, as lambs are torn by wild beasts. They were driven from their homesteads and farms, and sought to save themselves from starvation by robbery and violence against one another, their own internal anarchy adding to the miseries caused by others, until there was no food left in the whole land except whatever could be obtained by hunting.

CHAPTER 13: *During the reign of Theodosius the Younger, Palladius is sent to the Christians among the Scots. The Britons make an unsuccessful appeal to the Consul Aëtius* [A.D. 446]

IN the year of our Lord 423, Theodosius the Younger, next after Honorius and forty-fifth in succession from Augustus, ruled the Empire for twenty-six years. In the eighth year of his reign, the Roman Pontiff Celestine sent Palladius* to the Scots who believed in Christ to be their first bishop. In the twenty-third year of his reign, Aëtius, an illustrious patrician, became Consul for the third time together with Symmachus. To him the wretched remnant of the Britons sent a letter, which commences: 'To Aëtius, thrice Consul, come the groans of the Britons', and in the course of the letter they describe their calamities: 'The barbarians drive us into the sea, and the sea drives us back to the barbarians. Between these, two deadly alternatives confront us, drowning or slaughter.' But even this plea could not obtain help; for at the time Aëtius was already engaged in two serious wars with Blaedla and Attila, the kings of the Huns. And although Blaedla had been assassinated the previous year through the treachery of his brother Attila, the latter remained so dangerous an enemy to the State that he devastated nearly all Europe, invading and destroying cities and strongholds alike. During this period there was a famine at Constantinople, followed closely by a plague, and much of the walls of that city and fifty-seven towers fell into ruin. Many other cities fell into disrepair, and the polluting stench of rotting corpses spread disease among men and beasts alike.

CHAPTER 14: *The Britons, made desperate by famine, drive the Barbarians out of their land. There soon follows an abundance of corn, luxury, plague, and doom on the nation*

MEANWHILE the famine which left a lasting memory of its horrors to posterity distressed the Britons more and more. Many were compelled to surrender to the invaders; others, trusting in God's help where no human hand could save them, continued their resistance. Making frequent sallies from the mountains, caves, and forests, they began at length to inflict severe losses on the enemy who had plundered their country for so many years. Thereupon the Irish pirates departed to their homes unabashed, intending to return after a short interval, while the Picts remained inactive in the northern parts of the island, save for occasional raids and forays to plunder the Britons.

When the depredations of its enemies had ceased, the land enjoyed an abundance of corn without precedent in former years; but with plenty came an increase in luxury, followed by every kind of crime, especially cruelty, hatred of truth, and love of falsehood. If anyone happened to be more kindly or truthful than his neighbours, he became a target for all weapons of malice as though he were an enemy of Britain. And not only the laity were guilty of these things, but even the Lord's flock and their pastors. Giving themselves up to drunkenness, hatred, quarrels, and violence, they threw off the easy yoke of Christ. Suddenly a terrible plague struck this corrupt people, and in a short while destroyed so large a number that the living could not bury the dead. But not even the death of their friends or the fear of their own death was sufficient to recall the survivors from the spiritual death to which their crimes had doomed them. So it was that, not long afterwards, an even more terrible retribution overtook this wicked nation. For they consulted how they might obtain help to avoid or repel the frequent fierce attacks of their northern neighbours, and all agreed with the advice of their king, Vortigern, to call on the assistance of the Saxon peoples across the sea. This decision, as its results were to show, seems to have been ordained by God as a punishment on their wickedness.

CHAPTER 15: *The Angles are invited into Britain. At first they repel the enemy, but soon come to terms with them, and turn their weapons against their own allies*

IN the year of our Lord 449, Martian became Emperor with Valentinian, the forty-sixth in succession from Augustus, ruling for seven years. In his time the Angles or Saxons came to Britain at the invitation of King Vortigern in three longships, and were granted lands in the eastern part of the island on condition that they protected the country: nevertheless, their real intention was to subdue it. They engaged the enemy advancing from the north, and having defeated them, sent back news of their success to their homeland, adding that the country was fertile and the Britons cowardly. Whereupon a larger fleet quickly came over with a great body of warriors, which, when joined to the original forces, constituted an invincible army. These also received from the Britons grants of land where they could settle among them on condition that they maintained the peace and security of the island against all enemies in return for regular pay.

These new-comers were from the three most formidable races of Germany, the Saxons, Angles, and Jutes. From the Jutes are descended the people of Kent and the Isle of Wight and those in the province of the West Saxons opposite the Isle of Wight who are called Jutes to this day. From the Saxons – that is, the country now known as the land of the Old Saxons – came the East, South and West Saxons. And from the Angles – that is, the country known as Angulus, which lies between the provinces of the Jutes and Saxons and is said to remain unpopulated to this day – are descended the East and Middle Angles, the Mercians, all the Northumbrian stock (that is, those peoples living north of the river Humber), and the other English peoples. Their first chieftains are said to have been the brothers Hengist and Horsa. The latter was subsequently killed in battle against the Britons, and was buried in east Kent, where a monument bearing his name still stands. They were the sons of Wictgils, whose father was Witta, whose father was Wecta, son of Woden, from whose stock sprang the royal house of many provinces.

It was not long before such hordes of these alien peoples vied together to crowd into the island that the natives who had invited them began to live in terror. Then all of a sudden the Angles made an alliance with the Picts, whom by this time they had driven some distance away, and began to turn their arms against their allies. They began by demanding a greater supply of provisions; then, seeking to provoke a quarrel, threatened that unless larger supplies were forthcoming, they would terminate their treaty and ravage the whole island. Nor were they slow to carry out their threats. In short, the fires kindled by the pagans proved to be God's just punishment on the sins of the nation, just as the fires once kindled by the Chaldeans destroyed the walls and buildings of Jerusalem. For, as the just Judge ordained, these heathen conquerors devastated the surrounding cities and countryside, extended the conflagration from the eastern to the western shores without opposition and established a stranglehold over nearly all the doomed island. Public and private buildings were razed; priests were slain at the altar; bishops and people alike, regardless of rank, were destroyed with fire and sword, and none remained to bury those who had suffered a cruel death. A few wretched survivors captured in the hills were butchered wholesale, and others, desperate with hunger, came out and surrendered to the enemy for food, although they were doomed to lifelong slavery even if they escaped instant massacre. Some fled overseas in their misery; others, clinging to their homeland, eked out a wretched and fearful existence among the mountains, forests, and crags, ever on the alert for danger.

CHAPTER 16: *Under the leadership of Ambrosius, a Roman, the Britons win their first victory against the Angles* [c. A.D. 493]

WHEN the victorious invaders had scattered and destroyed the native peoples and returned to their own dwellings, the Britons slowly began to take heart and recover their strength, emerging from the dens where they had hidden themselves, and joining in prayer that God might help them to avoid complete extermination. Their leader at this time was Ambrosius Aurelianus, a man of good character and the sole survivor of Roman race from the catastrophe. Among the slain had been his own parents, who were of royal birth and title. Under his leadership the Britons took up arms, challenged their conquerors to battle, and with God's help inflicted a defeat on them. Thenceforward victory swung first to one side and then to the other, until the battle of Badon Hill, when the Britons made a considerable slaughter of the invaders. This took place about forty-four years after their arrival in Britain: but I shall deal with this later.

CHAPTER 17: *Bishop Germanus sails to Britain with Lupus: with God's help he quells two storms, one of the sea, the other of the Pelagians* [A.D. 429]

A FEW years before their arrival, the Pelagian heresy introduced by Agricola, son of Severianus a Pelagian prelate, had seriously infected the faith of the British Church. Although the British rejected this perverse teaching, so blasphemous against the grace of Christ, they were unable to refute its plausible arguments by controversial methods, and wisely decided to ask help from the bishops of Gaul in this spiritual conflict. These summoned a great synod, and consulted together as to whom they should send to support the Faith. Their unanimous choice fell upon the apostolic bishops Germanus of Auxerre and Lupus of Troyes, whom they appointed to visit the Britons and to confirm their belief in God's grace. The two bishops readily accepted the commands and decisions of Holy Church, and put to sea. They had safely sailed half-way on their voyage from Gaul with a favourable wind when they were suddenly subjected to the hostile power of devils, who were furious that such men as they should dare to recall the Britons to the way of salvation. They raised violent storms and turned day into night with black clouds. The sails were torn to shreds by the gale, the skill of the sailors was defeated, and the safety of the ship depended on prayer

rather than on seamanship. Germanus their leader and bishop,
spent and exhausted, had fallen asleep, when the storm
reached a fresh pitch of violence, as though relieved of its
opponent, and seemed about to overwhelm the vessel in the
surging waves. At this juncture, Lupus and his companions
roused their leader, and anxiously begged him to oppose the
fury of the elements. More resolute than they in the face of
imminent disaster, he called upon Christ and cast a few drops
of holy water on the waves in the Name of the Sacred Trinity,
encouraging his companions and directing them all to join
him in prayer. God heard their cry and their adversaries were
put to flight; the storm was stilled, the wind veered round to
help them on their course and, after a swift and peaceful passage, they arrived safely at their destination. Here great crowds
gathered from all quarters to greet the bishops, whose arrival
had been foretold even by the predictions of their opponents.
For when the evil spirits had been expelled by the bishops
from the persons of those whom they had possessed, they
disclosed their fears and revealed the origin of the storms
and perils they had raised, acknowledging themselves overcome by the merits and power of the saints.

Meanwhile, the island of Britain was rapidly influenced by
the reasoning, preaching, and virtues of these apostolic bishops, and the word of God was preached daily not only in the
churches, but in streets and fields, so that Catholics everywhere were strengthened and heretics corrected. Theirs was
the honour and authority of apostles by their holy witness,
the truth by their learning, the virtue by their merits. So the
majority of the people readily accepted their teaching, while
the authors of false doctrines made themselves scarce, grieving
like evil spirits over the people who were snatched from their
grasp. At length, after due deliberation, they dared to challenge
the saints and appeared with rich ornaments and magnificent
robes, supported by crowds of flattering followers. For they
preferred to hazard a trial of strength rather than submit in
shameful silence before the people whom they had subverted,

lest they should appear to admit defeat. An immense gathering had assembled there with their wives and children to watch and judge, but the contestants were greatly dissimilar in bearing. On one side human presumption, on the other divine faith; on one side pride, on the other piety; on one side Pelagius, on the other Christ. The holy bishops gave their adversaries the advantage of speaking first, which they did at great length, filling the time, and the ears of their audience, with empty words. The venerable bishops then fed the torrents of their eloquence from the springs of the Apostles and evangelists, confirming their own words by the word of God, and supporting their principal statements by quotation from the scriptures. The conceit of the Pelagians was pricked, their lies exposed, and unable to defend any of their arguments, they admitted their errors. The people, who were acting as their judges, were hardly restrained from violence, and confirmed their verdict with acclamation.

CHAPTER 18: *Germanus gives sight to the blind daughter of a tribune. He takes some relics from the tomb of Saint Alban, and deposits relics of the Apostles and other Martyrs*

IMMEDIATELY after this, a man who held the status of a tribune came forward with his wife and asked the bishops to cure his blind daughter, a child of ten. They directed him to take her to their opponents, but the latter, smitten by guilty consciences, joined their entreaties to those of the girl's parents and begged the bishops to heal her. Seeing their opponents yield, they offered a short prayer; then Germanus, being filled with the Holy Ghost, called on the Trinity, and taking into his hands a casket containing relics of the saints that hung around his neck, he applied it to the girl's eyes in the sight of them all. To the joy of the parents and the amazement of the crowd, the child's sight was emptied of darkness and filled with the light of truth. Thenceforward all erroneous arguments were expunged from the minds of the people, who eagerly accepted the teaching of the bishops.

Once this abominable heresy had been put down, its authors refuted, and the people established in the pure faith of Christ, the bishops paid a visit to the tomb of the blessed martyr Alban to return thanks to God through him. Germanus, who had with him relics of all the Apostles and several martyrs, first offered prayer, and then directed the tomb to be opened, so that he could deposit these precious gifts within it. For he thought it fitting that, as the equal merits of the saints had won them a place in heaven, so their relics should be gathered together from different lands into a common resting-place. And when he had reverently deposited these relics, Germanus took away with him a portion of earth from the place where the blessed martyr's blood had been shed. This earth was seen to have retained the martyr's blood, which had reddened the shrine where his persecutor had grown pale with fear. As a result of these events, a great number of people were converted to our Lord on the same day.

CHAPTER 19: *Germanus is detained by illness. He puts out a fire among houses by his prayer, and is healed of his sickness by a vision*

WHILE they were returning from this place, the ever-watchful Devil, having set his snares, contrived that Germanus should fall and break a leg, not knowing that his merits, like those of the blessed Job, would be enhanced by bodily affliction. While he was thus detained by illness, fire broke out in a cottage near his lodging, and after destroying the adjoining dwellings which at that place were thatched with reeds from the marshes, it was carried by the wind to the cottage where he lay. The people ran to pick up the bishop and carry him to a place of safety; but, full of trust in God, he reproved them and would not allow them to do so. In despair, the people ran off to fight the fire; but to afford clearer evidence of God's power, whatever the crowd endeavoured to save was destroyed. Meanwhile the flames leaped over the house where the saint lay disabled and helpless; but, although they raged all around it, the place that sheltered him stood untouched amid a sea of fire. The crowd was overjoyed at the miracle and praised God for this proof of his power, while innumerable poor folk kept vigil outside his cottage day and night hoping for healing of soul or body.

It is impossible to relate all that Christ effected through his servant, and what wonders the sick saint performed. And while he refused any treatment for his own illness, he saw beside him one night a being in shining robes, who seemed to reach out his hand and raise him up, ordering him to stand on his feet. From that moment his pain ceased, his former health was restored, and when dawn came he continued on his journey undaunted.

CHAPTER 20: *The two bishops obtain God's help in battle, and return home* [A.D. 429]

MEANWHILE the Saxons and Picts joined forces and made war on the Britons, whom necessity had compelled to arm; and since the latter feared that their strength was unequal to the challenge, they called on the saintly bishops for help. They came at once as they had promised, and put such heart into the timid people that their presence was worth a large army. Under these apostolic leaders, Christ himself commanded in the camp. It also happened that the holy season of Lent was beginning, and was so reverently kept under the bishops' direction that the people came each day for instruction and flocked to receive the grace of Baptism. Most of the army sought Holy Baptism, and in readiness for the Feast of our Lord's Resurrection a church was constructed of interlaced boughs and set up in that armed camp as though it were a city. Strong in faith and fresh from the waters of Baptism, the army advanced; and whereas they had formerly despaired of human strength, all now trusted in the power of God. The preparation and disposition of the British forces was reported to the enemy, who, anticipating an easy victory over an ill-equipped army, advanced rapidly, closely observed by the British scouts.

After the Feast of Easter, when the greater part of the British forces, fresh from the font, were preparing to arm and embark on the struggle, Germanus promised to direct the battle in person. He picked out the most active men and, having surveyed the surrounding country, observed a valley among the hills lying in the direction from which he expected the enemy to approach. Here he stationed the untried forces under his own orders. By now the main body of their remorseless enemies was approaching, watched by those whom he had placed in ambush. Suddenly Germanus, raising the standard, called upon them all to join him in a mighty shout. While the enemy advanced confidently, expecting to take the Britons unawares, the bishops three times shouted, 'Alleluia!' The whole army joined in this shout, until the surrounding hills echoed with the sound. The enemy column panicked, thinking that the very rocks and sky were falling on them, and were so terrified that they could not run fast enough. Throwing away their weapons in headlong flight, they were well content to escape naked, while many in their hasty flight were drowned in a river which they tried to cross. So the innocent British army saw its defeats avenged, and became an inactive spectator of the victory granted to it. The scattered spoils were collected, and the Christian forces rejoiced in the triumph of heaven. So the bishops overcame the enemy without bloodshed, winning a victory by faith and not by force.

Having restored peace to the island and overcome all its enemies, both visible and invisible, the bishops prepared to return home. Their own merits and the prayers of the blessed martyr Alban obtained them a peaceful voyage, and a propitious vessel restored them to their own welcoming people.

CHAPTER 21: *The Pelagian heresy revives, and Germanus returns to Britain with Severus. He heals a lame youth, and after denouncing or converting the heretics, restores the British Church to the Catholic Faith* [?A.D. 435–44]

AFTER no great interval, news came from Britain that certain people were again promulgating the Pelagian heresy. Once again all the clergy requested blessed Germanus to defend God's cause as before. Promptly assenting, he took ship and made a peaceful crossing to Britain with a favouring wind, taking with him a man of great holiness named Severus. Severus had been a disciple of the most blessed father Lupus, Bishop of Troyes; he subsequently became Bishop of Trier, and preached the Word in western Germany.

Meanwhile evil spirits throughout the land had been reluctantly compelled to foretell Germanus' coming, so that a local chieftain named Elaphius hurried to meet the saints before receiving any definite news. He brought with him his son, who in the very flower of his youth was crippled by a painful disease of the leg, whose muscles had so contracted that the limb was entirely useless. Accompanying Elaphius was the whole population of his province. The bishops on arrival were met by the ignorant folk, to whom they spoke and gave their blessing. And having assured themselves that the people as a whole remained loyal to the Faith as they had left them, and that the error was restricted to a minority, they sought out its adherents and rebuked them. Suddenly Elaphius threw himself at the bishops' feet, and presented to them his son, the sight of whose infirmity proclaimed his need louder than words. All were moved to pity at the spectacle, especially the bishops, who earnestly prayed God to show mercy. Blessed Germanus then asked the youth to sit down, and drawing out the leg bent with disease, he passed his healing hand over the afflicted area, and at his touch health swiftly returned. The withered limb filled, the muscles regained their power, and in the presence of them all the lad was restored healed to his parents. The people were amazed at this miracle, and the Catholic Faith was firmly implanted in all their hearts. Germanus then warned them to live better and to shun all error. And the false teachers, who by common consent had been condemned to banishment, were brought before the bishops to be taken to the Continent, so that the country might be rid of them and they themselves brought to recognize their error. Henceforward, the Faith was maintained uncorrupted in Britain for a long time.

Having settled all these matters, the blessed bishops returned home as successfully as they had come.

Germanus subsequently visited Ravenna to obtain peace for the people of Armorica.[1] There he was received with honour by the Emperor Valentinian and his mother Placidia, and while still in this city he departed to Christ. His body was carried back with a splendid escort to his own city and many signs of his holiness were shown. Not long afterwards, in the fifth year of Marcian's reign, Valentinian was murdered by supporters of the patrician Aëtius, whom he had executed, and with him fell the Empire of the West.

CHAPTER 22: *The Britons enjoy a respite from foreign invasions, but exhaust themselves in civil wars and plunge into worse crimes*

MEANWHILE Britain enjoyed a rest from foreign, though not from civil, wars. Amid the wreckage of deserted cities destroyed by the enemy, the citizens who had survived the enemy now attacked each other. So long as the memory of past disaster remained fresh, kings and priests, commoners

1. Brittany.

and nobles kept their proper rank. But when those who remembered died, there grew up a generation that knew nothing of these things and had experienced only the present peaceful order. Then were all restraints of truth and justice so utterly abandoned that no trace of them remained, and very few of the people even recalled their existence. Among other unspeakable crimes, recorded with sorrow by their own historian Gildas, they added this – that they never preached the Faith to the Saxons or Angles who dwelt with them in Britain. But God in his goodness did not utterly abandon the people whom he had chosen; for he remembered them, and sent this nation more worthy preachers of truth to bring them to the Faith.

CHAPTER 23 : *The holy Pope Gregory sends Augustine and other monks to preach to the English nation, and encourages them in a letter to persevere in their mission* [A.D. 596]

IN the year of our Lord 582, Maurice, fifty-fourth in succession from Augustus, became Emperor, and ruled for twenty-one years. In the tenth year of his reign, Gregory, an eminent scholar and administrator, was elected Pontiff of the apostolic Roman see, and ruled it for thirteen years, six months, and ten days. In the fourteenth year of this Emperor, and about the one hundred and fiftieth year after the coming of the English to Britain, Gregory was inspired by God to send his servant Augustine with several other God-fearing monks to preach the word of God to the English nation. Having undertaken this task in obedience to the Pope's command and progressed a short distance on their journey, they became afraid, and began to consider returning home. For they were appalled at the idea of going to a barbarous, fierce, and pagan nation, of whose very language they were ignorant. They unanimously agreed that this was the safest course, and sent back Augustine – who was to be consecrated bishop in the event of

66

their being received by the English – so that he might humbly request the holy Gregory to recall them from so dangerous, arduous, and uncertain a journey. In reply, the Pope wrote them a letter of encouragement, urging them to proceed on their mission to preach God's word, and to trust themselves to his aid. This letter ran as follows:

'GREGORY, Servant of the servants of God, to the servants of our Lord. My very dear sons, it is better never to undertake any high enterprise than to abandon it when once begun. So with the help of God you must carry out this holy task which you have begun. Do not be deterred by the troubles of the journey or by what men say. Be constant and zealous in carrying out this enterprise which, under God's guidance, you have undertaken: and be assured that the greater the labour, the greater will be the glory of your eternal reward. When Augustine your leader returns, whom We have appointed your abbot, obey him humbly in all things, remembering that whatever he directs you to do will always be to the good of your souls. May Almighty God protect you with His grace, and grant me to see the result of your labours in our heavenly home. And although my office prevents me from working at your side, yet because I long to do so, I hope to share in your joyful reward. God keep you safe, my dearest sons.

'Dated the twenty-third of July, in the fourteenth year of the reign of the most pious Emperor Maurice Tiberius Augustus, and the thirteenth year after his Consulship: the fourteenth indiction.'

CHAPTER 24: *Pope Gregory writes commending them to the Bishop of Arles*

T HE venerable Pontiff also wrote to Etherius, Archbishop of Arles, asking him to offer a kindly welcome to Augustine on his journey to Britain. This letter reads:

'To his most reverend and holy brother and fellow-bishop Etherius: Gregory, servant of the servants of God.

'Religious men should require no commendation to priests who exhibit the love that is pleasing to God; but since a suitable opportunity to write has arisen, We have written this letter to you, our brother, to certify that its bearer, God's servant Augustine, with his companions, of whose zeal we are assured, has been directed by us to proceed to save souls with the help of God. We therefore request Your Holiness to assist them with pastoral care, and to make speedy provision for their needs. And in order that you may assist them the more readily, we have particularly directed Augustine to give you full information about his mission, being sure that when you are acquainted with this, you will supply all their needs for the love of God. We also commend to your love the priest Candidus, our common son in Christ, whom we have transferred to a small patrimony in our church. God keep you safely, most reverend brother.

'Dated the twenty-third day of July, in the fourteenth year of the reign of the most pious Emperor Maurice Tiberius Augustus, and the thirteenth year after his Consulship: the fourteenth indiction.'*

CHAPTER 25: *Augustine reaches Britain, and first preaches in the Isle of Thanet before King Ethelbert, who grants permission to preach in Kent* [A.D. 597]

REASSURED by the encouragement of the blessed father Gregory, Augustine and his fellow-servants of Christ resumed their work in the word of God, and arrived in Britain. At this time the most powerful king there was Ethelbert, who reigned in Kent and whose domains extended northwards to the river Humber, which forms the boundary between the north and south Angles. To the east of Kent lies the large island of Thanet, which by English reckoning is six hundred hides* in extent; it is separated from the mainland by a waterway about three furlongs broad called the Wantsum, which joins the sea at either end and is fordable only in two places. It was here that God's servant Augustine landed with companions, who are said to have been forty in number. At the direction of blessed Pope Gregory, they had brought interpreters from among the Franks, and they sent these to Ethelbert, saying that they came from Rome bearing very glad news, which infallibly assured all who would receive it of eternal joy in heaven and an everlasting kingdom with the living and true God. On receiving this message, the king ordered them to remain in the island where they had landed, and gave directions that they were to be provided with all necessaries until he should decide what action to take. For he had already heard of the Christian religion, having a Christian wife of the Frankish royal house named Bertha, whom he had received from her parents on condition that she should have freedom to hold and practise her faith unhindered with Bishop Liudhard, whom they had sent as her helper in the faith.

After some days, the king came to the island and, sitting down in the open air, summoned Augustine and his companions to an audience. But he took precautions that they should not approach him in a house; for he held an ancient superstition that, if they were practisers of magical arts, they might have opportunity to deceive and master him. But the monks were endowed with power from God, not from the Devil, and approached the king carrying a silver cross as their standard and the likeness of our Lord and Saviour painted on a board. First of all they offered prayer to God, singing a litany for the eternal salvation both of themselves and of those to whom and for whose sake they had come. And when, at the king's command, they had sat down and preached the word of life to the king and his court, the king said: 'Your words and promises are fair indeed; but they are new and uncertain, and I cannot accept them and abandon the age-old beliefs that

I have held together with the whole English nation. But since you have travelled far, and I can see that you are sincere in your desire to impart to us what you believe to be true and excellent, we will not harm you. We will receive you hospitably and take care to supply you with all that you need; nor will we forbid you to preach and win any people you can to your religion.' The king then granted them a dwelling in the city of Canterbury, which was the chief city of all his realm, and in accordance with his promise he allowed them provisions and did not withdraw their freedom to preach. Tradition says that as they approached the city, bearing the holy cross and the likeness of our great King and Lord Jesus Christ as was their custom, they sang in unison this litany: 'We pray Thee, O Lord, in all Thy mercy, that Thy wrath and anger may be turned away from this city and from Thy holy house, for we are sinners. Alleluia.'

CHAPTER 26: *The life and doctrine of the primitive Church are followed in Kent: Augustine establishes his episcopal see in the king's city*

As soon as they had occupied the house given to them they began to emulate the life of the apostles and the primitive Church. They were constantly at prayer; they fasted and kept vigils; they preached the word of life to whomsoever they could. They regarded worldly things as of little importance, and accepted only the necessities of life from those they taught. They practised what they preached, and were willing to endure any hardship, and even to die for the truth which they proclaimed. Before long a number of heathen, admiring the simplicity of their holy lives and the comfort of their heavenly message, believed and were baptized. On the east side of the city stood an old church, built in honour of Saint Martin during the Roman occupation of Britain, where the Christian queen of whom I have spoken went to pray. Here they first assembled to sing the psalms, to pray, to say Mass, to preach, and to baptize, until the king's own conversion to the Faith gave them greater freedom to preach and to build and restore churches everywhere.

At length the king himself, among others, edified by the pure lives of these holy men and their gladdening promises, the truth of which they confirmed by many miracles, believed and was baptized. Thenceforward great numbers gathered each day to hear the word of God, forsaking their heathen rites and entering the unity of Christ's holy Church as believers. While the king was pleased at their faith and conversion, it is said that he would not compel anyone to accept Christianity; for he had learned from his instructors and guides to salvation that the service of Christ must be accepted freely and not under compulsion. Nevertheless, he showed greater favour to believers, because they were fellow-citizens of the kingdom of heaven. And it was not long before he granted his teachers in his capital of Canterbury a place of residence appropriate to their station, and gave them possessions of various kinds to supply their wants.

CHAPTER 27: *Augustine is consecrated bishop: he sends to inform Pope Gregory what has been achieved, and receives replies to his questions*

MEANWHILE God's servant Augustine visited Arles and, in accordance with the holy father Gregory's directions, was consecrated archbishop of the English nation by Etherius, archbishop of that city. On his return to Britain, he sent the priest Laurence and the monk Peter to Rome to inform the blessed Pope Gregory that the English had accepted the Faith of Christ, and that he himself had been consecrated bishop. At the same time, he sought advice on certain current problems. The Pope answered his enquiries without delay, and I have thought it proper to record these replies in my history.

I. The first question of Augustine, Bishop of the Church of Canterbury: What is to be the relation between the bishop and his clergy? And how are the offerings made by the faithful at the altar to be apportioned? And what are the functions of a bishop in his church?

Gregory, Pope of the City of Rome, replies: Holy Scripture, with which you are certainly well acquainted, offers us guidance in this matter, and in particular the letters of blessed Paul to Timothy, in which he carefully instructs him on a bishop's duties in the house of God. But it is the custom of the Apostolic See to instruct all newly consecrated bishops that all money received is to be allocated under four heads: one for the bishop and his household, for hospitality and other commitments; another for the clergy; a third for the poor; and a fourth for the upkeep of churches. In your case, my brother, having been trained under monastic rule, you should not live apart from your clergy in the church of the English, which by God's help has lately been brought to the Faith. You are therefore to follow the way of life practised by our forefathers of the primitive Church, among whom none said that anything which he possessed was his own, but they had all things common. If there are any clerics* who have not received Sacred Orders and who cannot accept a life of continence, let them marry and receive their stipends outside the common fund; for it is written of the fathers whom we have mentioned, that 'distribution was made unto every man according as he had need'. So give consideration to the provision of their stipends, and see that they observe the Church's discipline and live orderly, attend to the singing of the Psalter, and by God's help preserve themselves in thought, word, and deed from everything unlawful. But to those who live as a Community there should be no need for us to mention allocating portions, exercising hospitality, and showing mercy. Everything that can be spared is to be devoted to holy and religious purposes, as the Lord and Master of all bids; '*Give alms of such things as ye have; and behold, all things are clean unto you.*'

II. Augustine's second question: Since we hold the same Faith, why do customs vary in different Churches? Why, for instance, does the method of saying Mass differ in the holy Roman Church and in the Churches of Gaul?

Pope Gregory's reply: My brother, you are familiar with the usage of the Roman Church, in which you were brought up. But if you have found customs, whether in the Church of Rome or of Gaul or any other that may be more acceptable to God, I wish you to make a careful selection of them, and teach the Church of the English, which is still young in the Faith, whatever you have been able to learn with profit from the various Churches. For things should not be loved for the sake of places, but places for the sake of good things. Therefore select from each of the Churches whatever things are devout, religious, and right; and when you have bound them, as it were, into a Sheaf, let the minds of the English grow accustomed to it.

III. Augustine's third question: What punishment should be awarded to those who rob churches?

Pope Gregory's reply: The punishment must depend on the circumstances of the offender. For some commit theft although they have means of subsistence, and others out of poverty. Some, therefore, should be punished by fines, others by beating; some severely, and others more leniently. But when the punishment has to be severe, let it be administered in charity, not in anger; for the purpose of such correction is to save the wicked from hell-fire. We must maintain discipline among the faithful as good fathers among their children, whom they beat for wrongdoing, and yet choose for their heirs, while they preserve their possessions for the benefit of those whom they appear to treat harshly. So charity must always be our motive and indicate the means of correction, so that we may do nothing unreasonable. You may add that thieves are to restore whatever they have taken from churches, but God forbid that the Church should recover with interest any worldly goods she may lose, or seek any gain from these empty things.

IV. Augustine's fourth question: Is it permissible for two brothers to marry two sisters, provided that there be no blood ties between the families?

Pope Gregory's reply: This is quite permissible. There is nothing in holy Scripture that seems to forbid it.

V. Augustine's fifth question: To what degree may the faithful marry with their kindred? And is it lawful for a man to marry his step-mother or sister-in-law?

Pope Gregory's reply: An earthly law of the Roman state permits first-cousins to marry. But experience shows that such unions do not result in children, and sacred law forbids a man to '*uncover the nakedness of his kindred.*' Necessity therefore forbids a closer marriage than that between the third or fourth generation, while the second generation, as we have said, should wholly abstain from marriage. But to wed one's step-mother is a grave sin, for the Law says: '*Thou shalt not uncover the nakedness of thy father.*' Now the son cannot uncover the nakedness of his father; but since it says, '*They shall be one flesh*', whosoever presumes to wed his step-mother, who was one flesh with his father, thereby commits this offence. It is also forbidden to marry a sister-in-law, since by a former union she had become one with his own brother: it was for denouncing this sin that John the Baptist was beheaded and met his holy martyrdom. For John was not ordered to deny Christ, but was in fact put to death as a confessor of Christ. For since our Lord Jesus Christ said: '*I am the Truth*', John shed his blood for Christ in that he gave his life for the truth.

But since there are many among the English who, while they were still heathen, are said to have contracted these unlawful marriages, when they accept the Faith they are to be instructed that this is a grave offence and that they must abstain from it. Warn them of the terrible judgement of God lest for their bodily desires they incur the pains of eternal punishment. Nevertheless, they are not on that account to be deprived of the Communion of the Body and Blood of Christ, lest they appear to be punished for sins committed unknowingly before

they received the purification of Baptism. For in these days
the Church corrects some things strictly, and allows others
out of leniency; others again she deliberately glosses over and
tolerates and by so doing often succeeds in checking an evil of
which she disapproves. But all who come to the Faith are to be
warned against doing these things, and should any subsequently be guilty of them, they are to be forbidden to receive
the Communion of the Body and Blood of our Lord. For
while these offences may to some extent be condoned in those
who acted in ignorance, they must be severely punished in
those who presume to sin knowingly.

VI. Augustine's sixth question: If a long journey is involved,
so that bishops cannot easily assemble, is it permissible for a
bishop to be consecrated without other bishops being
present?

Pope Gregory's reply: In the church of the English where
as yet you are the only bishop, you cannot do otherwise than
consecrate a bishop without other bishops being present. For
when do bishops from Gaul pay a visit, so that they can be
present as witnesses to the consecration? It is our wish, brother,
that you should so establish bishops that they are not un-
necessarily far apart: so that at a bishop's consecration other
pastors, whose presence is certainly desirable, may be readily
summoned. Therefore, when in God's good time bishops are
appointed in various places at no great distance from one
another, no consecration is to take place except in the presence
of three or four bishops. For in spiritual matters we may often
with advantage follow the customs of the world, so that we
may arrange things carefully and wisely. When a wedding is
celebrated, married folk are invited, so that those who have
already travelled some way down the path of marriage may
share the joy of the new couple. So, at this spiritual consecration, when a man is joined to God in the sacred ministry,
why should not those be invited who will take pleasure in the
elevation of the new bishop, or offer their prayers to God for
his protection?

VII. Augustine's seventh question: What are to be our relations with the bishops of Gaul and Britain?

Pope Gregory's reply: We give you no authority over the bishops of Gaul, for since the time of my early predecessors the Bishop of Arles has received the *pallium*★, and his authority is to be in no way impaired. If, therefore, you have occasion to cross over into the province of Gaul, you are to consult with the Bishop of Arles how to correct any faults among the bishops; and should he be remiss in administering discipline, inspire him with your own zeal. We have already written to him, requesting him to offer you every assistance whenever you visit Gaul and to ensure that his bishops observe no customs contrary to the laws of God our Maker. Although we give you no authority over the bishops of Gaul, you should nevertheless advise, encourage and show them a good example. Recall the minds of any wrong-doers to the pursuit of holiness, for it is written in the Law: '*When thou comest into the standing corn of thy neighbour, then thou mayest pluck the ears with thine hand; but thou shalt not move a sickle into thy neighbour's standing corn.*' Similarly, you may not use the sickle of authority in the field entrusted to another man, but use your good influence to separate the Lord's wheat from the chaff of their sins, and by your teaching and persuasion assimilate them into the body of the Church. But no official action is to be taken without the authority of the Bishop of Arles, so that the long-established institutions of our fathers may not fall into disuse. All the bishops of Britain, however, we commit to your charge. Use your authority to instruct the unlearned, to strengthen the weak, and correct the misguided.

VIII. Augustine's eighth question: May an expectant mother be baptized? How soon after childbirth may she enter church? And how soon after birth may a child be baptized if in danger of death? How soon after child-birth may a husband have relations with his wife? And may a woman properly enter church at the time of menstruation? And may she receive Communion at these times? And may a man enter

church after relations with his wife before he has washed? Or
receive the sacred mystery of Communion? These uncouth
English people require guidance on all these matters.

Pope Gregory's reply: I have no doubt, my brother, that
questions such as these have arisen, and I think I have already
answered you; but doubtless you desire my support for your
statements and rulings. Why should not an expectant mother
be baptized? – the fruitfulness of the flesh is no offence in the
sight of Almighty God. For when our first parents sinned in
the Garden, they justly forfeited God's gift of immortality.
But although God deprived man of immortality for his sin,
he did not destroy the human race on that account, but of his
merciful goodness left man his ability to continue the race.
On what grounds, then, can Almighty God's free gift to
man be excluded from the grace of Holy Baptism? For it
would be foolish to suppose that his gift of grace is contrary to the sacred mystery by which all guilt is washed
away.

As to the interval that must elapse after childbirth before a
woman may enter church, you are familiar with the Old
Testament rule: that is, for a male child thirty-three days and
for a female, sixty-six. But this is to be understood as an alle-
gory, for were a woman to enter church and return thanks in
the very hour of her delivery, she would do nothing wrong.
The fault lies in the bodily pleasure, not in the pain; the
pleasure is in the bodily union, the pain is in the birth, so that
Eve, the mother of us all, was told: '*In sorrow thou shalt bring
forth children.*' If, then, we forbid a woman who is delivered of
a child to enter church, we make this penalty into a sin. There
is no obstacle to the Baptism either of a woman who has been
delivered, or of a newborn babe, even if it is administered to
her in the very hour of her delivery, or to the child at the hour
of its birth, provided that there be danger of death. For as the
grace of this sacred mystery is to be offered with great
deliberation to the living and conscious, so is it to be administered without delay to the dying; for if we wait to offer them

this mystery of redemption, it may be too late to find anyone to be redeemed.

A man should not approach his wife until her child is weaned. But a bad custom has arisen in the behaviour of married people that women disdain to suckle their own children, and hand them over to other women to nurse. This custom seems to have arisen solely through incontinency; for when women are unwilling to be continent, they refuse to suckle their children. So those who observe this bad custom of giving their children to others to nurse must not approach their husbands until the time of their purification has elapsed. For even apart from childbirth, women are forbidden to do so during their monthly courses, and the Old Law prescribed death for any man who approached a woman during this time. But a woman should not be forbidden to enter church during these times; for the workings of nature cannot be considered culpable, and it is not just that she should be refused admittance, since her condition is beyond her control. We know that the woman who suffered an issue of blood, humbly approaching behind our Lord, touched the hem of his robe and was at once healed of her sickness. If, therefore, this woman was right to touch our Lord's robe, why may not one who suffers nature's courses be permitted to enter the church of God? And if it is objected that the woman in the Gospels was compelled by disease while these latter are bound by custom, then remember, my brother, that everything that we suffer in this mortal body through the infirmity of its nature is justly ordained by God since the Fall of man. For hunger, thirst, heat, cold, and weariness originate in this infirmity of our nature; and our search for food against hunger, drink against thirst, coolness against heat, clothing against cold, and rest against weariness is only our attempt to obtain some remedy in our weakness. In this sense the menstrual flow in a woman is an illness. So, if it was a laudable presumption in the woman who, in her disease, touched our Lord's robe, why may not the same concession be granted to all women who endure the weakness of their nature?

A woman, therefore, should not be forbidden to receive the mystery of Communion at these times. If any out of a deep sense of reverence do not presume to do so, this is commendable; but if they do so, they do nothing blameworthy. Sincere people often acknowledge their faults even when there is no actual fault, because a blameless action may often spring from a fault. For instance, eating when we are hungry is no fault, but being hungry originates in Adam's sin; similarly, the monthly courses of women are no fault, because nature causes them. But the defilement of our nature is apparent even when we have no deliberate intention to do evil, and this defilement springs from sin; so may we recognize the judgement that our sin has brought on us. And so may man, who sinned willingly, bear the punishment of his sin unwillingly. Therefore, when women after due consideration do not presume to approach the Sacrament of the Body and Blood of the Lord during their courses, they are to be commended. But if they are moved by devout love of this holy mystery to receive it as pious custom suggests, they are not to be discouraged. For while the Old Testament makes outward observances important, the New Testament does not regard these things so highly as the inward disposition, which is the sole true criterion for allotting punishment. For instance, the Law forbids the eating of many things as unclean, but in the Gospel our Lord says: '*Not that which goeth into the mouth defileth a man; but that which cometh out of the mouth, this defileth a man.*' He also said: '*Out of the mouth proceed evil thoughts.*' Here Almighty God clearly shows us that evil actions spring from the root of evil thoughts. Similarly, Saint Paul says: '*Unto the pure all things are pure; but unto them that are defiled and unbelieving is nothing pure.*' And later, he indicates the cause of this corruption, adding: '*For even their mind and conscience is defiled.*' If, therefore, no food is unclean to one of a pure mind, how can a woman who endures the laws of nature with a pure mind be considered impure?

It is not fitting that a man who has approached his wife

should enter church before he has washed, nor is he to enter at once, though washed. The ancient Law prescribed that a man in such cases should wash, and forbade him to enter a holy place before sunset. But this may be understood spiritually; for when a man's mind is attracted to those pleasures by lawless desire, he should not regard himself as fitted to join in Christian worship until these heated desires cool in the mind, and he has ceased to labour under wrongful passions. And although various nations have differing views on this matter and observe different customs, it was always the ancient Roman usage for such a man to seek purification and out of reverence to refrain awhile from entering a holy place. In making this observation, we do not condemn marriage itself, but since lawful intercourse must be accompanied by bodily desire, it is fitting to refrain from entering a holy place, since this desire itself is not blameless. For David, who said: '*Behold, I was shapen in iniquity, and in sin did my mother conceive me*', was not himself born of any illicit union, but in lawful wedlock. But knowing himself to have been conceived in iniquity, he grieved that he had been born in sin, like a tree bearing in its branches the sap of evil drawn up from its root. In saying this, he does not term the bodily union of married people iniquity, but the desire of such union. For there are many things that are lawful and legitimate, and yet in the doing of them we are to some extent contaminated. For example, we often correct faults under stress of anger and thereby disturb our peace of mind; and though we are right to do so, it is not good that we should lose our peace of mind in the process. He who said: '*Mine eye is troubled because of anger*'[1] had been roused by the crimes of evil men, and because only a quiet mind can rest in the light of contemplation, he regretted that his eye was troubled by anger, so that he was disquieted and prevented from contemplating heavenly things so long as he was distracted by indignation at the wicked doings of men.

1. In the Authorized Version this passage (Psalm 6. 7) reads: 'Mine eye is consumed because of grief.'

So while anger against evil is commendable, it is harmful to a man because in being disturbed by it he is conscious of some guilt. Lawful intercourse should be for the procreation of off-spring, and not for mere pleasure; to obtain children, and not to satisfy lust. But if any man is not moved by a desire for pleasure, but only by a desire for children, he is to be left to his own judgement either as to entering church, or to receiving the Communion of the Body and Blood of our Lord; for we have no right to debar one who does not yield to the fires of temptation. But when lust takes the place of desire for children, the mere act of union becomes something that the pair have cause to regret; and although the holy teachings give them permission, yet this carries a warning with it. For when the Apostle Paul said: '*If they cannot contain, let them marry*', he at once added, '*I speak this by permission, and not of command-ment.*' This concession makes it lawful, yet not good; so when he spoke of permission, he indicated that it was not blameless.

It should be carefully considered that, when God was about to speak to the people on Mount Sinai, he first ordered them to abstain from women. And if such a degree of bodily purity was required in those who were to hear the word of God when he spoke to men through a subject creature, how much the more should women preserve themselves in purity of body when about to receive the Body of Almighty God himself, lest they be overwhelmed by the very greatness of this inestimable mystery? For this reason the priest instructed David that, if his men were clean in this respect, they might be given the shewbread, which would have been entirely forbidden had not David first certified that they had kept themselves from women. Similarly the man who has cleansed himself with water after intercourse with his wife is allowed to approach the mystery of Holy Communion, since he may enter church in accordance with this decision.

IX. Augustine's ninth question: May a man receive communion after a sexual illusion in a dream; or, if a priest, may he celebrate the holy mysteries?

Pope Gregory's reply: The Testament of the Old Law, as I have already mentioned, speaks of such a man as unclean and does not permit him to enter church until evening and after purification. But this is to be understood spiritually in another sense; for a man may be under a delusion and tempted to impurity in a dream, because, having yielded to temptation, he is defiled by real mental imaginings. Then he must cleanse himself with water, thus washing away his sinful thoughts with tears. And, unless the fire of temptation dies earlier, he should regard himself as unclean until evening. But we should carefully examine the origin of such illusions in the mind of a sleeper; for sometimes they arise from over-eating, sometimes from excess or lack of bodily vigour, and sometimes from impure thoughts. When such illusion occurs through excess or lack of bodily vigour, it need not be feared, because it is to be deplored rather as something the mind has unwittingly suffered than as something it has done. But when a greedy appetite runs riot and overloads the repositories of the bodily fluids, the mind is to blame, although not to the extent that a man must be forbidden to receive the holy mystery, or to say mass when a feast-day requires it, or when necessity demands that he administer the sacrament in the absence of another priest. But if there are others who can perform this ministry, then this illusion caused by greed need not debar a man from receiving the holy mystery unless the mind of the sleeper has been excited by impure thoughts; but I think that humility should move him to refrain from offering the holy mysteries under these circumstances. For there are some who are not mentally disturbed by impure thoughts, although subject to these illusions. In these things there is just one thing that shows that the mind is not innocent even in its own judgement: although it remembers nothing that occurs during sleep, yet it does remember its greedy appetites. But if the sleeper's illusion springs from indecent thoughts when awake, his guilt stands clear in his mind and he recognizes the source of his sin, because he has unconsciously experienced what has been in his conscious thoughts. But the question arises whether an evil thought merely suggests itself to a man, or whether he proceeds to take pleasure in it, or, worse still, to assent to it. For all sin is consummated in three ways, that is, by suggestion, pleasure, and consent. Suggestion comes through the devil, pleasure through the flesh, and consent through the will. The Serpent suggested the first sin, and Eve, as flesh, took physical pleasure in it, while Adam, as spirit, consented; and great discernment is needed if the mind, in judging itself, is to distinguish between suggestion and pleasure, and between pleasure and consent. For when the Evil Spirit suggests a sin, no sin is committed unless the flesh takes pleasure in it; but when the flesh begins to take pleasure, then sin is born; and if deliberate consent is given, sin is complete. The seed of sin, therefore, is in suggestion, its growth in pleasure, and its completion in consent. It often happens, however, that what the Evil Spirit sows in the mind and the flesh anticipates with pleasure, the soul rejects. And although the body cannot experience pleasure without the mind, yet the mind, in contending against the desires of the body, is to some extent unwillingly chained to them, having to oppose them for conscience sake, and strongly regretting its bondage to bodily desires. It was for this reason that Paul, that great soldier in God's army, confessed with sorrow: '*I see another law in my members warring against the law of my mind, and bringing me into captivity to the law of sin, which is in my members.*' Now if he was a captive, he fought but little; yet he did fight. So he was both captive and also fighting with the law of the mind, to which the law of the body is opposed. And if he fought thus, he was no captive. So one may say that a man is both captive and free; free through the law of right which he loves, and captive through the law of bodily pleasure, of which he is an unwilling victim.

S UCH were the blessed Pope Gregory's replies to the questions of the most reverend Bishop Augustine. The Pope
also wrote a letter to the Bishop of Arles, which was delivered
to Vergilius, successor to Etherius. This ran as follows:

'To our most reverend and holy brother Vergilius, our
fellow-bishop: Gregory, servant of the servants of God.

'It is well established that brethren who visit us on their
own initiative should be warmly welcomed, since most visitors are invited out of affection. Therefore, if Bishop Augustine, who is brother to us both, happens to visit you, I beg you
to receive him with proper affection and kindness, so that he
may be encouraged by your goodwill and that others may
learn how brotherly love is to be cultivated. And since it often
happens that an independent observer sees what needs correction sooner than the man on the spot, I ask that, should he
bring to your notice any wrong-doing among clergy or others,
you make careful enquiry into these matters with his help. In
this way you will show yourself strict and alert against all abuses
that offend God and incur His displeasure, so that the guilty
may be corrected, the innocent vindicated, and others mend
their ways. God keep you safe, most reverend brother.

'Dated the twenty-second day of June, in the nineteenth
year of our most pious Lord and Emperor Maurice Tiberius
Augustus, and the eighteenth year after his Consulship: the
fourth indiction.

CHAPTER 29: *Gregory sends Augustine the* pallium, *a letter, and several clergy* [A.D. 601]

H EARING from Bishop Augustine that he had a rich
harvest but few to help him gather it, Pope Gregory sent
with his envoys several colleagues and clergy, of whom the

principal and most outstanding were Mellitus, Justus, Paulinus, and Rufinianus. They brought with them everything necessary for the worship and service of the Church, including sacred vessels, altar coverings, church ornaments, vestments for priests and clergy, relics of the holy Apostles and martyrs, and many books. Gregory also sent a letter to Augustine, telling him that he had dispatched the *pallium* to him, and giving him directions on the appointment of bishops in Britain. This letter runs as follows:

'To our most reverend and holy brother and fellow-bishop Augustine: Gregory, servant of the servants of God.

'While Almighty God alone can grant His servants the ineffable joys of the kingdom of heaven, it is proper that we should reward them with earthly honours, and encourage them by such recognition to devote themselves to their spiritual labours with redoubled zeal. And since the new Church of the English has now, through the goodness of God and your own efforts, been brought to the grace of God, we grant you the privilege of wearing the *pallium* in that Church whenever you perform the solemnities of the Mass. You are to consecrate twelve bishops in different places, who will be subject to your jurisdiction: the bishop of the city of London will thenceforward be consecrated by his own synod, and will receive the honour of the *pallium* from this apostolic See which, by divine decree, we at present occupy. We wish you also to send a bishop of your own choice to the city of York, and if that city with the adjoining territory accepts the word of God, this bishop is to consecrate twelve other bishops, and hold the dignity of Metropolitan. If we live to see this, we intend to grant him the *pallium* also, but he is to remain subject to your authority. After your death, however, he is to preside over the bishops whom he has consecrated and to be wholly independent of the Bishop of London. Thenceforward, seniority of consecration is to determine whether the Bishop of London or York takes precedence; but they are to consult one another and take united action in all matters concerning

the Faith of Christ, and take and execute all decisions without
mutual disharmony.

'You, my brother, are to exercise authority in the Name of
our Lord and God Jesus Christ both over those bishops whom
you shall consecrate, and any who shall be consecrated by the
Bishop of York, and also over all the British bishops. Let Your
Grace's words and example show them a pattern of right
belief and holy life, so that they may execute their office in
right belief and practice and, when God wills, attain the kingdom of heaven. God keep you safe, most reverend brother.

'Dated the twenty-second of June, in the nineteenth year
of our most pious Lord and Emperor Maurice Tiberius
Augustus, and the nineteenth after his Consulship: the fourth
indiction.'

CHAPTER 30: *A copy of the letter sent by Pope Gregory to
Abbot Mellitus on his departure for Britain* [A.D. 601]

WHEN these messengers had left, the holy father Gregory
sent after them letters worthy of our notice, which
show most clearly his unwearying interest in the salvation of
our nation. The letter runs as follows:

'To our well loved son Abbot Mellitus: Gregory, servant
of the servants of God.

'Since the departure of those of our fellowship who are
bearing you company, we have been seriously anxious, because we have received no news of the success of your journey.
Therefore, when by God's help you reach our most reverend
brother, Bishop Augustine, we wish you to inform him that
we have been giving careful thought to the affairs of the
English, and have come to the conclusion that the temples of
the idols among that people should on no account be destroyed. The idols are to be destroyed, but the temples themselves are to be aspersed with holy water, altars set up in them,
and relics deposited there.* For if these temples are well-built,

they must be purified from the worship of demons and dedicated to the service of the true God. In this way, we hope that the people, seeing that their temples are not destroyed, may abandon their error and, flocking more readily to their accustomed resorts, may come to know and adore the true God. And since they have a custom of sacrificing many oxen to demons, let some other solemnity be substituted in its place, such as a day of Dedication or the Festivals of the holy martyrs whose relics are enshrined there. On such occasions they might well construct shelters of boughs for themselves around the churches that were once temples, and celebrate the solemnity with devout feasting. They are no longer to sacrifice beasts to the Devil, but they may kill them for food to the praise of God, and give thanks to the Giver of all gifts for the plenty they enjoy. If the people are allowed some worldly pleasures in this way, they will more readily come to desire the joys of the spirit. For it is certainly impossible to eradicate all errors from obstinate minds at one stroke, and whoever wishes to climb to a mountain top climbs gradually step by step, and not in one leap. It was in this way that the Lord revealed Himself to the Israelite people in Egypt, permitting the sacrifices formerly offered to the Devil to be offered thenceforward to Himself instead. So He bade them sacrifice beasts to Him, so that, once they became enlightened, they might abandon one element of sacrifice and retain another. For, while they were to offer the same beasts as before, they were to offer them to God instead of to idols, so that they would no longer be offering the same sacrifices. Of your kindness, you are to inform our brother Augustine of this policy, so that he may consider how he may best implement it on the spot. God keep you safe, my very dear son.

'Dated the seventeenth of June, in the nineteenth year of the reign of our most pious Lord and Emperor Maurice Tiberius Augustus, and the eighteenth after his Consulship: the fourth indiction.'

At the same time, hearing that Augustine had performed miracles, Pope Gregory sent him a letter in which he warned him not to fall into the peril of pride on this account. He wrote:

'My very dear brother, I hear that Almighty God has worked great wonders through you for the nation which He has chosen. Therefore let your feeling be one of fearful joy and joyful fear at God's heavenly gifts – joy that the souls of the English are being drawn through outward miracles to inward grace; fear lest the frail mind becomes proud because of these wonderful events. For when it receives public recognition, it is liable to fall through senseless conceit. We should remember how the disciples returned from their preaching full of joy, and said to their heavenly Master: '*Lord, even the devils are subject unto us, through thy name.*' But they received the prompt rejoinder: '*In this rejoice not. But rather rejoice because your names are written in heaven.*' For when the disciples rejoiced at these miracles, they were thinking of their transitory personal joy; but Christ recalled them from personal to universal, and from transitory to eternal joy, saying: '*In this rejoice, because your names are written in heaven.*' For God's chosen do not all work miracles, yet the names of all are written in heaven. For those who are disciples of the truth should rejoice only in that good thing which they share with all men, and which they shall enjoy for ever.

'Finally, dearest brother, in all the outward actions which by God's help you perform, always strictly examine your inner dispositions. Clearly understand your own character, and how much grace is in this nation for whose conversion God has given you the power to work miracles. And if you remember that you have ever offended our Creator by word or action, let the memory of your sin crush any temptation to pride that may arise in your heart. And bear in mind that whatever powers to perform miracles you have received or shall receive from God are entrusted to you solely for the salvation of your people.'

CHAPTER 32: *Pope Gregory sends letters and gifts to King Ethelbert*

P OPE GREGORY also sent a letter to King Ethelbert with many gifts of different kinds, wishing to bestow earthly honours on this king who by his exertions and zeal, and to his great joy, had been brought to knowledge of heavenly glory. A copy of this letter follows.

'To our excellent son, the most glorious King Ethelbert, King of the English: the Bishop Gregory.

'The reason why Almighty God raises good men to govern nations is that through them He may bestow the gifts of His mercy on all whom they rule. We know that this is so in the case of the English nation, over whom you reign so gloriously, so that by means of the good gifts that God grants to you He may bless your people as well. Therefore, my illustrious son, zealously foster the grace that God has given you, and press on with the task of extending the Christian Faith among the people committed to your charge. Make their conversion your first concern; suppress the worship of idols, and destroy their shrines; raise the moral standards of your subjects by your own innocence of life, encouraging, warning, persuading, correcting, and showing them an example by your good deeds. God will most surely grant you His rewards in heaven if you faithfully proclaim His Name and truth upon earth; and He whose honour you seek and uphold among your peoples will make your own name glorious to posterity.

'So it was that the devout Emperor Constantine in his day turned the Roman State from its ignorant worship of idols by his own submission to our mighty Lord and God Jesus Christ, and with his subjects accepted Him with all his heart. The result is that his glorious reputation has excelled that of all his predecessors, and he has outshone them in reputation as greatly as he surpassed them in good works. Now, therefore, let Your Majesty make all speed to bring to your subject princes and peoples the knowledge of the One God, Father, Son and Holy Spirit, so that your own merit and repute may excel that of all the former kings of your nation. And when you have thus cleansed your subjects from their sins, you will bear the load of your own sins with greater confidence before the judgement seat of God.

'Our most reverend brother Bishop Augustine has been trained under monastic Rule, has a complete knowledge of holy scripture, and, by the grace of God, is a man of holy life. Therefore I beg you to listen to his advice ungrudgingly, follow it exactly and store it carefully in your memory; for if you listen to him when he speaks in God's name, God himself will listen more readily to the prayers he utters on your behalf. But if you ignore his advice – which God forbid – and disregard him when he speaks for God, how should God pay attention when he speaks for you? Work sincerely and wholeheartedly with him in fervent faith, and support his efforts with all the strength God has given you, so that you may receive a place in the kingdom of Christ, Whose Faith you profess and uphold in your own realm.

'We would also have Your Majesty know what we have learned from the words of Almighty God in holy Scripture, that the end of this present world is at hand and the everlasting kingdom of the Saints is approaching.* When the end of the world is near, unprecedented things occur – portents in the sky, terrors from heaven, unseasonable tempests, wars, famines, pestilences, and widespread earthquakes. Not all these things will happen during our own lifetimes, but will all ensue in due course. Therefore, if any such things occur in your own country, do not be anxious, for these portents of the end are sent to warn us to consider the welfare of our souls and remember our last end, so that, when our Judge comes, He may find us prepared by good lives. I have mentioned these matters in this short letter, my illustrious son, in the hope that as the Christian Faith grows more strong in your kingdom, our correspondence with you may become more frequent. So my pleasure in addressing you will keep pace with the joy in my heart at the glad news of the complete conversion of your people.

'I have sent some small presents, which will not appear small to you, since you will receive them with the blessing of the blessed Apostle Peter. May Almighty God continue to perfect you in His grace, prolong your life for many years, and after this life receive you among the citizens of our heavenly home. May the grace of heaven preserve Your Majesty in safety.

'Dated the twenty-second day of June, in the nineteenth year of our most pious lord and Emperor Maurice Tiberius Augustus, and the eighteenth after his Consulship: the fourth indiction.'

CHAPTER 33: *Augustine repairs the Church of Our Saviour and builds a monastery of Saint Peter the Apostle. A note on Peter, its first Abbot* [A.D. 602]

HAVING been granted his episcopal see in the royal capital, as already recorded, Augustine proceeded with the king's help to repair a church which he was informed had been built long ago by Roman Christians. This he hallowed in the Name of our Saviour, God, and Lord Jesus Christ,* and established there a dwelling for himself and his successors. He also built a monastery a short distance to the east of the city, where at his suggestion King Ethelbert erected from the foundations a church dedicated to the blessed Apostles Peter and Paul, enriching it with many gifts. It was here that the bodies of Augustine and all the Archbishops of Canterbury

and of the Kings of Kent were to rest. This church was not
consecrated by Augustine himself, however, but by
Laurence his successor.

The first abbot of this monastery was the priest Peter, who
was sent on a mission to Gaul and was drowned at sea in a
bay called Amfleat,[1] where the local inhabitants buried him
without honour. But, as evidence of his holy life, Almighty
God caused a heavenly light to appear over his grave every
night, until the local people saw it and, realizing that a holy
man lay buried there, made enquiries as to whose the body
might be. Then they took up the body and interred it in a
church in the city of Boulogne with the honours due to so
great a man.

CHAPTER 34: *Ethelfrid, King of the Northumbrians, defeats
the Scots and drives them out of England* [A.D. 603]

ABOUT this time, Ethelfrid, a very powerful and ambitious king, ruled the kingdom of the Northumbrians. He
ravaged the Britons more cruelly than all other English
leaders, so that he might well be compared to Saul the King
of Israel, except of course that he was ignorant of true religion.
He overran a greater area than any other king or ealdorman,
exterminating or enslaving the inhabitants, making their
lands either tributary to the English or ready for English
settlement. One might fairly apply to him the words of the
patriarch Jacob's blessing of his son: *'Benjamin shall ravin as
a wolf; in the morning he shall devour the prey, and at night he
shall divide the spoil.'*

Alarmed at his advance, Aidan, king of those Scots who
lived in Britain, came against him with a large and strong
army, but was defeated and fled with very few, having lost
almost his entire army at a famous place known as Degsastan,
that is, Degsa's Stone. In this battle, Ethelfrid's brother Theod-

1. Ambleteuse.

bald and all his following were killed. Ethelfrid won this fight
in the year of our Lord 603, the eleventh of his reign, which
lasted twenty-four years. It was also the first year of the reign
of Phocas, who then occupied the throne of the Roman
Empire. From that day until the present, no king of the Scots
in Britain has dared to do battle with the English.

BOOK TWO

CHAPTER 1: *On the death of Pope Gregory*

ABOUT this time, in the year of our Lord 605, having ruled the apostolic Roman Church most illustriously for thirteen years, six months, and ten days, the blessed Pope Gregory died and was taken up to his eternal home in heaven. And it is fitting that he should receive fuller mention in this history, since it was through his zeal that our English nation was brought from the bondage of Satan to the Faith of Christ, and we may rightly term him our own apostle. For during his pontificate, while he exercised supreme authority over all the churches of Christendom that had already long since been converted, he transformed our still idolatrous nation into a church of Christ. So we may rightly describe him by the term apostle; for if he is not an apostle to others, yet doubtless he is to us, and we are *the seal of his apostleship in the Lord*.

Gregory was Roman-born, son of Gordian, and descended from ancestors not only noble but devout. Among them was Felix, once bishop of the same apostolic see, a man of high distinction in the Church of Christ, and Gregory maintained this family tradition by the nobility and devotion of his religious life. By God's grace, he turned his aptitude for worldly success wholly to the attainment of heavenly glory. For he suddenly retired from secular life and sought admission to a monastery. There he entered upon a life of such perfection in grace that in later years he used to recall with tears how his mind was set on high things, soaring above all that is transitory, and how he was able to devote himself entirely to thoughts of heaven. Remaining in the body, he could yet transcend its limitations in contemplation, and looked forward to death, which most men regard as a punishment, as the gateway to life and reward of his labours. He used to mention this, not in order to call attention to his increase in virtue, but lamenting rather the decrease in virtue that he believed himself to have suffered through his pastoral responsibilities. One day, in private conversation with his deacon Peter, Gregory described his former spiritual state, then sadly continued: 'My pastoral responsibilities now compel me to have dealings with worldly men, and after the unclouded beauty of my former peace, it seems that my mind is bespattered with the mire of daily affairs. For when it has squandered itself in attention to the worldly affairs of numberless people, even though it turns inward again to meditate on spiritual things, it does so with unmistakably lessened powers. So when I compare what I now endure with what I have lost, and when I weigh that loss, my burden seems greater than ever.'

Holy Gregory spoke in this way from deep humility. Yet we cannot but believe that he lost none of his monastic perfection through his pastoral cares, and indeed made greater spiritual progress by his labours for the conversion of souls than in his former peaceful life, especially since, even when he became Pope, he ordered his house as a monastery. When he was first summoned from his monastery, ordained to the ministry of the altar, and sent to Constantinople as representative of the apostolic see, he never abandoned his spiritual exercises even amid the concourse of an earthly palace. For some of his fellow-monks were so devoted to him that they accompanied him to the Imperial city, and he began to maintain a regular religious observance with them. In this way, as he records, their example proved an anchor-cable that held him fast to the peaceful shore of prayer while he was tossed on the restless waves of worldly affairs, and his studies in their company enabled him to refresh a mind distracted by earthly concerns. By their fellowship he was not only strengthened against the temptations of the world, but inspired to ever greater spiritual activity.

When these companions urged him to write a mystical commentary on the often obscure book of Job, he could not refuse a task imposed on him by brotherly affection, which would be of help to many people. So in a work of thirty-five sections he gave a marvellously clear exposition, showing first the literal meaning of the book, then how it refers to the sacraments of Christ and the Church, and in what sense it applies to each one of the faithful. He began this work when Papal representative in the Imperial city, and completed it in Rome after he became Pope. During his stay in Constantinople he encountered a new heresy about our state at the resurrection and aided by the grace of Catholic truth crushed it in the very moment of birth. For Eutychius, bishop of that city, was proclaiming that our bodies will then be impalpable, of finer texture than wind and air: but when Gregory heard this, he proved both by the light of reason and by the example of our Lord's Resurrection that this opinion is utterly opposed to orthodox belief. For the Catholic belief is that the body, when transfigured in the glory of immortality, is indeed made finer by the operation of spiritual power, but remains palpable by reason of its nature. This is exemplified in our Lord's risen body, of which he said to the disciples: 'Handle Me, and see; for a spirit hath not flesh and bones as ye see Me have.' In defence of the Faith, our venerable father Gregory contested this rising heresy so effectively that, with the help of the devout Emperor Tiberius Constantine, it was entirely suppressed, and no one has since been found to revive it.

Gregory also wrote a notable book, *The Pastoral Office*, in which he describes in clear terms the qualities essential in those who rule the Church, showing how they should live; with what discernment they should instruct their various pupils; and with what constant awareness they should daily call to mind their own frailty. He also compiled forty *Homilies* on the Gospel, which he divided into two volumes of equal size. He wrote four books of *Dialogues*, in which, at the request of his deacon Peter, he assembled the most splendid achievements of saints in Italy known or reported to him, to serve as patterns of holy life for posterity. So, whereas in his *Commentaries* he showed what virtues we should strive for, in describing the miracles of the saints he made clear the splendour of those virtues. In twenty-two homilies he also revealed the illumination latent in the early and latter parts of the prophet Ezekiel, which had hitherto remained very obscure. Further, he compiled a book of answers in reply to the questions of Saint Augustine, first bishop of the English nation, which I have already mentioned and quoted in full in this history. In conjunction with the bishops of Italy he also compiled the short *Synodical Book*, which deals with the administration of the Church. To these must be added his personal letters. The extent of his writings is all the more amazing when one considers that throughout his youth, to quote his own words, he was often in agony from gastric pain, perpetually worn out by internal exhaustion and frequently troubled by a slow but chronic fever. But in all these afflictions he reflected that holy scripture says: '*The Lord scourgeth every son whom He receiveth*', and the greater his worldly sufferings, the greater his assurance of eternal joy.

Much might be said of his imperishable genius, which was unimpaired even by the most severe physical afflictions; for while other popes devoted themselves to building churches and adorning them with gold and silver, Gregory's sole concern was to save souls. Whatever money he had he bestowed zealously to relieve the poor, in order that '*his righteousness might endure for ever, and his horn be exalted with honour*'. Like Job, he might justly claim, '*When the ear heard me, then it blessed me; and when the eye saw me, it gave witness to me, because I delivered the poor that cried, and the fatherless, and him that had none to help him. The blessing of him that was ready to perish came upon me, and I caused the widow's heart to sing for joy. I put*

*on righteousness, and it clothed me; my judgement was as a robe
and a diadem. I was eyes to the blind, and feet was I to the lame.
I was a father to the poor; and the cause which I knew not I searched
out. And I brake the jaws of the wicked, and plucked the spoil out
of his teeth.'* And again, *'I have not withheld the poor from their
desire, nor caused the eye of the widow to fail; nor have I eaten
my morsel myself alone, and the fatherless hath not eaten thereof.
For in my youth compassion grew up with me, and it came forth
with me from my mother's womb.'*

Among his deeds of kindness and justice, this also finds a
place, that he saved our nation from the grasp of the ancient
Enemy by the preachers whom he sent us, and brought it
into the abiding liberty of God. He was full of joy at its conversion and salvation, as he mentions with fitting commendation in his Commentary on Job: 'The tongue of Britain,
which formerly knew only the utterance of barbarity, has
some time since begun to cry the Hebrew *Alleluia* to the praise
of God. The once restless sea now lies quiet beneath the feet
of His saints, and its ungovernable rages, which no earthly
princes could tame by the sword, are now quelled at the simple
word of His priests in the fear of God. Heathen nations who
never trembled before armed hosts now accept and obey the
teachings of the humble. For now that the grace of the knowledge of God has enlightened them and His heavenly words
are received and miracles too are published abroad, the fear of
God restrains them from their former wickedness, and they
desire with all their hearts to win the prize of eternal life.'
In these words Gregory proclaims that the holy Augustine
and his companions guided the English nation to knowledge
of the truth not only by their preaching but also by the display
of miracles.

Among many other matters, blessed Pope Gregory decreed
that Mass should be said over the tombs of the holy Apostles
Peter and Paul in their churches. He also introduced into the
Canon of the Mass three petitions filled with the utmost
perfection: *Order our days in Thy peace, preserve us from eternal*

damnation, and number us in the flock of Thine elect, Through Christ our Lord.

Gregory ruled the Church during the reigns of the Emperors Maurice and Phocas, and in the second year of the latter's reign he passed from this life and entered the true life of heaven. His body was laid to rest on March the twelfth in the church of Saint Peter the Apostle before the sacristy, whence he will one day rise in glory with other shepherds of Holy Church. On his tomb was inscribed this epitaph:

> Receive, O earth, the body that you gave,
> Till God's lifegiving power destroy the grave.
> Over his heaven-bound soul death holds no sway
> Who steps through death into a fairer day.
> The life of this high Pontiff, here at rest,
> With good deeds past all reckoning was blest.
> He fed the hungry, and he clothed the chill,
> And by his teaching shielded souls from ill.
> Wisdom was in his words, and all he wrought
> Was as a pattern, acting what he taught.
> To Christ he led the Angles, by God's grace
> Swelling Faith's armies with a new-won race.
> O holy pastor, all your work and prayer
> To God you offered with a shepherd's care.
> Triumphant now you reap your just reward,
> Raised to high place, the consul of the Lord.

I must here relate a story, handed down to us by the tradition of our forebears, which explains Gregory's deep desire for the salvation of our nation. We are told that one day some merchants who had recently arrived in Rome displayed their many wares in the market-place. Among the crowd who thronged to buy was Gregory, who saw among other merchandise some boys exposed for sale. These had fair complexions, fine-cut features, and beautiful hair. Looking at them with interest, he enquired from what country and what part of the world they came. 'They come from the island of Britain,' he was told, 'where all the people have this

99

appearance.' He then asked whether the islanders were Christians, or whether they were still ignorant heathens. 'They are pagans,' he was informed. 'Alas!' said Gregory with a heartfelt sigh: 'how sad that such bright-faced folk are still in the grasp of the Author of darkness, and that such graceful features conceal minds void of God's grace! What is the name of this race?' 'They are called Angles,' he was told. 'That is appropriate,' he said, 'for they have angelic faces, and it is right that they should become joint-heirs with the angels in heaven. And what is the name of the province from which they have been brought?' 'Deira,' was the answer. 'Good. They shall indeed be rescued *de ira* – from wrath – and called to the mercy of Christ. And what is the name of their king?' 'Aelle,' he was told. 'Then,' said Gregory, making play on the name, 'it is right that their land should echo the praise of God our Creator in the word *Alleluia*.'

Approaching the Pope of the apostolic Roman see – for he was not yet Pope himself – Gregory begged him to send preachers of the word to the English people in Britain to convert them to Christ, and declared his own eagerness to attempt the task should the Pope see fit to direct it. This permission was not forthcoming, for although the Pope himself was willing, the citizens of Rome would not allow Gregory to go so far away from the city. But directly Gregory succeeded to the Papacy himself, he put in hand this long cherished project. He sent other missionaries in his place; but it was his prayers and encouragement that made their mission fruitful. And I have thought it fitting to include this traditional story in the history of our Church.

CHAPTER 2: *Augustine urges the British bishops to cement Catholic unity, and performs a miracle in their presence. Retribution follows their refusal* [A.D. 603]

Meanwhile, with the aid of King Ethelbert, Augustine summoned the bishops and teachers of the nearest

British province* to a conference at a place still known to the
English as Augustine's Oak, which lies on the border between
the Hwiccas and the West Saxons. He began by urging them
to establish brotherly relations with him in Catholic unity, and
to join with him in God's work of preaching the Gospel to
the heathen.

Now the Britons did not keep Easter at the correct time,
but between the fourteenth and twentieth days of the moon
– a calculation depending on a cycle of eighty-four years.
Furthermore, certain other of their customs were at variance
with the universal practice of the Church. But despite protracted discussions, neither the prayers nor the advice nor the
censures of Augustine and his companions could obtain the
compliance of the Britons, who stubbornly preferred their
own customs to those in universal use among Christian
Churches. Augustine then brought this lengthy and fruitless
conference to a close, saying: 'Let us ask our Lord, *who makes
men to be of one mind* in His Father's house, to grant us a sign
from heaven and show us which tradition is to be followed,
and by what roads we are to hasten our steps towards His
kingdom. Bring in some sick person, and let the beliefs and
practice of those who can heal him be accepted as pleasing to
God and to be followed by all.' On the reluctant agreement of
his opponents, a blind Englishmen was led in and presented to
the British priests, from whose ministry he obtained no healing or benefit. Then Augustine, as the occasion demanded,
knelt in prayer to the Father of our Lord Jesus Christ, implor-
ing that the man's lost sight might be restored and prove the
means of bringing the light of spiritual grace to the minds of
countless believers. Immediately the blind man's sight was
restored, and all acknowledged Augustine as the true herald of
the light of Christ. The Britons declared that, while they had
learnt that what Augustine taught was the true way of righteousness, they could not abandon their ancient customs without the consent and approval of their own people, and therefore
asked that a second and fuller conference might be held.

This was arranged, and seven British bishops and many very learned men are said to have attended, who came mainly from their most famous monastery which the English call Bancornaburg,[1] then ruled by Abbot Dinoot. Those summoned to this council first visited a wise and prudent hermit, and enquired of him whether they should abandon their own traditions at Augustine's demand. He answered: 'If he is a man of God, follow him.' 'But how can we be sure of this?' they asked. 'Our Lord says, *Take My yoke upon you and learn of Me, for I am meek and lowly in heart,*' he replied. 'Therefore if Augustine is meek and lowly in heart, it shows that he bears the yoke of Christ himself, and offers it to you. But if he is haughty and unbending, then he is not of God, and we should not listen to him.' Then they asked, 'But how can we know even this?' 'Arrange that he and his followers arrive first at the place appointed for the conference,' answered the hermit. 'If he rises courteously as you approach, rest assured that he is the servant of Christ and do as he asks. But if he ignores you and does not rise, then, since you are in the majority, do not comply with his demands.'

The British bishops carried out his suggestion, and it happened that Augustine remained seated in his chair. Seeing this, they became angry, accusing him of pride and taking pains to contradict all that he said. Augustine then declared: 'There are many points on which your customs conflict with ours, or rather with those of the universal Church. Nevertheless, if you will agree with me on three points, I am ready to countenance all your other customs, although they are contrary to our own. These points are: to keep Easter at the correct time;* to complete the Sacrament of Baptism, by which we are reborn to God, according to the rites of the holy, Roman, and apostolic Church; and to join with us in preaching the word of God to the English.' But the bishops refused these things, nor would they recognize Augustine as their archbishop, saying among themselves that if he would not rise to greet them

1. Bangor-is-Coed, co. Flint.

in the first instance, he would have even less regard for them once they submitted to his authority. Whereupon Augustine, that man of God, is said to have answered with a threat that was also a prophecy: if they refused to accept peace with fellow-Christians, they would be forced to accept war at the hands of enemies; and if they refused to preach to the English the way of life, they would eventually suffer at their hands the penalty of death. And, by divine judgement, all these things happened as Augustine foretold.

Some while after this, the powerful king Ethelfrid, whom I have already mentioned, raised a great army at the City of Legions – which the English call Legacestir[1], but which the Britons more correctly name Carlegion – and made a great slaughter of the faithless Britons. Before battle was joined, he noticed that their priests were assembled apart in a safer place to pray for their soldiers, and he enquired who they were and what they had come there to do. Most of these priests came from the monastery of Bangor, where there are said to have been so many monks that although it was divided into seven sections, each under its own head, none of these sections contained less than three hundred monks, all of whom supported themselves by manual work. Most of these monks, who had kept a three-day fast, had gathered to pray at the battle, guarded by a certain Brocmail, who was there to protect them from the swords of the barbarians while they were intent on prayer. As soon as King Ethelfrid was informed of their purpose, he said: 'If they are crying to their God against us, they are fighting against us even if they do not bear arms.' He therefore directed his first attack against them, and then destroyed the rest of the accursed army, not without heavy loss to his own forces. It is said that of the monks who had come to pray about twelve hundred perished in this battle, and only fifty escaped by flight. Brocmail and his men took to their heels at the first assault, leaving those whom they should have protected unarmed and exposed to the sword-

1. Chester.

strokes of the enemy. Thus, long after his death, was fulfilled Bishop Augustine's prophecy that the faithless Britons, who had rejected the offer of eternal salvation, would incur the punishment of temporal destruction.

CHAPTER 3: *Augustine consecrates Mellitus and Justus as bishops: his own death* [A.D. 604]

IN the year of our Lord 604, Augustine, Archbishop of Britain, consecrated two bishops, Mellitus and Justus. Mellitus was appointed to preach in the province of the East Saxons, which is separated from Kent by the river Thames, and bounded on the east by the sea. Its capital is the city of London, which stands on the banks of the Thames, and is a trading centre for many nations who visit it by land and sea. At this time Sabert, Ethelbert's nephew through his sister Ricula, ruled the province under the suzerainty of Ethelbert, who, as already stated, governed all the English peoples as far north as the Humber. When this province too had received the faith through the preaching of Mellitus, King Ethelbert built a church dedicated to the holy Apostle Paul in the city of London, which he appointed as the episcopal see of Mellitus and his successors. Augustine also consecrated Justus as bishop of a Kentish city which the English call Hrofescaestir[1] after an early chieftain named Hrof. This lies nearly twenty-four miles west of Canterbury, and a church in honour of Saint Andrew the Apostle was built here by King Ethelbert, who made many gifts to the bishops of both these churches as well as to Canterbury; he later added lands and property for the maintenance of the bishop's household.

When our father Augustine, the beloved of God, died, his body was laid to rest just outside the church of the holy Apostles Peter and Paul, since the church was not yet completed or consecrated. But as soon as it was dedicated, his body

1. Rochester.

was brought inside and buried in the north porch with great honour. This is also the last resting-place of all succeeding archbishops except Theodore and Bertwald, whose bodies lie inside the church, no space remaining in the porch. Almost in the centre of the church stands an altar dedicated in honour of blessed Pope Gregory, at which a priest of the place says solemn mass in their memory each Saturday. On the tomb of Augustine is inscribed this epitaph:

'Here rests the Lord Augustine, first Archbishop of Canterbury, who, having been sent here by blessed Gregory, Pontiff of the City of Rome, and supported by God with miracles, guided King Ethelbert and his people from the worship of idols to the Faith of Christ. He ended the days of his duty in peace, and died on the twenty-sixth day of May in the above King's reign.'

CHAPTER 4: *Laurence and his fellow-bishops urge the Scots to maintain the unity of the Church, particularly in the observance of Easter: Mellitus visits Rome* [A.D. 605]

AUGUSTINE was succeeded in the archbishopric by Laurence, whom he had consecrated during his own lifetime; for he feared that even a short interval without a pastor might cause a setback to the newly established Church. In so doing, he followed the precedent set by the Church's first Pastor, blessed Peter, Prince of the Apostles, who, having established the Church in Rome, is said to have consecrated Clement as his assistant and successor. On receiving the dignity of archbishop, Laurence gave constant encouragement and a holy example to his flock, working tirelessly to perfect the edifice of the Church whose foundations he had seen so nobly laid. Nor was his interest limited to the Church newly recruited from the English; for he sought also to extend his pastoral care to the original inhabitants of Britain, and to the Scots of Ireland adjacent to this island of Britain. For having

learned that in their own country the life and practice of the
Scots and of the Britons were in many respects unorthodox –
particularly in the observance of Easter, which, as previously
explained, they did not keep at the right time, but between
the fourteenth and twentieth days of the moon – he wrote
them a letter jointly with his fellow-bishops, urging them to
join in maintaining the unity, peace, and Catholic customs of
the Christian Church established throughout the world. This
letter commences:

'To our dear brothers the lord bishops and abbots throughout Scottish lands: from Laurence, Mellitus, and Justus,
servants of the servants of God.

'When, in accordance with its custom, which holds good
throughout the world, the apostolic see sent us to the western
lands to preach the Gospel to the heathen peoples, we came to
this island of Britain. Until we realized the true situation, we
had a high regard for the devotion both of the Britons and of
the Scots, believing that they followed the customs of the
universal Church. On further acquaintance with the Britons,
we imagined that the Scots must be better. We have now,
however, learned through Bishop Dagan on his visit to this
island, and through Abbot Columbanus in Gaul, that the Scots
are no different from the Britons in their practices. For when
Bishop Dagan visited us, he refused not only to eat with us but
even to take his meal in the same house as ourselves.'

Laurence and his fellow-bishops also wrote a dignified
letter to the British bishops, in which he tried to bring them
into Catholic unity; but the present state of affairs shows how
little he succeeded.

At this time Mellitus, Bishop of London, visited Rome
to acquaint the Pope with the affairs of the Church of the
English. This most reverend Pope had summoned a council
of the bishops of Italy to draw up regulations for monastic
life and discipline, and Mellitus sat with them at this council,
which took place on the twenty-seventh of February 610 in
the eighth year of the Emperor Phocas. The presence of

Mellitus enabled him to subscribe to all the regular decisions of the council and confirm them with his authority, and to convey them to the Churches of the English for their acceptance and promulgation on his return to Britain. He also brought back letters from the Pope both to God's beloved Archbishop Laurence and all his clergy, and to King Ethelbert and his people. This Pope was Boniface [IV], third bishop of Rome after Gregory, who persuaded the Emperor Phocas to give the Christian Church the Roman temple anciently known as the *Pantheon*, as though it were emblematic of all the gods. After solemn purification, Boniface consecrated it as the Church of the Holy Mother of God and all Christian Martyrs; and once its company of devils had been cast out, it became a memorial to the Company of Saints.

CHAPTER 5: *At the deaths of Ethelbert and Sabert their successors revive idolatry: on this account, both Mellitus and Justus leave Britain* [A.D. 616]

IN the year of our Lord 616 – the twenty-first year after Augustine and his companions were dispatched to preach to the English nation – King Ethelbert of the Kentish folk died after a glorious earthly reign of fifty-six years, and entered the eternal joys of the kingdom of heaven. He was the third English king to hold sway over all the provinces south of the river Humber, but he was the first to enter the kingdom of heaven. The first king to hold such overlordship was Aelle, King of the South Saxons; the second was Caelin, King of the West Saxons, known in the speech of his people as Ceaulin; the third, as I have mentioned, was Ethelbert, King of the Kentish folk; the fourth was Redwald, King of the East Angles, who even in the lifetime of Ethelbert was winning pre-eminence for his own people. The fifth was Edwin, King of the Northumbrians, that is, the people living north of the Humber, who was a powerful king, and ruled all the peoples of Britain, both Angles and Britons, with the exception of the Kentish folk. He also brought under English rule the British Mevanian Isles,[1] which lie between Ireland and Britain. The sixth was Oswald, also King of the Northumbrians but a most Christian one, who maintained the same frontiers; the seventh was his brother Oswy,* who for a while ruled the same territory, and to a large extent conquered and made tributary the Picts and Scots in the northern parts of Britain. But I shall speak of these kings later.

King Ethelbert died on the twenty-fourth of February, twenty-one years after embracing the Faith, and was buried in Saint Martin's Porch in the Church of the blessed Apostles Peter and Paul, where Bertha his queen also rests. Among the many benefits that his wisdom conferred on the nation, he introduced with the consent of his counsellors a code of law inspired by the example of the Romans, which was written in English, and remains in force to this day. The first of his laws is designed to protect those whose persons and doctrines he had embraced, and prescribes what satisfaction must be made by any person who steals property from the Church, the bishop, or other clergy.

Ethelbert was son of Irminric, son of Octa, and after his grandfather Oeric, surnamed Oisc, the kings of the Kentish folk are commonly known as Oiscings. The father of Oeric was Hengist, who first came to Britain with his son Oeric at the invitation of Vortigern, as I have already related.

The death of Ethelbert and the accession of his son Eadbald proved to be a severe setback to the growth of the young Church; for not only did he refuse to accept the Faith of Christ, but he was also guilty of such fornication as the Apostle Paul mentions as being unheard of even among the heathen, in that he took his father's (second) wife as his own. His immorality was an incentive to those who, either out of fear or favour to the king his father, had submitted to the discipline

1. Man and Anglesey.

of faith and chastity, to revert to their former uncleanness. However, this apostate king did not escape the scourge of God's punishment; for he was subject to frequent fits of insanity and possessed by an evil spirit.

The death of the Christian King Sabert of the East Saxons aggravated the upheaval; for, when he departed for the heavenly kingdom he left three sons, all pagans, to inherit his earthly kingdom. These were quick to profess idolatry, which they had pretended to abandon during the lifetime of their father, and encouraged their people to return to the old gods. It is told that when they saw Bishop Mellitus offering solemn Mass in church, they said with barbarous presumption: 'Why do you not offer us the white bread which you used to give to our father Saba (for so they used to call him), while you continue to give it to the people in church?' The Bishop answered, 'If you will be washed in the waters of salvation as your father was, you may share in the consecrated bread, as he did; but so long as you reject the water of life, you are quite unfit to receive the Bread of Life.' They retorted: 'We refuse to enter that font and see no need for it; but we want to be strengthened with this bread.' The Bishop then carefully and repeatedly explained that this was forbidden, and that no one was admitted to receive the most holy Communion without the most holy cleansing of Baptism. At last they grew very angry, and said: 'If you will not oblige us by granting such an easy request, you shall no longer remain in our kingdom.' And they drove him into exile, and ordered all his followers to leave their borders.

After his expulsion, Mellitus came to Kent to consult with his fellow-bishops Laurence and Justus on the best course of action; and they decided that it would be better for all of them to return to their own country and serve God in freedom, rather than to remain impotently among heathen who had rejected the Faith. Mellitus and Justus left first and settled in Gaul to await the outcome of events. But the kings who had driven out the herald of truth did not long remain unpunished for their worship of demons; for they and their army fell in battle against the West Saxons. Nevertheless, the fate of the instigators did not cause their people to abandon their evil practices, or to return to the simple faith and love to be found in Christ alone.

CHAPTER 6: *Laurence is reproved by Saint Peter, and converts King Eadbald to Christ. Mellitus and Justus are recalled* [A.D. 616]

ON the very night before Laurence too was to follow Mellitus and Justus from Britain, he ordered his bed to be placed in the Church of the blessed Apostles Peter and Paul, of which we have spoken several times. Here after long and fervent prayers for the sadly afflicted Church he lay down and fell asleep. At dead of night, blessed Peter, Prince of the Apostles, appeared to him, and set about him for a long time with a heavy scourge, demanding with apostolic sternness why he was abandoning the flock entrusted to his care, and to which of the shepherds he would commit Christ's sheep left among the wolves when he fled. 'Have you forgotten my example?' asked Peter. 'For the sake of the little ones whom Christ entrusted to me as proof of His love, I suffered chains, blows, imprisonment, and pain. Finally, I endured death, the death of crucifixion, at the hands of unbelievers and enemies of Christ, so that at last I might be crowned with Him.' Deeply moved by the words and scourging of blessed Peter, Christ's servant Laurence sought audience with the king early next morning, and removing his garment, showed him the marks of the lash. The king was astounded, and enquired who had dared to scourge so eminent a man; and when he learned that it was for his own salvation that the archbishop had suffered so severely at the hands of Christ's own Apostle, he was greatly alarmed. He renounced his idolatry, gave up his unlawful wife, accepted the Christian Faith, and was baptized, henceforward promoting the welfare of the Church with every means at his disposal.

The king also sent to Gaul and recalled Mellitus and Justus, giving them free permission to return and set their churches in order: so, the year after they left, they returned. Justus came back to his own city of Rochester; but the people of London preferred their own idolatrous priests, and refused to accept Mellitus as bishop. And since the king's authority in the realm was not so effective as that of his father, he was powerless to restore the bishop to his see against the refusal and resistance of the pagans. After his conversion, however, he and his people were zealous to observe the teachings of our Lord, and in the monastery of the most blessed Prince of the Apostles he built a church to the Holy Mother of God, which was consecrated by Archbishop Mellitus.

CHAPTER 7: *The prayers of Bishop Mellitus put out a fire in his city* [A.D. 619]

ON the second day of February in the same king's reign, the blessed Archbishop Laurence passed to the kingdom of heaven, and was buried in the monastery church of the holy Apostle Peter next to his predecessor. Mellitus, Bishop of London, became the third Archbishop of Canterbury in the succession of Augustine, while Justus, who was still living, ruled the Church of Rochester. While these bishops were guiding the Church of the English with great care and energy, they received letters of encouragement from Boniface, Bishop of the apostolic Roman see, who succeeded Deusdedit in the year of our Lord 619. And although Mellitus became crippled with the gout, his sound and ardent mind overcame his troublesome infirmity, ever reaching above earthly things to those that are heavenly in love and devotion. Noble by birth, he was even nobler in mind.

I record one among many instances of his virtue. One day

the city of Canterbury was set on fire through carelessness, and the spreading flames threatened to destroy it. Water failed to extinguish the fire, and already a considerable area of the city was destroyed. As the raging flames were sweeping rapidly towards his residence, the bishop, trusting in the help of God where man's help had failed, ordered himself to be carried into the path of its leaping and darting advance. In the place where the flames were pressing most fiercely stood the Church of the Four Crowned Martyrs.* Hither the bishop was borne by his attendants, and here by his prayers this infirm man averted the danger which all the efforts of strong men had been powerless to check. For the southerly wind, which had been spreading the flames throughout the city, suddenly veered to the north, thus saving the places that lay in their path: then it dropped altogether, so that the fires burned out and died. Thus Mellitus, the man of God, afire with love for him, because it had been his practice by constant prayers and teaching to fend off storms of spiritual evil from himself and his people, was deservedly empowered to save them from material winds and flames.

Having ruled the Church five years, Mellitus likewise departed to the heavenly kingdom in the reign of King Eadbald, and was laid to rest with his predecessors in the same monastery church of the holy Apostle Peter on the twenty-fourth day of April, in the year of our Lord 624.

CHAPTER 8: *Pope Boniface [V] sends the* pallium *with a letter to Justus, Mellitus' successor* [A.D. 624]

JUSTUS, Bishop of Rochester, at once succeeded Mellitus as archbishop. He consecrated Romanus as Bishop of Rochester in his place, having received authority to consecrate bishops from Pope Boniface, successor to Pope Deusdedit. This letter of authority runs as follows:

'BONIFACE, to his well beloved brother Justus. The con-

tents of your letter and the success granted to your work are
double evidence of your devotion and diligence in spreading
the Gospel of Christ. Almighty God has not been unmindful
of the honour due to His Name, or of the reward due to your
labours; for He has faithfully promised the preachers of the
Gospel, *"Lo, I am with you alway, even unto the end of the
world."* This promise He has of His mercy especially fulfilled
in your own ministry, opening the hearts of the nations to
receive the mystery of the Gospel through your preaching.
For He has crowned the wonderful progress of your good
work with His blessing, and has granted a plentiful increase
to the faithful employment of the talents entrusted to you,
which will set your seal on many generations to come. This is
the just reward of the constancy with which you have held to
your appointed mission, while with commendable patience
you await the redemption of this nation, so that it may profit
through the merits of those who work for its salvation; for
our Lord Himself has said, *"He that endureth to the end shall
be saved."* By your patient hope and courageous endurance
you have been saved, so that you may cleanse the hearts of
the heathen from the ills implanted by nature and by superstition, and obtain mercy for them from their Saviour.
We learn, furthermore, from the letters of our son King
Ethelwald,[1] how your profound knowledge of God's holy
word has guided him to a real conversion and acceptance of
the true Faith. We firmly trust in God's patience and mercy,
and are confident that your preaching and ministry will effect
a complete conversion of his own people and also of their
neighbours. In this way, as the Scripture says, will you receive
the reward of a task well done from the Lord and Giver of all
good things, and the universal profession of the nations, after
receiving the mysteries of the Christian Faith, will proclaim:
*"Their sound is gone out through all the earth, and their words to
the end of the world."*

   'Moved by your devotion, my brother, we are sending

1. i.e. Eadbald.

you by the bearer of this letter the *pallium*, which we grant you the privilege of wearing only when you celebrate the Holy Mysteries. We also grant you authority, under the guiding mercy of our Lord, to consecrate bishops as occasion may require, in order that the Gospel of Christ may be diffused by the mouths of many preachers among all nations as yet unconverted. We are confident that you will maintain with whole-hearted sincerity this dignity granted you by the favour of the Apostolic See, bearing in mind all that is symbolized by this highest of honours which you have received to wear on your shoulders. And, as you implore God's mercy, endeavour so to live and labour that when you stand before the judgement seat of God, you may display this honour which we grant you not only unstained but enhanced by the witness of all the souls which you have won.

'God keep you in safety, my dearest brother.'

CHAPTER 9: *The reign of King Edwin: Paulinus comes to preach the Gospel to him, and first administers the Sacrament of Baptism to his daughter and others* [A.D. 625]

AT this time, the people of the Northumbrians, the English living north of the Humber, under Edwin their king received the Faith through the ministry of Paulinus, whom I have already mentioned. As a sign that he would come to the Faith and the heavenly kingdom, King Edwin received wide additions to his earthly realm, and brought under his sway all the territories inhabited either by English or by Britons, an achievement unmatched by any previous English king. He also brought the Isles of Anglesey and Man under English rule: of these, the southern island is the larger and more fertile, and by English reckoning, extends to nine hundred and sixty hides, while the other island extends to rather more than three hundred.

The Northumbrian people's acceptance of the Faith of

Christ came about through their king's alliance with the kings of Kent by his marriage to Ethelberga, known as Tata, a daughter of King Ethelbert. Edwin sent an embassy of nobles to her brother Eadbald, then king of the Kentish folk, to request her hand in marriage, but received the reply that it was not permissible for a Christian maiden to be given in marriage to a heathen husband, lest the Christian Faith and Sacraments be profaned by her association with a king who was wholly ignorant of the worship of the true God. When Edwin's messengers returned with this reply, he gave an assurance that he would place no obstacles in the way of the Christian Faith, and would afford complete freedom to Ethelberga and her attendants, both men and women, priests and servants, to live and worship in accordance with Christian belief and practice. He also professed himself willing to accept the religion of Christ if, on examination, his advisers decided that it appeared more holy and acceptable to God than their own.

On this understanding, the maiden was betrothed and sent to Edwin; and in accordance with the agreement Paulinus, a man beloved of God, was consecrated bishop, so that he could accompany the princess as her chaplain and by daily Mass and instruction preserve her and her companions from corruption by their association with the heathen.

Paulinus was consecrated bishop by Archbishop Justus on July 21st, 625, and came to Edwin with the princess as her spiritual counsellor in the marriage. But he was further determined to bring the nation to which he was sent to the knowledge of the Christian truth, and to fulfil the Apostle's saying, '*to espouse her to one husband, that he might present her as a chaste virgin to Christ*'. Therefore, directly he entered the province he began to toil unceasingly not only by God's help to maintain the faith of his companions unimpaired, but if possible to bring some of the heathen to grace and faith by his teaching. But although he laboured long, yet as the Apostle says, '*the god of this world blinded the minds of them which believed not, lest the light of the glorious Gospel of Christ should shine unto them*'.

During the following year, an assassin named Eumer was sent into the province by Cuichelm, King of the West Saxons, in order to rob Edwin both of his kingdom and his life. This man had a double-edged, poisoned dagger, to ensure that if the wound itself were not mortal, the poison would complete its work. On Easter Day Eumer arrived at the royal residence by the Derwent, and was admitted into the king's presence on the pretext of delivering a message from his master. And while he was artfully delivering his pretended message, he suddenly sprang up, and drawing the dagger from beneath his clothes, attacked the king. Swift to see the king's peril, Lilla, his counsellor and best friend, having no shield to protect the king, interposed his own body to receive the blow; but even so, it was delivered with such force that it wounded the king through the body of his warrior. The assassin was immediately attacked on all sides, but killed yet another of the king's men named Fordhere in the ensuing struggle.

On the same holy night of Easter Day, the queen was delivered of a daughter, to be named Eanfled; and as the king thanked his gods in the presence of Bishop Paulinus for the birth of his daughter, the bishop gave thanks to Christ, and told the king that it was Christ who had given the queen a safe and painless delivery in response to his prayers. The king was greatly pleased at his words, and promised that if God would grant him life and victory over the king his enemy who had sent the assassin, he would renounce his idols and serve Christ; and as a pledge that he would keep his word he gave his infant daughter to Paulinus to be consecrated to Christ. Accordingly, on the Feast of Pentecost this infant, together with twelve others of her household, was the first of the Northumbrians to receive Baptism.

When the king had recovered from the assassin's wound, he summoned his forces, marched against the West Saxons, and in the ensuing campaign either slew or forced to surrender all those who had plotted his murder. Returning home victorious, the king would not receive the Sacrament of Christian Baptism at once or without due consideration, although he had already abandoned idol-worship when he promised that he would serve Christ. But he wished first to receive a full course of instruction in the Faith from the venerable Paulinus, and to discuss his proper course with those of his counsellors on whose wisdom he placed most reliance. For the king was by nature a wise and prudent man, and often sat alone in silent converse with himself for long periods, turning over in his inmost heart what he should do and which religion he should follow.

CHAPTER 10: *Pope Boniface writes to the king, urging him to accept the Faith*

ABOUT this time, the king received a letter from Boniface, Bishop of the apostolic Roman see, urging him to accept the Faith. Here follows a copy of this letter, sent by the blessed and apostolic Pope Boniface of the Church and City of Rome to the illustrious Edwin, King of the English:

'To the illustrious Edwin, King of the English: Boniface, Bishop, servant of the servants of God.

'The words of man can never express the power of the supreme Divinity, abiding in His own greatness, invisible, inscrutable, eternal, such that no human intelligence can understand or define how great it is. Nevertheless, God's humanity having opened the doors of man's heart to admit Him, mercifully infuses into their minds by secret inspiration some knowledge of Himself. Accordingly, we have undertaken to extend our priestly responsibility to disclose to you the fullness of the Christian Faith, in order that we may impart to your senses also the Gospel of Christ, which our Saviour commanded to be preached to all nations, and may offer you the medicine of salvation.

'The clemency of the Divine Majesty, who by His Word

alone created and established the heavens and the earth, the
sea and all that in them is, has ordained the laws by which
they subsist; and by the counsel of His co-eternal Word in the
unity of the Holy Spirit He has formed man after His own
image and likeness from the dust of the earth. He has further
granted him a most excellent prerogative, placing him above
all other creatures in order that he may inherit eternal life by
obedience to His commandments. This God – Father, Son,
and Holy Spirit – the undivided Trinity – is adored and
worshipped by the human race from east to west, which con-
fesses Him by the faith that brings salvation as Creator of all
things and Maker of all men. To him are subject all imperial
power and authority; for it is by him that kingship is conferred. Of His bountiful mercy and for the well-being of all
his creatures, He has been pleased to warm with His Holy
Spirit the frozen hearts of the most distant nations of the
world in a most wonderful manner to knowledge of Himself.

'We presume that Your Majesty has heard in fuller detail,
as from a neighbouring territory, how our Redeemer in His
mercy has brought light to our excellent son Eadbald and the
nations subject to him. We therefore trust that Heaven's
mercy will grant this wonderful gift to you as it has to him,
more especially as we understand that your gracious Queen
and true partner is already endowed with the gift of eternal
life through the regeneration of Holy Baptism. In this letter
we affectionately urge Your Majesties to renounce idol-
worship, reject the mummery of temples and the deceitful
flattery of omens, and believe in God the Father Almighty,
and in His Son Jesus Christ, and in the Holy Spirit. This Faith
will free you from Satan's bondage, and through the libera-
tive power of the holy and undivided Trinity you will inherit
eternal life.

'The profound guilt of those who perversely cling to pernicious superstition and idolatrous worship is clearly shown
by the damnable example of those they adore. Of such the
Psalmist says: "*All the gods of the nations are idols; but the Lord*

made the heavens." And again: *"Eyes have they, but they see not: they have ears, but they hear not: noses have they, but they smell not; they have hands, but they handle not; feet have they, but they walk not. They that make them are like unto them; so is everyone that trusteth in them."* How can such objects have power to help you, when they are made for you from perishable materials by the labour of your own subjects and servants? Even their inanimate resemblance to living shapes is due solely to man's craftsmanship. Unless you move them they cannot move, but are like a stone fixed in its place: they are manufactured, but have no intelligence, being utterly insensible and having no power to hurt or help. We cannot understand how people can be so deluded as to worship as gods objects to which they themselves have given the likeness of a body.

'Accept therefore the sign of the Holy Cross, by which the entire human race has been redeemed, and exorcize from your heart the damnable crafts and devices of the Devil, who jealously opposes all the workings of God's goodness. Overthrow and destroy these artificial gods of your own making; and the very destruction of these things, which never drew the breath of life and could never receive understanding from their makers, will itself afford you clear evidence of the nothingness of these objects of your former worship. Consider, you yourselves, to whom God has given the breath of life, are nobler than these man-made things; for Almighty God has ordered your descent through countless generations from the first man that He created. Therefore accept the knowledge of your Creator, who breathed into your frame the breath of life, and who sent His only-begotten Son for your redemption, that He might deliver you from original sin and the evil power of the Devil, and grant you the prize of Heaven.

'Accept the message of the Christian teachers and the Gospel that they proclaim. Believe in God the Father Almighty, and in Jesus Christ His Son and in the Holy Spirit, the inseparable Trinity. Spurn the temptations of the Devil, and reject all the suggestions of our malicious and deceitful enemy. Thus, born again by water and the Holy Spirit, you will be empowered by God's generous aid to abide in the splendour of eternal glory with Him in whom you shall come to believe.

'We impart to you the blessing of your protector, blessed Peter, Prince of the Apostles. With it we send you a tunic with a golden ornament, and a cloak from Ancyra, asking Your Majesty to accept these gifts with the same goodwill as that with which we send them.'

CHAPTER 11: *The Pope writes to the Queen, urging her to exert her influence to obtain the king's salvation*

THE Pope also wrote to Queen Ethelberga as follows. A copy of the letter of the blessed and apostolic Boniface, Pope of the City of Rome, to Ethelberga, Queen of King Edwin:

'To his illustrious daughter, Queen Ethelberga, from Bishop Boniface, servant of the servants of God.

'In His great providence, our loving Redeemer has offered a saving remedy to the human race, which He has saved from the Devil's enslaving tyranny by the shedding of His own precious Blood. Christ has made His Name known to the nations in various ways, so that they may acknowledge their Creator by accepting the mysteries of the Christian Faith. God in His mercy has revealed this truth to Your Majesty's own mind in your own mystical cleansing and regeneration. We have been greatly encouraged by God's goodness in granting you, through your own profession of faith, an opportunity to kindle a spark of the true religion in your husband; for in this way He will more swiftly inspire not only the mind of your illustrious Consort to love of Him, but the minds of your subjects as well.

'We have been informed by those who came to report the laudable conversion of our glorious son King Eadbald that Your Majesty, who has also received the wonderful sacrament of the Christian Faith, shows a shining example of good works, pleasing to God. We also know that you carefully shun idol-worship and the allurements of temples and divinations; and that, having given your allegiance to Christ, you are unshakeably devoted to the love of our Redeemer and labour constantly to propagate the Christian Faith. Out of pastoral affection, we particularly enquired about your illustrious husband and learned that he still serves abominable idols and is slow to listen to the teaching of the preachers. It has caused us deep grief to hear that your partner remains a stranger to the knowledge of the most high and undivided Trinity. Our paternal responsibility moves us to urge Your Christian Majesty, imbued with the force of divine inspiration, not to avoid the duty imposed on us in season and out of season, in order that, with the assistance and strength of our Lord and Saviour Jesus Christ, the King also may be added to the Christian fold. Only in this way will you enjoy the full privileges of marriage in perfect union; for the Scripture says, *"The two shall become one flesh."* But how can it be called a true union between you, so long as he remains alienated from the daylight of your Faith by the barrier of dark and lamentable error?

'Let it therefore be your constant prayer that God of His mercy will bless and enlighten the King, so that you, who are united in one flesh by the ties of bodily affection, may after this fleeting life remain united for ever in the bond of faith. My illustrious daughter, persevere in using every effort to soften his heart by teaching him the commandments of God. Help him to understand the excellence of the mystery that you have accepted by believing and the marvellous worth of the reward that you have been accounted worthy to receive in this new birth. Melt the coldness of his heart by teaching him about the Holy Spirit, so that the warmth of divine faith

may set his mind on fire through your constant encouragement and remove the numbing and deadening errors of
paganism. If you do this, the witness of the Holy Spirit will
most certainly be fulfilled in you, that "*the unbelieving
husband shall be saved through the believing wife.*" For this is why
you have received our Lord's merciful goodness, in order that
you may restore to your Redeemer with increase the fruits
of faith and of the boundless blessings entrusted to you. We
shall not cease from constant prayer that God will assist and
guide you to accomplish this.

'Having mentioned this matter, as fatherly duty and
affection demands, we beg you to inform us, as soon as a
suitable messenger is available, what measure of success God's
goodness grants you in the conversion of your husband and
the people over whom you reign. Good news will greatly
relieve our mind, which anxiously awaits the longed-for salvation of you and yours. And when we see the glory of the
divine atonement spreading ever more widely among you, we
shall give glad and heartfelt thanks to God, the Giver of all
good things, and to blessed Peter, Prince of the Apostles.

'We impart to you the blessing of your protector, blessed
Peter, Prince of the Apostles. With it we send you a silver
mirror, together with a gold and ivory comb, asking Your
Majesty to accept these gifts with the same goodwill as that
with which we send them.'

CHAPTER 12: *King Edwin is moved to accept the Faith by a
vision seen during his exile* [A.D. 625]

SUCH was the letter written by Pope Boniface on the salvation of King Edwin and his people. But the principal
factor influencing the king to study and accept the truths of
salvation was a heavenly vision which God in his mercy had
once granted the king when he was an exile at the court of
Redwald, King of the Angles. For although Paulinus found

it difficult to bring the king's proud mind to accept the
humility of the way of salvation or to acknowledge the mystery of the life-giving Cross, he nevertheless continued, by
words of exhortation addressed to men and words of sup-
plication addressed to the divine compassion, to strive for the
conversion of the king and his nation. It seems most likely
that Paulinus finally learnt in the spirit the nature of the
vision previously vouchsafed to the king. Whereupon he lost
no time in urging the king to implement the promise that he
had made at the time of the vision, and which he had undertaken to fulfil should he be delivered out of his troubles
and ascend the throne of the kingdom.

Now the vision was this. When his predecessor Ethelfrid
was persecuting him, Edwin wandered as an unknown
fugitive for many years through many lands and kingdoms,
until at length he came to Redwald and asked him for protection against the plots of his powerful enemy. Redwald gave
him a ready welcome and promised to do everything he asked.
But as soon as Ethelfrid heard that he had arrived in that province and that he and his companions were living at the king's
court as his friends, he sent messengers to offer Redwald a
large sum of money to murder him. Obtaining no satisfaction, he sent a second and third time, offering even heavier
bribes and threatening war if his demand were refused. At
length Redwald, either intimidated by his threats or corrupted
by his bribes, agreed to his demand and promised either to
kill Edwin or to surrender him to Ethelfrid's envoys. This plot
was discovered by a loyal friend of Edwin, who went to his
room early one night when he was about to retire and, calling
him out, warned him of the king's wicked intentions, adding:
'If you are willing, I will guide you at this very hour out of
this province and take you to some place where neither
Redwald nor Ethelfrid can find you.' Edwin replied: 'Thank
you for your goodwill. But I cannot act as you suggest. I cannot be the first to break the agreement that I have made with
so great a king, who has so far done me no harm nor shown

any hostility towards me. If I must die, I would rather die by his hand than by a hand less noble. For what refuge remains for me, who have already wandered for so many years in every corner of Britain, trying to escape the machinations of my enemies?' When his friend had left, Edwin remained, sitting sadly alone outside the palace, tossed upon conflicting tides of thought, and not knowing what to do or where to turn.

He had remained for a long time in silent thought, tormented by inward fires that brought no light, when suddenly, at dead of night, he saw a man approaching whose face and appearance were strange to him and whose unexpected arrival caused him considerable alarm. But the stranger came up and greeted him, asking why he was sitting sadly on a stone, wakeful and alone at an hour when everyone else was at rest and asleep. Edwin asked what concern it might be of his whether he passed the night indoors or out of doors. In reply, the man said: 'Don't think that I am unaware why you are sad and sleepless and why you are keeping watch outside alone. I know very well who you are, what your troubles are, and what impending evils you dread. But tell me this: what reward will you give the man, whoever he may be, who can deliver you from your troubles and persuade Redwald not to harm you or betray you to death at the hands of your enemies?' Edwin answered that he would give any reward in his power in return for such an outstanding service. Then the other went on: 'And what if he also promised, and not in vain, that you should become king, crush your enemies, and enjoy greater power than any of your forbears, greater indeed than any king who has ever been among the English nation?' Heartened by these enquiries, Edwin readily promised that, in return for such blessings, he would give ample proofs of his gratitude. The stranger then asked a third question: 'If the man who can truthfully foretell such good fortune can also give you better and wiser guidance for your life and salvation than anything known to your parents and kinsfolk, will you

promise to obey him and follow his salutary advice?' Edwin
at once promised that he would faithfully follow the guidance
of anyone who could save him out of so many troubles and
raise him to a throne. On this assurance, the man who
addressed him laid his right hand on Edwin's head, saying:
'When you receive this sign, remember this occasion and our
conversation, and do not delay the fulfilment of your promise.' Hereupon, it is said, he vanished, and Edwin realized
that it was not a man but a spirit who had appeared to him.

The young prince was still sitting there alone, greatly
heartened by what he had heard, but puzzling over the identity and origin of the being who had talked with him, when
his loyal friend approached with a cheerful greeting, and said:
'Get up and come inside. You can now cast aside your cares and
sleep without fear; for the king has had a change of heart. He
now intends you no harm, and means to keep the promise that
he made you. For when he privately told the queen of his
intention to deal with you as I warned, she dissuaded him, saying that it was unworthy in a great king to sell his best friend
in the hour of need for gold, and worse still to sacrifice his
royal honour, the most valuable of all possessions, for love of
money.' In brief, the king did as she advised, and not only
refused to surrender the exiled prince to the envoys of his
enemy but assisted him to recover his kingdom. As soon as
the envoys had gone home, he raised a great army to make war
on Ethelfrid and allowing him no time to summon his full
strength, encountered him with a great preponderance of
force and killed him. In this battle, which was fought in
Mercian territory on the east bank of the river Idle, Raegenhere,
son of Redwald, also met his death. So Edwin, as his vision
had foretold, not only escaped the plots of his enemy but
succeeded to his throne at his death.

While king Edwin hesitated to accept the word of God at
Paulinus' preaching, he used to sit alone for hours, as I have
said, earnestly deliberating what he should do and what
religion he should follow. On one of these occasions, the

man of God came to him and, laying his right hand on his head, enquired whether he remembered this sign. The king trembled and would have fallen at his feet; but Paulinus raised him and said in a friendly voice: 'God has helped you to escape from the hands of the enemies whom you feared, and it is through His bounty that you have received the kingdom that you desired. Remember the third promise that you made, and hesitate no longer. Accept the Faith and keep the commands of Him who has delivered you from all your earthly troubles and raised you to the glory of an earthly kingdom. If you will henceforward obey His will, which he reveals to you through me, he will save you likewise from the everlasting doom of the wicked and give you a place in His eternal kingdom in heaven.'

CHAPTER 13 : *Edwin holds a council with his chief men about accepting the Faith of Christ. The high priest destroys his own altars* [A.D. 627]

WHEN he heard this, the king answered that it was his will as well as his duty to accept the Faith that Paulinus taught, but said that he must still discuss the matter with his principal advisers and friends,* so that, if they were in agreement with him, they might all be cleansed together in Christ the Fount of Life. Paulinus agreed, and the king kept his promise. He summoned a council of the wise men, and asked each in turn his opinion of this strange doctrine and this new way of worshipping the godhead that was being proclaimed to them.

Coifi, the Chief Priest, replied without hesitation: 'Your Majesty, let us give careful consideration to this new teaching; for I frankly admit that, in my experience, the religion that we have hitherto professed seems valueless and powerless. None of your subjects has been more devoted to the service of our gods than myself; yet there are many to whom you show greater favour, who receive greater honours, and who are more successful in all their undertakings. Now, if the gods had any power, they would surely have favoured myself, who have been more zealous in their service. Therefore, if on examination you perceive that these new teachings are better and more effectual, let us not hesitate to accept them.'

Another of the king's chief men signified his agreement with this prudent argument, and went on to say: 'Your Majesty, when we compare the present life of man on earth with that time of which we have no knowledge, it seems to me like the swift flight of a single sparrow through the banqueting-hall where you are sitting at dinner on a winter's day with your thanes and counsellors. In the midst there is a comforting fire to warm the hall; outside, the storms of winter rain or snow are raging. This sparrow flies swiftly in through one door of the hall, and out through another. While he is inside, he is safe from the winter storms; but after a few moments of comfort, he vanishes from sight into the wintry world from which he came. Even so, man appears on earth for a little while; but of what went before this life or of what follows, we know nothing. Therefore, if this new teaching has brought any more certain knowledge, it seems only right that we should follow it.' The other elders and counsellors of the king, under God's guidance, gave similar advice.

Coifi then added that he wished to hear Paulinus' teaching about God in greater detail; and when, at the king's bidding, this had been given, he exclaimed: 'I have long realized that there is nothing in our way of worship; for the more diligently I sought after truth in our religion, the less I found. I now publicly confess that this teaching clearly reveals truths that will afford us the blessings of life, salvation, and eternal happiness. Therefore, Your Majesty, I submit that the temples and altars that we have dedicated to no advantage be immediately desecrated and burned.' In short, the king granted blessed Paulinus full permission to preach, renounced idolatry, and professed his acceptance of the Faith of Christ.

And when he asked the Chief Priest who should be the first to
profane the altars and shrines of the idols, together with the
enclosures that surrounded them, Coifi replied: 'I will do this
myself; for now that the true God has granted me knowledge,
who more suitably than I can set a public example and destroy
the idols that I worshipped in ignorance?' So he formally
renounced his empty superstitions and asked the king to give
him arms and a stallion – for hitherto it had not been lawful
for the Chief Priest to carry arms or to ride anything but a
mare – and, thus equipped, he set out to destroy the idols.
Girded with a sword and with a spear in his hand, he mounted
the king's stallion and rode up to the idols. When the crowd
saw him, they thought he had gone mad; but without
hesitation, as soon as he reached the temple, he cast into it the
spear he carried and thus profaned it. Then, full of joy at his
knowledge of the worship of the true God, he told his companions to set fire to the temple and its enclosures and destroy
them. The site where these idols once stood is still shown, not
far east of York, beyond the river Derwent, and is known
today as Goodmanham. Here it was that the Chief Priest,
inspired by the true God, desecrated and destroyed the altars
that he had himself dedicated.

CHAPTER 14: *Edwin and his people accept the Faith, and are
baptized by Paulinus* [A.D. 627]

So King Edwin, with all the nobility of his kingdom and
a large number of humbler folk, accepted the Faith
and were washed in the cleansing waters of Baptism in the
eleventh year of his reign, which was the year of our Lord
627, and about one hundred and eighty years after the first
arrival of the English in Britain. The king's Baptism took
place at York on Easter Day, the 12th of April, in the church
of Saint Peter the Apostle, which the king had hastily built of
timber* during the time of his instruction and preparation for

Baptism; and in this city he established the see of his teacher and bishop Paulinus. Soon after his Baptism, at Paulinus' suggestion, he gave orders to build on the same site a larger and more noble basilica of stone, which was to enclose the little oratory he had built before. The foundations were laid, and the walls of a square church began to rise around this little oratory; but before they reached their appointed height, the cruel death of the king left the work to be completed by Oswald his successor. Thenceforward for six years, until the close of Edwin's reign, Paulinus preached the word in that province with the king's full consent and approval, and as many as were predestined to eternal life believed and were baptized. Among these were Osfrid and Eadfrid, sons of King Edwin, who were both born to him in exile of Coenburg, daughter of Cearl, King of the Mercians.

At a later date, other children of his by Queen Ethelberga were also baptized: these included a son, Ethelhun; a daughter, Ethelthryd; and another son, Wuscfrea. The two former were snatched from life while still wearing their white baptismal robes, and were buried in the church at York. Yffi, son of Osfrid, was also baptized, and many others of noble and princely rank. Indeed, so great was the fervour of faith and desire for baptism among the Northumbrian people that Paulinus is said to have accompanied the king and queen to the royal residence at Ad-Gefrin[1] and remained there thirty-six days constantly occupied in instructing and baptizing. During this period, he did nothing from dawn to dusk but proclaim Christ's saving message to the people, who gathered from all the surrounding villages and countryside; and when he had instructed them, he washed them in the cleansing waters of Baptism in the nearby River Glen. This residence was abandoned by the later kings, who built another at a place called Maelmin.

These events took place in the province of Bernicia. In the province of Deira, where Paulinus often stayed with the king,

1. Yeavering, in Glendale.

he baptized in the River Swale, which flows near the village of Catterick; for during the infancy of the church in those parts it was not yet possible to build oratories or baptisteries. A basilica was built at the royal residence of Campodonum;[1] but this, together with all the buildings of the residence, was burned by the pagans who killed King Edwin, and later kings replaced this seat by another in the vicinity of Loidis.[2] The stone altar of this church survived the fire, and is preserved in the monastery that lies in Elmet Wood and is ruled by the most reverend priest and abbot Thrydwulf.

CHAPTER 15: *The Province of the East Angles accepts the Christian Faith* [A.D. 627]

So great was Edwin's zeal for the true Faith that he persuaded King Earpwald, son of Redwald, King of the East Angles, to abandon his superstitious idolatry and accept the Faith and Sacraments of Christ with his whole province. His father Redwald had in fact long before this received Christian Baptism in Kent, but to no good purpose; for on his return home his wife and certain perverse advisers persuaded him to apostatize from the true Faith. So his last state was worse than the first: for, like the ancient Samaritans, he tried to serve both Christ and the ancient gods, and he had in the same temple an altar for the holy Sacrifice of Christ side by side with an altar on which victims were offered to devils. Aldwulf, king of that province, who lived into our own times, testifies that this temple was still standing in his day and that he had seen it when a boy. This King Redwald was a man of noble descent but ignoble in his actions: he was son of Tytila, and grandson of Wuffa, after whom all kings of the East Angles are called Wuffings.

Not long after Earpwald's acceptance of Christianity, he

1. Possibly Doncaster, or Slack near Huddersfield.
2. Leeds.

was killed by a pagan named Ricbert, and for three years the province relapsed into heathendom, until Earpwald's brother Sigbert succeeded to the kingship. Sigbert was a devout Christian and a man of learning, who had been an exile in Gaul during his brother's lifetime, and was there converted to the Christian Faith, so that when he began his reign, he laboured to bring about the conversion of his whole realm. In this enterprise he was nobly assisted by Bishop Felix, who came to Archbishop Honorius from the Burgundian region, where he had been brought up and ordained, and, by his own desire, was sent by him to preach the word of life to this nation of the Angles. Nor did he fail in his purpose; for, like a good farmer, he reaped a rich harvest of believers. He delivered the entire province from its age-old wickedness and infelicity, brought it to the Christian Faith and works of righteousness and – in full accord with the significance of his own name – guided it towards eternal felicity. His episcopal see was established at Dunwich; and after ruling the province as its bishop for seventeen years, he ended his days there in peace.

CHAPTER 16: *Paulinus preaches the Word of God in the Province of Lindsey. The reign of King Edwin* [A.D. 628]

PAULINUS also preached the word of God to the province of Lindsey, which lies immediately south of the Humber, and extends to the sea. His first convert was Blaecca, Reeve of the city of Lincoln, with all his family. In this city he also built a stone church of fine workmanship, which today, either through neglect or enemy damage, has lost its roof, although the walls are still standing. And each year miracles of healing occur in this place for the benefit of those who seek it in faith. When Justus had departed to Christ, it was in this church that Paulinus consecrated Honorius as bishop in his stead, as I will describe in due course.

The priest Deda, abbot of the monastery of Partney and a most reliable authority, when relating the story of the Faith in this province, told me that one of the oldest inhabitants had described to him how he and many others had been baptized by Paulinus in the presence of King Edwin, and how the ceremony took place at noon in the river Trent, close to the city which the English call Tiowulfingacaestir. He used to paint a verbal portrait of Paulinus as a tall man having a slight stoop, with black hair, an ascetic face, a thin hooked nose, and a venerable and awe-inspiring presence. Paulinus was also assisted in his ministry by the deacon James, a man of great energy and repute in Christ's Church, who lived until our own day.

So peaceful was it in those parts of Britain under King Edwin's jurisdiction that the proverb still runs that a woman could carry her new-born babe across the island from sea to sea without any fear of harm. Such was the king's concern for the welfare of his people that in a number of places where he had noticed clear springs adjacent to the highway he ordered posts to be erected with brass bowls hanging from them, so that travellers could drink and refresh themselves. And so great was the people's affection for him, and so great the awe in which he was held, that no one wished or ventured to use these bowls for any other purpose. So royally was the king's dignity maintained throughout his realm that whether in battle or on a peaceful progress on horseback through city, town, and countryside in the company of his thanes, the royal standard was always borne before him. Even when he passed through the streets on foot, the standard known to the Romans as a *Tufa*,* and to the English as a *Tuf*, was carried in front of him.

At this time, Honorius had succeeded Boniface as Bishop of the apostolic see. Learning that the Northumbrian people and their king had been converted to the Faith and confession of Christ by the labours of Paulinus, he sent him the *pallium* and with it a letter of encouragement to King Edwin, urging him with fatherly affection to ensure that his people maintained and made progress in the true Faith that they had received. This letter ran as follows:

'To his most excellent son, the most illustrious Edwin, King of the English, from Bishop Honorius, servant of the servants of God, Greeting.

'Your sincere Christian character, afire with ardent faith in the worship of your Creator, has shone out far and wide. It has been spoken of throughout the world and has reaped a rich harvest for your labours. For you who are kings acknowledge your kingship when by your worship of God you express belief in your own king and creator according to the true teaching which you have received about Him and, so far as human nature allows, serve Him with a sincere and devout mind. And what more can we offer God than our perseverance in doing good, our worship and confession of Him as Creator of the human race, and the zealous fulfilment of our vows? Accordingly, most noble son, our paternal love rightly moves us to urge you to labour with vigilant mind and constant prayer to preserve yourself wholly in that state of grace to which God in His mercy has called you. He who in this world has deigned to deliver you from all error, and led you to the knowledge of His Name, will thus also prepare a place for you in our heavenly home. Make a regular study of the writings of your teacher and my master Gregory of apostolic memory, and constantly bear in mind the loving teaching which he so gladly gave for the benefit of your souls, so that his prayers may obtain an increase in your

kingdom and people, and bring you blameless to Almighty
God.

'We are glad to accede to your requests on behalf of your
bishops without delay, and in so doing we pay tribute to the
sincerity of your own faith, which has often been most highly
praised by the bearers of this letter. Accordingly, we have
sent two *pallia*, one to each of the Metropolitans, Honorius
and Paulinus, so that, whenever either of them shall be summoned from this world to his Maker, the survivor may have
our authority to appoint another bishop in his place. We
have been induced to grant this privilege not only out of
regard for you, but also in the realization of the great and wide
provinces that separate us, so that we may show our recognition of your devotion in all matters and accede to your pious
wishes.

'May the grace of God preserve Your Majesty in safety.'

CHAPTER 18: *On succeeding Justus in the See of Canterbury*
[A.D. 627–31], *Honorius receives the* pallium *and a letter
from Pope Honorius* [A.D. 634]

MEANWHILE, Archbishop Justus was taken up into the
heavenly kingdom on November the tenth, and
Honorius was elected to the see in his place. He therefore
came to Paulinus to be ordained and, meeting him at Lincoln,
was there consecrated fourth successor to Augustine in the
See of Canterbury. Pope Honorius sent him the *pallium* and
a letter confirming the arrangement already made in his
letter to King Edwin: namely, that on the death of either of
the Archbishops of Canterbury or York, the survivor was to
have authority to appoint a successor in place of the deceased
archbishop, which privilege would obviate the necessity of
a wearisome sea and land journey to Rome on every occasion
for consecration. I have thought it proper to include the text
of the letter in this history.

'HONORIUS, to his well-beloved brother Honorius.

'Among the many good gifts which the mercy of our Redeemer has deigned to grant His servants, His generous love is never more evident than when He permits us to display our mutual love in brotherly converse, as it were face to face. For this blessing we constantly give thanks to His Divine Majesty and earnestly pray that He will confirm your loving labours in preaching the Gospel with constant and lasting results and that, in following the rule of your master and patron the holy Gregory, you may bear much fruit, so that, through your ministry, God will bless His Church with ever-increasing strength; that the souls already won by you and your predecessors, beginning with the Lord Gregory, may be established and grow ever stronger in faith and good works, and in reverence and love for God; and that in due time the promises of our Lord Jesus Christ may be fulfilled in you, and His voice summon you to eternal joy, saying: *"Come to Me, all ye that labour and are heavy-laden, and I will give you rest."* And again, *"Well done, thou good and faithful servant; because thou hast been faithful over a few things, I will make thee ruler over many things. Enter thou into the joy of thy Lord."* Our constant love urges us to offer you these preliminary words of encouragement, dearest brothers, and we shall not fail hereafter to grant any privileges that we think likely to benefit your churches.

'In response to your request and that of our sons your kings, we hereby, in the name of blessed Peter, Prince of the Apostles, grant that whenever God's mercy shall summon either of you to Himself, the survivor shall have authority to appoint a bishop in his place. As proof of this authority we have sent to each of your Lordships the *pallium* to wear at such a consecration, so that by our permission and direction you may perform it in a manner acceptable to God. The great expanses of land and sea that separate us make it necessary for us to grant you this authority, in order that troubles may not arise on every such occasion in your churches, but rather the devotion of the people committed to your charge may be further enlarged. God keep you in safety.

'Given the eleventh day of June, in the twenty-fourth year of the reign of our Lord Heraclius Augustus, and the twenty-third after his consulship: and in the twenty-third year of his son Constantine, and the third after his consulship: and in the third year of the most illustrious Caesar Heraclius, his son: the seventh indiction: the year of our Lord 634.'

CHAPTER 19: *Pope Honorius* [A.D. 634], *and later Pope John* [A.D. 640], *write letters to the Scots about Easter and the Pelagian heresy*

POPE HONORIUS also wrote to the Scots, whom he learned to be in error about the observance of Easter, as I mentioned earlier. He earnestly warned them not to imagine that their little community, isolated at the uttermost ends of the earth, had a wisdom exceeding that of all churches ancient and modern throughout the world, and he urged them not to keep a different Easter, contrary to paschal calculations and the synodical decrees of all the bishops of the world.

Similarly John [IV], who succeeded Severinus, successor to Honorius, while still pontiff elect, sent them authoritative and learned letters to correct this error, showing clearly how Easter Day must be sought between the fifteenth and twenty-first days of the moon, as was agreed at the Council of Nicaea. In this letter he particularly warned them to beware of and suppress the heresy of Pelagius, which, he learned, was reviving among them. The letter begins as follows:

'To our well-beloved and holy Tomianus,* Columbanus, Cromanus, Dimnaus, and Baithanus, bishops: to Cromanus, Ernianus, Laistranus, Scellanus, and Segenus, priests: to Saranus and the other Scottish teachers and abbots. Greetings from Hilarus, Arch-priest and Guardian (during its vacancy) of the holy Apostolic See: John, deacon and (Pope) elect in the

Name of God: John, First Secretary and Guardian of the holy Apostolic See: and John, servant of God, Counsellor of the Apostolic See.

'Certain letters addressed to Pope Severinus, of blessed memory, remained unanswered at the time of his death. Therefore, lest any pressing matters should remain long unconsidered, we opened them and learned that certain persons in your province are attempting to revive a new heresy from an old one, contrary to the orthodox faith, and that in the dark cloud of their ignorance they refuse to observe our Easter on which Christ was sacrificed, arguing that it should be observed with the Hebrew Passover on the fourteenth day of the moon.'

From the beginning of this letter it is evident that this heresy had arisen only in very recent times and that the error was restricted to a limited number of persons in the nation. Having therefore explained the proper calculation of Easter, they add this on Pelagianism:

'We learn also that the pernicious Pelagian heresy has once again revived among you, and we strongly urge you to expel the venom of this wicked superstition from your minds. You cannot be unaware that this detestable heresy has already been condemned; for not only has it been suppressed these two hundred years, but it is daily laid under the ban of our perpetual anathema. We therefore beg you not to rake up the ashes of controversies long since burned out. For who can do other than condemn the insolent and impious assertion that man can live without sin of his own free will and not of God's grace? In the first place, it is blasphemous folly to say that any man is sinless; for no one can be sinless save the one Mediator between God and man, the Man Jesus Christ, who was conceived and born without sin. All other men are born in original sin and bear unmistakeable evidence of Adam's fall, even when they are innocent of actual sin. For, as the prophet says, *"Behold, I was shapen in iniquity; and in sin did my mother conceive me."'*

137

THE glorious reign of Edwin over English and Britons alike lasted seventeen years, during the last six of which, as I have said, he laboured for the kingdom of Christ. Then the British King Cadwalla* rebelled against him, supported by Penda, a warrior of the Mercian royal house, who from then onwards ruled that nation with varying success for twenty-two years. In a fierce battle on the field called Haethfelth[1] on the twelfth of October 633, when he was 48 years old, Edwin was killed, and his entire army destroyed or scattered. In the same battle, Osfrid, a gallant young warrior, one of Edwin's sons, was killed before his father. Another son, Eadfrid, was compelled to submit to Penda, who subsequently in breach of a solemn promise put him to death during the reign of Oswald.

At this time a terrible slaughter took place among the Northumbrian church and nation, the more horrible because it was carried out by two commanders, one of whom was a pagan and the other a barbarian more savage than any pagan. For Penda and all his Mercians were idol-worshippers ignorant of the name of Christ; but Cadwalla, although he professed to call himself a Christian, was utterly barbarous in temperament and behaviour. He was set upon exterminating the entire English race in Britain, and spared neither women nor innocent children, putting them all to horrible deaths with ruthless savagery, and continuously ravaging their whole country. He had no respect for the newly established religion of Christ. Indeed even in our own days the Britons pay no respect to the faith and religion of the English and have no more dealings with them than with the heathen. The head of King Edwin was carried to York and subsequently placed in the church of the blessed Apostle Peter, which he had begun to build, but which his successor Oswald completed, as I have

1. Hatfield, near Doncaster.

related above. It rested in the porch dedicated to the holy Pope Gregory, from whose disciples he had received the word of life.

As a result of this disaster, the affairs of the Northumbrians were in such utter disorder that flight offered the sole hope of safety. Paulinus took Queen Ethelberga, whom he had previously accompanied to the province, and returned by sea to Kent, where he was most honourably received by Archbishop Honorius and King Eadbald. On his journey he was escorted by Bassus, a gallant warrior of King Edwin, and brought with him Eanfled, Edwin's daughter, and Wuscfrea his son; also Yffi, son of Osfrid his son, whom his mother, fearing Eadbald and Oswald, later sent over to Gaul to be brought up by her friend, King Dagobert. The two children, however, both died in infancy and were buried in church with the honour due to royal children and innocents in Christ. Paulinus also brought away with him many precious things belonging to King Edwin, among them a great cross of gold and a golden chalice hallowed for the use of the altar. These are still preserved and can be seen in the church at Canterbury.

At this time, the church of Rochester was in great need of a pastor, since Romanus its bishop, who had been sent by Archbishop Justus to Pope Honorius as his representative, had been drowned at sea off Italy. Therefore, at the request of Archbishop Honorius and King Eadbald, Paulinus assumed this charge, which he held until he too departed to the kingdom of heaven with the glorious fruit of his labours. When he died he left in the church of Rochester the *pallium* that he had received from the Roman Pontiff.

Paulinus left behind his deacon James to care for the church of York. James was a holy churchman who remained a long time in that church, teaching and baptizing, and snatching much prey from the clutches of our old enemy the Devil. The village close to Catterick, where he usually lived, bears his name to this day. He had a wide knowledge of church music; and when peace was at length restored to the province and

the number of believers increased, he began to teach many
people to sing the music of the Church after the Uses of Rome
and Canterbury. At last, old and *full of days* as the Scripture
says, he went the way of his fathers.

BOOK THREE

CHAPTER 1: *King Edwin's immediate successors abandon their people's Faith and lose their kingdom: the most Christian King Oswald restores both* [A.D. 633–4]

AFTER Edwin's death in battle, the kingdom of Deira, to which his family belonged and where he began his reign, devolved upon Osric, son of Edwin's uncle Elfric, who had been baptized into the Christian Faith by Paulinus. But the kingdom of Bernicia – for the kingdom of the Northumbrians had anciently been divided into these two provinces – fell to Eanfrid, son of Ethelfrid, who claimed descent from the royal family of that province.

During the whole of Edwin's reign the sons of Ethelfrid his predecessor together with many young nobles lived in exile among the Scots or Picts and were there instructed in the teachings of the Scottish Church and received the grace of Baptism. But on the death of their enemy Edwin, they received permission to return to their own land, and Eanfrid, as eldest son, inherited the crown of Bernicia. As soon as they had obtained control of their earthly kingdoms, however, both these kings apostatized from the faith of the kingdom of heaven which they had accepted, and reverted to the corruption and damnation of their former idolatry.

Not long afterwards they were justly punished by meeting their death at the hands of the godless Cadwalla, king of the Britons. First Osric next summer was rashly besieging him in a strong city when Cadwalla, making a sudden sally with his entire force, caught him off his guard and destroyed him with his whole army. After this, for a full year, Cadwalla

ruled the Northumbrian provinces, not as a victorious king
but as a savage tyrant, ravaging them with ghastly slaughter
until at length he also destroyed Eanfrid, who had unwisely
visited him to negotiate peace accompanied only by twelve
picked soldiers. This year remains accursed and hateful to all
good men, not only on account of the apostasy of the English
kings, by which they divested themselves of the sacraments
of the Faith, but also because of the savage tyranny of the
British king. Hence all those calculating the reigns of kings
have agreed to expunge the memory of these apostate kings
and to assign this year to the reign of their successor King
Oswald, a man beloved of God. This king, after the death of
his brother Eanfrid, mustered an army small in numbers but
strong in the faith of Christ; and despite Cadwalla's vast forces,
which he boasted of as irresistible, the infamous British leader
was killed at a place known by the English as Denisesburn,
that is, the Brook of Denis.

CHAPTER 2: *Before engaging the heathen in battle, King
   Oswald sets up a wooden cross: a young man is later healed
   by a portion of it, and innumerable other miracles take place*
[A.D. 634]

WHEN King Oswald was about to give battle to the
heathen, he set up the sign of the holy cross and, kneel-
ing down, asked God that He would grant his heavenly aid
to those who trusted in Him in their dire need. The place is
pointed out to this day and held in great veneration. It is told
that, when the cross had been hurriedly made and a hole dug
to receive it, the devout king with ardent faith took the cross
and placed it in position, holding it upright with his own
hands until the soldiers had thrown in the earth and it stood
firm. This done he summoned his army with a loud shout,
crying, 'Let us all kneel together, and ask the true and living
God Almighty of His mercy to protect us from the arrogant

savagery of our enemies, since He knows that we fight in a just cause to save our nation.' The whole army did as he ordered and, advancing against the enemy at the first light of dawn, won the victory that their faith deserved. At this spot where the king prayed, innumerable miracles of healing are known to have been performed, which serve as a reminder and a proof of the King's faith. Even to this day many folk take splinters of wood from this holy cross, which they put into water, and when any sick men or beasts drink of it or are sprinkled with it, they are at once restored to health.

This place is called in English *Hefenfelth*, meaning 'the heavenly field', which name, bestowed upon it long ago, was a sure omen of events to come, portending that there the heavenly sign would be set up, a heavenly victory won, and heavenly wonders shown. It lies on the northern side of the wall which the Romans built from sea to sea, as I have related, to protect Britain from the attacks of the barbarous peoples. The brothers of the church of Hexham, which lies not far away, have long been accustomed to make a yearly pilgrimage here on the eve of the anniversary of Oswald's death in order to keep vigil for the welfare of his soul, to recite the psalter, and to offer the Holy Sacrifice for him at dawn. By a further development of this good custom, the brothers have recently built a church on the spot, which has made it honoured and hallowed above all others. This is very fitting, for we know that there was no emblem of the Christian Faith, no church, and no altar in the whole of Bernicia until the new Christian leader Oswald, moved by his devotion to the Faith, set up this standard of the holy cross before giving battle to his relentless enemies.

It is not irrelevant to mention one of the many miracles that have taken place at this cross. A few years ago, one of the brothers of the church of Hexham named Bothelm, who is still living, was walking unwarily on the ice at night, when he suddenly fell and fractured an arm. He suffered such agonizing pain from it that he could not even raise his hand to his mouth. At length, hearing that another brother had decided to go up next day to the site of the cross, he begged him to bring back a piece of its revered wood, saying that by this means he trusted that God would grant him healing. The brother carried out his request, and as he returned at night when the brothers were seated at their evening meal, he passed the sick man a bit of the old moss that grew on the surface of the cross. Being at table, the brother had nowhere to keep the proffered gift, so he thrust it next his breast, and when he retired, forgot to take it out. But, waking up in the middle of the night, he felt something cold at his side, and thrusting in his hand to feel what it was, found that his arm was whole and sound as if he had never suffered such great pain.

CHAPTER 3: *Oswald asks the Scots to send him a bishop: when Aidan arrives, he grants him the island of Lindisfarne as his episcopal see* [A.D. 635]

As soon as he became king, Oswald greatly wished that all the people whom he ruled should be imbued with the grace of the Christian Faith, of which he had received such signal proof in his victory over the heathen. So he sent to the Scottish elders among whom he and his companions had received the sacrament of Baptism when in exile, asking them to send him a bishop by whose teaching and ministry the English people over whom he ruled might receive the blessings of the Christian Faith and the sacraments. His request was granted without delay, and they sent him Bishop Aidan, a man of outstanding gentleness, holiness, and moderation. He had *a zeal in God, but not according to knowledge*, in that he kept Easter in accordance with the customs of his own nation, which, as I have several times observed, was between the fourteenth and twentieth days of the moon. For the northern province of the Scots and all the Picts still observed these customs, believing that they were following the teachings of the holy and praiseworthy father Anatolius, although the true facts are evident to any scholar. But the Scots in the south of Ireland had already conformed to the injunctions of the Bishop of the apostolic see, and learnt to observe Easter at the canonical time.

On Aidan's arrival, the king appointed the island of Lindisfarne to be his see at his own request. As the tide ebbs and flows, this place is surrounded by sea twice a day like an island, and twice a day the sand dries and joins it to the mainland. The king always listened humbly and readily to Aidan's advice and diligently set himself to establish and extend the Church of Christ throughout his kingdom. And while the bishop, who was not fluent in the English language, preached the Gospel, it was most delightful to see the king himself interpreting the word of God to his ealdorman and thanes; for he himself had obtained perfect command of the Scottish tongue during his long exile. Henceforward many Scots arrived day by day in Britain and proclaimed the word of God with great devotion in all the provinces under Oswald's rule, while those of them who were in priest's orders ministered the grace of Baptism to those who believed. Churches were built in several places, and the people flocked gladly to hear the word of God, while the king of his bounty gave lands and endowments to establish monasteries, and the English, both noble and simple, were instructed by their Scots teachers to observe a monastic life.

For most of those who came to preach were monks, Aidan himself being a monk sent from the island of Hii,[1] whose monastery was for a long time the principal monastery of nearly all the northern Scots and all the Picts and exercised a widespread authority.* The island itself belongs to Britain, and is separated from the mainland only by a narrow strait; but the Picts living in that part of Britain gave it to the Scots monks long ago, because they received the Faith of Christ through their preaching.

1. Iona.

CHAPTER 4: *How the Picts received the Faith of Christ*
[A.D. 565]

IN the year of our Lord 565, when Justin the Younger succeeded Justinian and ruled as Emperor of Rome, a priest and abbot named Columba, distinguished by his monastic habit and life, came from Ireland to Britain to preach the word of God in the provinces of the northern Picts, which are separated from those of the southern Picts by a range of steep and desolate mountains.[1]

The southern Picts, who live on this side of the mountains, are said to have abandoned the errors of idolatry long before this date and accepted the true Faith through the preaching of Bishop Ninian,* a most reverend and holy man of British race, who had been regularly instructed in the mysteries of the Christian Faith in Rome. Ninian's own episcopal see, named after Saint Martin and famous for its stately church, is now held by the English, and it is here that his body and those of many saints lie at rest. The place belongs to the province of Bernicia and is commonly known as *Candida Casa*, the White House,[2] because he built the church of stone, which was unusual among the Britons.

Columba* arrived in Britain in the ninth year of the reign of the powerful Pictish king, Bride son of Meilochon; he converted that people to the Faith of Christ by his preaching and example, and received from them the island of Iona on which to found a monastery. Iona is a small island, with an area of about five hides according to English reckoning, and his successors hold it to this day. It was here that Columba died and was buried at the age of seventy-seven, some thirty-two years after he had come into Britain to preach. Before he came to Britain, he had founded a noble monastery in Ireland known in the Scots language as *Dearmach*, the Field of Oaks,[3] because of the oak forest in which it stands. From both of these monasteries Columba's disciples went out and

1. The Grampians.　　2. Whithorn.　　3. Durrow.

146

founded many others in Britain and Ireland; but the monastery on the isle of Iona, where his body lies, remains the chief of them all.

Iona is always ruled by an abbot in priest's orders, to whose authority the whole province, including the bishops, is subject, contrary to the usual custom.* This practice was established by its first abbot Columba, who was not a bishop himself, but a priest and monk. His life and sayings are said to have been recorded in writing by his disciples. But whatever type of man he may have been, we know for certain that he left successors distinguished for their purity of life, their love of God, and their loyalty to the monastic rule. In observing the great Feast of Easter they followed doubtful rules; for being so isolated from the rest of the world, there was no one to acquaint them with the synodical decrees about the keeping of Easter. But they diligently followed whatever pure and devout customs they learned in the prophets, the Gospels, and the writings of the Apostles. They held to their own manner of keeping Easter for another 150 years, until the year of our Lord 715.

In that year the most reverend and holy father, Bishop Egbert, an Englishman, who had spent many years of exile in Ireland for love of Christ, and was most learned in the scriptures, and renowned for lifelong holiness came and corrected their error, and they changed to the right canonical customs for observing Easter. This error was that they kept Easter not, as some supposed, on the fourteenth day of the moon, as do the Jews, but on the Sunday of the wrong week. For as Christians they knew well that the Resurrection of our Lord took place on the first day after the Sabbath and should always be kept on that day. But being barbarous and simple, they had not learned when this first day after the Sabbath, which is now called the Lord's Day, should occur. Yet, since they did not fail in the fervent grace of charity, they were worthy to learn the full truth in this matter, in accordance with the Apostle's promise, when he said: '*And if in anything*

ye be otherwise minded, God shall reveal even this unto you.' But
I shall speak of this more fully in its proper place.

CHAPTER 5: *The Life of Bishop Aidan* [DIED A.D. 651]

IT was from this island and from this community of monks
(while the abbot and priest Segenus was ruling there) that
Aidan was sent, when he had been made bishop, to preach the
Faith of Christ to a province of the English. Among other evidences of holy life, he gave his clergy an inspiring example of
self-discipline and continence, and the highest recommenda-
tion of his teaching to all was that he and his followers lived
as they taught. He never sought or cared for any worldly
possessions, and loved to give away to the poor who chanced
to meet him whatever he received from kings or wealthy folk.
Whether in town or country, he always travelled on foot
unless compelled by necessity to ride; and whatever people
he met on his walks, whether high or low, he stopped and
spoke to them. If they were heathen, he urged them to be
baptized; and if they were Christians, he strengthened their
faith, and inspired them by word and deed to live a good life
and to be generous to others.

His life is in marked contrast to the apathy of our own
times, for all who walked with him, whether monks or layfolk, were required to meditate, that is, either to read the
scriptures or to learn the Psalms. This was their daily occupation wherever they went; and if, on rare occasions, he was
invited to dine with the king, he went with one or two clerics,
and when he had eaten sparingly, he left as soon as possible
to read or pray with them. Many devout men and women
of that day were inspired to follow his example, and adopted
the practice of fasting until None on Wednesdays and
Fridays throughout the year, except during the fifty days
after Easter. If wealthy people did wrong, he never kept
silent out of respect or fear, but corrected them outspokenly.

Nor would he offer money to influential people, although he offered them food whenever he entertained them as host. But, if the wealthy ever gave him gifts of money, he either distributed it for the needs of the poor, as I have mentioned, or else used it to ransom any who had unjustly been sold as slaves. Many of those whom he had ransomed in this way later became his disciples; and when they had been instructed and trained, he ordained them to the priesthood.

It is said that when King Oswald originally asked the Scots to send a bishop to teach the Faith of Christ to himself and his people, they sent him another man of a more austere disposition. After some time, meeting with no success in his preaching to the English, who refused to listen to him, he returned home and reported to his superiors that he had been unable to achieve anything by teaching to the nation to whom they had sent him, because they were an ungovernable people of an obstinate and barbarous temperament. The Scots fathers therefore held a great conference to decide on the wisest course of action; for while they regretted that the preacher whom they had sent had not been acceptable to the English, they still wished to meet their desire for salvation. Then Aidan, who was present at the conference, said to the priest whose efforts had been unsuccessful: 'Brother, it seems to me that you were too severe on your ignorant hearers. You should have followed the practice of the Apostles, and begun by giving them the milk of simpler teaching, and gradually nourished them with the word of God until they were capable of greater perfection and able to follow the loftier precepts of Christ.' At this the faces and eyes of all who were at the conference were turned towards him; and they paid close attention to all he said, and realized that here was a fit person to be made bishop and sent to instruct the ignorant and unbelieving, since he was particularly endowed with the grace of discretion, the mother of virtues. They therefore consecrated him bishop, and sent him to preach. Time was to show that Aidan was remarkable not only for discretion, but for the other virtues as well.

SUCH then was the bishop who brought knowledge of the Faith to King Oswald and the English people under his rule. Thus instructed, Oswald not only learned to hope for the kingdom of heaven, which had been unknown to his ancestors, but was also granted by Almighty God, Creator of heaven and earth, an earthly kingdom greater than they enjoyed. For at length he brought under his sceptre all the peoples and provinces of Britain speaking the four languages, British, Pictish, Scottish, and English.

Although he reached such a height of power, Oswald was always wonderfully humble, kindly, and generous to the poor and strangers. The story is told how on the Feast of Easter one year, Oswald sat down to dine with Bishop Aidan. A silver dish of rich food was set before him, and they were on the point of raising their hands to bless the food, when the servant who was appointed to relieve the needs of the poor came in suddenly and informed the king that a great crowd of needy folk were sitting in the road outside begging alms of the king. Oswald at once ordered his own food to be taken out to the poor, and the silver dish to be broken up and distributed among them. The bishop, who was sitting beside him, was deeply moved to see such generosity, and taking hold of the king's right hand, exclaimed. 'May this hand never wither with age.' Later events proved that his prayer was heard; for when Oswald was killed in battle, his hand and arm were severed from his body, and they remain uncorrupted to this day. They are preserved as venerated relics in a silver casket at the church of Saint Peter in the royal city, which is called after a former queen named Bebba.[1]

Through King Oswald's diplomacy the provinces of Deira and Bernicia, formerly hostile to each other, were peacefully united and became one people. Oswald was nephew to King

1. Bebbanburh, now Bamburgh.

Edwin by his sister Acha; and it is fitting that so great a predecessor should have had so worthy a man of his own blood to maintain his religion and his throne.

CHAPTER 7: *The West Saxons accept the Faith through the teaching of Birinus and his successors Agilbert and Leutherius* [A.D. 635]

A that time, during the reign of Cynigils, the West Saxons, anciently known as the Gewissae, accepted the Faith of Christ through the preaching of Bishop Birinus. He had come to Britain at the direction of Pope Honorius [I], having promised in his presence that he would sow the seeds of our holy Faith in the most inland and remote regions of the English, where no other teacher had been before him. He was accordingly consecrated bishop by Asterius, Bishop of Genoa, at the Pope's command; but when he had reached Britain and entered the territory of the Gewissae, he found them completely heathen, and decided that it would be better to begin to preach the word of God among them rather than seek more distant converts. He therefore evangelized that province, and when he had instructed its king, he baptized him and his people. It happened at the time that the most holy and victorious Oswald was present, and greeted King Cynigils as he came from the font, and offered him an alliance most acceptable to God, taking him as his godson and his daughter as wife. The two kings gave Bishop Birinus the city of Dorcic[1] for his episcopal see, and there he built and dedicated several churches and brought many people to God by his holy labours. He also died and was buried there; and many years later, when Haeddi* was bishop, his body was translated to Venta[2] and laid in the church of the blessed Apostles Peter and Paul.

On the death of Cynigils, his son Coenwalh succeeded to

1. Dorchester (Oxon.).   2. Winchester.

the throne, but refused to accept the Faith and sacraments of
the heavenly kingdom. Not long afterwards he lost his earthly
kingdom also. For he put away his wife, who was sister of
Penda, King of the Mercians, and took another woman. This
led to war, and Coenwalh was driven out of his kingdom by
Penda and took refuge with Anna, King of the East Angles.
There he lived in exile for three years, during which he
learned the Christian Faith and received Baptism. For Anna
his host was a good man and blessed with good and holy
children, as I shall mention later.

When Coenwalh had been restored to his kingdom, there
arrived in the province a bishop from Gaul named Agilbert,
who had been studying the scriptures in Ireland for many
years. This bishop came to the king and voluntarily undertook to evangelize the country. Appreciating his learning and
enthusiasm, the king asked him to accept an episcopal see and
remain in the province as his chief bishop. Agilbert acceded
to the king's request and presided as bishop for many years.
Later, however, the king, who understood only Saxon, grew
tired of the bishop's foreign speech, and invited to the province a bishop of his own tongue called Wini, who had also
been consecrated in Gaul; and dividing his kingdom into two
dioceses, he gave Wini the city of Venta – known by the
Saxons as Wintancæstir – as his see. This action gravely
offended Agilbert, as the king had not consulted him in the
matter, and he returned to Gaul, where he became Bishop of
Paris and ended his days there at an advanced age. Not many
years after Agilbert's departure from Britain, Wini was also
driven from his bishopric by the king, and took refuge with
Wulfhere, King of the Mercians, to whom he offered money
for the Bishopric of London, which he held till his death.
So for a considerable time the province of the West Saxons
remained without any bishop.

During this interval King Coenwalh often suffered great
damage to his kingdom from his enemies. Eventually he
remembered that he had formerly been driven from his

throne because of his infidelity and had been restored to it
after his acceptance of the Christian Faith, and realized that his
kingdom was now justly deprived of God's protection because it had no bishop. He therefore sent messengers to Agilbert in Gaul, offering him satisfaction and requesting him to
return to his bishopric. But Agilbert sent his regrets and said
that it was impossible for him to return, since he was now
responsible for his own bishopric and city of Paris. But, not
wishing to reject such an urgent appeal for help, he sent in his
place his nephew, the priest Leutherius,[1] to be consecrated as
his bishop if the king were agreeable, recommending him as
worthy of a bishopric. Both king and people welcomed
Leutherius with honour, and asked Theodore, then Archbishop of Canterbury, to consecrate him their bishop. He was
accordingly consecrated at Canterbury, and for many years
wisely ruled the West Saxon see alone with the full support
of the synod.

CHAPTER 8: *Earconbert, King of Kent, orders the destruction
of idols. His daughter Earcongota and his kinswoman
Ethelberga dedicate themselves to God as nuns* [A.D. 640]

IN the year of our Lord 640, King Eadbald of Kent departed
this life, and his son Earconbert succeeded to the government of the realm, which he ruled most nobly for over
twenty-four years and some months. He was the first of the
English kings to give orders for the complete abandonment
and destruction of idols throughout his realm, and for the
observance of the Lenten fast, enforcing his decrees by suitable
penalties for disobedience. His daughter Earcongota, who
shared her father's zeal, was a nun of outstanding virtue, who
served God in a convent in Frankish territory founded by the
noble Abbess Fara at a place called Brie:* for as yet there were
few monasteries built in English territory,* and many who

1. A Latinized form of the name Hlothere.

wished to enter conventual life went from Britain to the
Frankish realm or Gaul for the purpose. Girls of noble family
were also sent there for their education, or to be betrothed
to their heavenly Bridegroom, especially to the houses of
Brie, Chelles, and Andelys; among such girls were Saethryd,
step-daughter of King Anna of East Anglia, already mentioned, and Ethelberga his own daughter. Although foreigners, both were of such merit that they became Abbesses
of Brie. Sexburg, Anna's eldest daughter, and wife to King
Earconbert of Kent, was the mother of Earcongota, who
deserves especial mention.

To this day the people of the district tell stories of the wonderful deeds and miracles of the nun Earcongota; but I must
restrict myself to a brief account of her passing to the heavenly
kingdom. When she felt her call approaching, she set out to
visit the cells of all the infirm handmaids of Christ, especially
those who were of a great age or were most esteemed for their
holiness of life, and humbly commending herself to their
prayers, she revealed to them how she had received intimation
of her coming death. She told how, in a vision, she had seen a
company of men in white robes entering the monastery, and
when she asked them what they were looking for and what
they wanted, they replied: 'We have been sent to bring away
with us the golden coin that was brought here from Kent.'
And on the very night when, as dawn drew near, she left the
darkness of this world and entered the light of heaven, many
brethren of the monastery,* who lived in separate buildings,
said that they had clearly heard choirs of angels singing and a
sound like that of a great throng entering the monastery. And
when they came out to discover what it might be, they saw a
great light coming down from heaven, which carried away
the holy soul of Earcongota, freed from the bonds of the body,
to the eternal joys of heaven. Other miracles are reported to
have taken place in the monastery that night; but these I leave
to her own people to recount, while I turn to other matters.
The venerable body of this virgin and spouse of Christ was

laid to rest in the church of the blessed Protomartyr Saint Stephen. Three days later it was decided to take up the stone slab covering the grave, and replace the body at a greater depth. While this was taking place, a perfume of such fragrance rose from below that it seemed to all the brethren and sisters standing round as though a store of balm had been unsealed.

Ethelberga, aunt of Earcongota, also preserved with strict self-discipline the glory of the perpetual virginity beloved by God, and the extent of her holiness became even more apparent after her death. For while she was abbess she began building within her monastery a church in honour of all the Apostles, in which she wished to be buried; but when the work was only half done, she was prevented by death from completing it and was buried within the church in a spot that she had chosen. After her death the brethren became wholly occupied in other matters, and the building of the church was discontinued for seven years. At the end of this period they decided to abandon an undertaking that had proved too great for their resources, and to remove the abbess' bones to another church that was already completed and consecrated. When they opened the tomb, they found the body untouched by decay as it had been by the corruption of sinful desires. So having washed it, and clothed it in fresh garments, they removed it to the church of Saint Stephen the Martyr. Her feast-day is kept there with great splendour on the seventh of July.

CHAPTER 9: *Miraculous cures take place at the site of Oswald's death. A traveller's horse is cured, and a paralytic girl healed*

OSWALD, the most Christian king of the Northumbrians, reigned for nine years, if we include the fatal year made abhorrent by the callous impiety of the British king Cadwalla and the insane apostasy of the English kings (Osric and Eanfrid): for it has been generally agreed that the names of these apostates should be erased from the list of Christian kings and the year of their reign ignored. At the end of this period Oswald fell in a fierce battle fought at the place called in English Maserfelth[1] against the same heathen Mercians and their heathen king, who had also slain his predecessor Edwin. He died on the fifth of August 642, when he was thirty-eight years of age.

Oswald's great devotion and faith in God was made evident by the miracles that took place after his death. For at the place where he was killed fighting for his country against the heathen, sick men and beasts are healed to this day. Many people took away the very dust from the place where his body fell, and put it in water, from which sick folk who drank it received great benefit. This practice became so popular that, as the earth was gradually removed, a pit was left in which a man could stand. But it is not to be wondered at that the sick received healing at the place of his death; for during his lifetime he never failed to provide for the sick and needy and to give them alms and aid. Many miracles are reported as having occurred at this spot, or by means of the earth taken from it; but I will content myself with two, which I have heard from my elders.

Not long after Oswald's death, a man happened to be riding near the place when his horse suddenly showed signs of distress. It stopped and hung its head, foaming at the mouth, and as its pains increased, it collapsed on the ground. The rider dismounted, removed the saddle, and waited to see whether the beast was going to recover or to die. At length, having tossed this way and that in great pain for a considerable time, it rolled on to the spot where the great king had died. Immediately the pain ceased, and the horse stopped its wild struggles; then, having rolled on its other side, as tired beasts do, it got up fully recovered and began to graze. The

1. Probably Oswestry.

traveller, an observant man, concluded that the place where his horse was cured must possess especial sanctity, and when he had marked it, he mounted and rose on to the inn where he intended to lodge. On his arrival he found a girl, the niece of the landlord, who had long suffered from paralysis; and when members of the household in his presence were deploring the girl's disease, he began to tell them about the place where his horse had been cured. So they put the girl into a cart, took her to the place, and laid her down. Once there she fell asleep for a short while; and, on awaking, she found herself restored to health. She asked for water and washed her face; then she tidied her hair, adjusted her linen headgear, and returned home on foot in perfect health with those who had brought her.

CHAPTER 10: *How the earth from this place has power over fire*

ABOUT this time another man, a Briton by race, is said to have been crossing the ground where this battle had been fought, and noticing that one spot was more green and beautiful than the rest of the field, he came to the wise conclusion that there could be no other explanation for this exceptional greenness but that some person of greater sanctity than anyone else in the army had been slain there. So he took away some of the earth wrapped up in a linen cloth, thinking that, as the event proved, it might have power to heal the sick. Proceeding on his journey, he arrived that night at a village and entered a house where some neighbours were having a feast. He was welcomed by the owners of the house, and when he had hung the cloth containing the earth on a beam of the wall, he sat down to share their meal. They had sat eating and drinking for a long while around a blazing fire in the centre of the room, when sparks flew up into the roof of the house, which was made of wattles thatched with hay, and quickly burst into flame. When the fuddled revellers realized this, they rushed out of the burning house in terror, powerless to extinguish the blaze. The house burned down, and only the beam from which the earth hung remained whole and untouched by the flames. When they saw this miracle, they were all astonished, and after making careful enquiry, they found that the man had taken the earth from the place where Oswald's blood had been shed. These marvels were reported far and wide, and many folk began to visit the place each day and obtained healing for themselves and their families.

CHAPTER 11: *A heavenly light appears all night over Oswald's tomb, and folk are healed from demonic possession*

IT would not be right to omit mention of the favours and miracles that were shown when Oswald's bones were discovered and translated into the church where they are now enshrined. This took place through the devout interest of Queen Osthryd of the Mercians, daughter of his brother Oswy who succeeded him on the throne, as I shall mention in due course.

In the province of Lindsey there is a noble monastery called Beardaneu,[1] which was greatly loved, favoured, and enriched by the queen and her husband Ethelred. She wished that the honoured bones of her uncle should be reinterred there. But when the waggon carrying the bones arrived towards evening at the abbey, the monks were reluctant to admit it; for although they acknowledged Oswald's holiness, they were influenced by old prejudices against him even after his death, because he originally came from a different province and had ruled them as an alien king. So it came about that the king's bones remained outside the gates all night, with only a large awning spread over the waggon in which they lay. But a sign from heaven showed them that the bones should be

1. Bardney Abbey, Lincs.

welcomed with respect by all the faithful: for throughout the night a pillar of light shone skywards from the waggon, and was seen by nearly all the inhabitants of the province of Lindsey. Early next morning, therefore, the monks who had previously refused to admit it, began to pray earnestly that the holy relics so dear to God should find a resting-place in their midst. Accordingly the bones were washed and laid in a casket made for the purpose, which was placed in the church with fitting honour. And to furnish a lasting memorial of the royal saint, they hung the king's banner of purple and gold over his tomb. The water in which the bones had been washed was poured away in a corner of the cemetery, and from that time on the very earth that had received this venerated water had the saving power to expel devils from the bodies of those who were possessed.

Some while later, when Queen Osthryd was staying in the monastery, the venerable Ethelhild, abbess of a neighbouring house, visited her to pay her respects. This lady, who is still living, is sister of Bishop Ethelwin of Lindsey and of Abbot Aldwin of Partney, which lies not far away. While she was talking with the queen, the conversation turned to Oswald, and the abbess told her how she had herself seen the light reaching heavenwards from Oswald's relics on that night. And the queen informed her how the dust from the pavement, on which the water that had washed the bones had been spilt, had already healed many sick people. The abbess then asked that she might be given some of this healing dust; and when it had been given her, she tied it up in a cloth, and put it into a little casket which she took away with her. Some while later, a guest visited her abbey who was often horribly tormented by an evil spirit during the night hours. This man was hospitably welcomed, and had retired to bed after supper, when he was suddenly possessed by the devil and began to cry out, grind his teeth, foam at the mouth, and toss his limbs in wild contortions. No one could hold or bind him, so a servant ran and knocked at the abbess' door to inform her. She opened the monastery gate herself and went out with one of the nuns to the men's quarters, where she called one of the priests to accompany her to the sufferer. On their arrival, they found a crowd already present, none of whom had been able to control the man's wild convulsions. The priest therefore employed exorcism and did all he could to allay the sufferer's frenzy; but all his efforts were useless. When there seemed no hope left of easing his frenzy, the abbess suddenly remembered this dust, and told a maidservant to go at once and fetch the casket containing it. As soon as she returned from her errand and entered the porch of the house where the possessed man lay writhing, he immediately became silent, laying down his head as though to sleep, and relaxing his whole body. 'All in rapt silence stood, with gaze intent,'[1] watching anxiously to see the outcome of this affair. After some while, the man who had been so tormented sat up with a deep sigh, saying: 'I am now restored to health and in my right mind.' They eagerly asked him what had happened, and he replied: 'As soon as the maid carrying the casket approached the porch of the house, all the evil spirits who were tormenting me went away and left me and were nowhere to be seen.' Then the abbess gave him a portion of the dust, and after the priest had offered prayers, the man spent a quiet night and was never again troubled by the old enemy.

CHAPTER 12: *A little boy is cured of ague at Saint Oswald's tomb*

SOME while after this, there was a little boy in the monastery who had been seriously troubled by ague. One day he was anxiously awaiting the hour of an attack, when one of the brothers came in to him and said: 'My boy, shall I tell you how you may be cured of this complaint? Get up, and go to Oswald's tomb in the church. Remain there quietly and

---

1. Virgil: *Aeneid* ii. 1.

mind you don't stir from it until the time that your fever is due
to leave you. Then I will come and fetch you.' The boy did as
the brother advised, and while he sat by the saint's tomb the
fever dared not touch him: furthermore, it was so completely
scared that it never recurred, either on the second or the third
day, or ever after. A brother of that monastery who told me
this story added that the boy who had been so miraculously
cured was by then a young man and still living in the monastery. But it need cause no surprise that the prayers of this
king, who now reigns with God, should be acceptable to
him, since when he was a king on earth he always used to
work and pray fervently for the eternal kingdom.

It is said that Oswald often remained in prayer from the
early hour of Lauds until dawn, and that through his practice
of constant prayer and thanksgiving to God he always sat
with his hands palm upwards on his knees. It is also said, and
has become proverbial, that his life even closed in prayer; for
when he saw the enemy forces surrounding him and knew
that his end was near, he prayed for the souls of his soldiers.
'God have mercy on their souls, said Oswald as he fell' is now
a proverb. As I have already mentioned, his bones were taken
up and buried in the Abbey of Bardney; but the king who
slew him ordered that his head and hands with the forearms
be hacked off and fixed on stakes. The following year,
Oswald's successor Oswy came to the place with his army
and removed them, placing the head in the church at Lindisfarne,* and the hands and arms in his own royal city of
Bamburgh.

CHAPTER 13 : *A man in Ireland is recalled from death's door
by means of Oswald's relics*

THE fame of this illustrious hero was not confined to
Britain, for the rays of his beneficent light shone far
overseas, and reached Germany and Ireland. The most rever-

end Bishop Acca* tells how, on a journey to Rome, Bishop Wilfrid and he stayed awhile with the most holy Wilbrord, then Archbishop of the Frisians, and how he heard him speak of the miracles that had been done by the relics of the venerated king in his own province. Wilbrord also told them that when he was still a priest in Ireland, and living the life of a pilgrim out of love for his heavenly home, stories of the king's holiness were already current far and wide. I include in this history one of the stories that he told.

'At the time of the great plague that swept Britain and Ireland,' he said, 'one of its many victims was a scholar of Scottish race, who was well read in literature but utterly uninterested and careless in the matter of his eternal salvation. When he realized that his death was near, he began to fear that as soon as he died his sins would drag him down to hell. As I was in the neighbourhood, he sent for me and said with tears in his voice, sighing and trembling: "You can see how this disease has tightened its hold and brought me to the point of death. I have no doubt that after the death of my body I shall immediately be condemned to the eternal death of the soul and endure all the torments of hell; for although I have made a great study of the scriptures, I have for a long time devoted myself to evil-doing rather than to keeping God's Commandments. But, if God's mercy allows me to survive, I solemnly resolve to amend my evil ways and will completely reform my character and way of life in submission to the will of God. I am fully aware that I do not deserve any prolongation of my life, nor can I expect it, unless it pleases God to pardon a wretched sinner through the intercession of those who have served Him faithfully. I have heard the well-known story of your most saintly King Oswald, whose wonderful faith and virtue have become renowned even after his death by the working of miracles. I therefore beg you, if you possess any of his relics, to bring them to me, and perhaps God will have pity on me for his sake." I told him: "I have a portion of the stake to which the king's head was fixed by the heathen after his death, and if you will make a sincere act of faith, God of His mercy and through the merits of this great saint may grant you a long term of earthly life and render you fitted to enter into life eternal." The man then assured me that he had complete faith in this. Then I blessed some water, and put in it a chip of this oak, and gave it to the sick man to drink. He quickly began to feel better, and having recovered from his illness, he lived many years after. He gave his heart and life entirely to God, and wherever he went he proclaimed the mercy of our kind Creator and the glory of His faithful servant Oswald.'

CHAPTER 14: *On the death of Paulinus, Ithamar succeeds to his Bishopric of Rochester. An account of the wonderful humility of King Oswin, who was treacherously murdered by Oswy* [A.D. 642–651]

WHEN Oswald departed to the kingdom of heaven, his brother Oswy, a young man of about thirty, succeeded to his earthly throne and ruled for twenty-eight troubled years. He was attacked both by the pagan Mercians, who had already killed his brother, and also by his own son Alchfrid and his nephew Ethelwald, son of his brother and predecessor. In the year of our Lord 644, the second year of Oswy's reign, the most reverend father Paulinus, formerly Bishop of York and subsequently Bishop of Rochester, died on the tenth of October, after an episcopate lasting nineteen years, two months, and twenty-one days. He was buried in the sacristy of the church of the blessed Apostle Andrew, which had been founded and built in Rochester by King Ethelbert. In his place Archbishop Honorius consecrated Ithamar, a man of Kent, but as worthy and learned as his predecessors.

During the first part of his reign, Oswy shared the royal dignity with Oswin, who came of Edwin's royal line and

was son of the above-mentioned Osric. This prince, who was
a man of great holiness and piety, ruled the province of Deira
most prosperously for seven years and was deeply loved by
all. But even with him Oswy, who ruled the province of
Bernicia, that is, the northern part of the Transhumbrian
people, could not live peaceably; and when their differences
grew more acute, he most treacherously murdered him. For,
when the kings had raised armies against each other, Oswin
realized that his opponent's forces were far stronger than his
own, and decided not to risk an engagement but to await a
more favourable opportunity. So he disbanded the army that
he had raised at Wilfaresdun, that is, Wilfar's Hill, ten miles
north-west of the village of Cataract,[1] and sent all his men to
their homes. He himself, accompanied by a single trusted
soldier named Tondhere, went back and lay concealed in the
house of the nobleman Hunwald, whom he regarded as his
greatest friend. Alas, it was far otherwise: for Hunwald betrayed Oswin and his man to Oswy, who amid universal
disgust ordered his commander Ethelwin to put them both
to death. This crime took place on the twentieth of August at
In-Getlingum[2] in the ninth year of his reign, and here at a later
date, in atonement for this crime, a monastery was built in
which prayers were to be offered to God daily for the souls
of the two kings, both slayer and slain alike.

King Oswin was a man of handsome appearance and lofty
stature, pleasant in speech and courteous in manner. He was
generous to high and low alike, and soon won the affection
of everyone by his regal qualities of mind and body, so that
nobles came from almost every province to enter his service.
But among his other especial endowments of virtue and
moderation the greatest was what one may describe as the
singular blessing of humility, of which a single instance will
be sufficient.

He had given Bishop Aidan a very fine horse, in order that

1. Catterick.
2. Gilling, Yorks.

he could ride whenever he had to cross a river or undertake any difficult or urgent journey, although the bishop ordinarily travelled on foot. Not long afterwards, when a poor man met the bishop and asked for alms, the bishop immediately dismounted and ordered the horse with all its royal trappings to be given to the beggar; for he was most compassionate, a protector of the poor and a father to the wretched. When this action came to the king's ears, he asked the bishop as they were going in to dine: 'My lord bishop, why did you give away the royal horse which was necessary for your own use? Have we not many less valuable horses or other belongings which would have been good enough for beggars, without giving away a horse that I had specially selected for your personal use?' The bishop at once answered, 'What are you saying, Your Majesty? Is this child of a mare more valuable to you than this child of God?' At this they went in to dinner, and the bishop sat down in his place; but the king, who had come in from hunting, stood warming himself by the fire with his attendants. As he stood by the fire, the king turned over in his mind what the bishop had said; then suddenly unbuckling his sword and handing it to a servant, he impulsively knelt at the bishop's feet and begged his forgiveness, saying: 'I will not refer to this matter again, nor will I enquire how much of our bounty you give away to God's children.' The bishop was deeply moved, and immediately stood up and raised him to his feet, assuring him of his high regard and begging him to sit down to his food without regrets. At the bishop's urgent request, the king sat down and began to be merry; but Aidan on the contrary grew so sad that he began to shed tears. His chaplain asked him in his own language, which the king and his servants did not understand, why he wept. Aidan replied: 'I know that the king will not live very long; for I have never before seen a humble king. I feel that he will soon be taken from us, because this nation is not worthy of such a king.' Not very long afterwards, as I have related, the bishop's foreboding was borne out by the king's death. And Bishop Aidan himself was taken from this world only eleven days after his beloved king, and received the eternal reward of his labours from our Lord on the thirty-first of August 651.

CHAPTER 15: *Bishop Aidan foretells a coming storm, and gives seafarers holy oil to calm the waves* [c. A.D. 651]

ALMIGHTY God made known the greatness of Aidan's merits by the evidence of miracles, of which it must suffice to mention three in his memory. A priest named Utta, a truthful and serious man, who on that account was generally respected by all, even by worldly princes, was sent to Kent to bring back Eanfled as wife for King Oswy: she was the daughter of King Edwin and had been taken to Kent when her father was killed. Intending to make the outward journey by land and to return with the princess by sea, he went to Bishop Aidan and asked him to pray for him and his companions as they set out on their long journey. When Aidan had blessed them and commended them to God, he gave them some holy oil, saying: 'When you set sail, you will encounter a storm and contrary winds. Remember then to pour the oil that I am giving you on to the sea, and the wind will immediately drop, giving you a pleasant, calm voyage and a safe return home.' Everything happened as the bishop foretold. In a rising gale, the sailors dropped anchor, hoping to ride out the storm. This proved impossible; for the roaring seas broke into the ship from every side, and it began to fill. Everyone felt that his last hour had come, when at last the priest remembered the bishop's words. He took out the flask of oil, and poured some of it over the sea, which immediately ceased its raging as Aidan had foretold. So it came about that the man of God through the spirit of prophecy both foretold the storm and, although absent, calmed its fury. The story of this miracle is no groundless fable; for it was related to me by Cynimund, a most faithful priest of our own church [Jarrow], who had it from the mouth of the priest Utta, on and through whom the miracle was performed.

CHAPTER 16: *Aidan's prayers save the royal city when fired by the enemy*

ANOTHER notable miracle of the same father Aidan is told by those in a position to know the facts. While he was bishop, Penda and his enemy army of Mercians spread ruin far and wide throughout the lands of the Northumbrians and reached the very gates of the royal city, which takes its name from Bebba, a former queen. Unable to enter it either by force or after a siege. Penda attempted to set fire to it. Pulling down all the neighbouring villages, he carried to Bamburgh a vast quantity of beams, rafters, wattled walls, and thatched roofs, piling it high around the city wall on the landward side. Directly the wind became favourable, he set fire to this mass, intending to destroy the city. Now, while all this was happening, the most reverend Bishop Aidan was living on Farne Island, which lies nearly two miles from the city and which was his retreat when he wished to pray alone and undisturbed: indeed, his lonely hermitage can be seen there to this day. When the saint saw the column of smoke and flame wafted by the winds above the city walls, he is said to have raised his eyes and hands to heaven, saying with tears: 'Lord, see what evil Penda does!' No sooner had he spoken than the wind shifted away from the city, and drove back the flames on to those who had kindled them, so injuring some and unnerving all that they abandoned their assault on a city so clearly under God's protection.

DEATH came to Aidan when he had completed sixteen years of his episcopate, while he was staying at a royal residence near the capital. Having a church and lodging there, Aidan often used to go and stay at the place, travelling about the surrounding countryside to preach. This was his practice at all the king's country-seats, for he had no personal possessions except his church and a few fields around it. When he fell ill, a tent was erected for him on the west side of the church, so that the tent was actually attached to the church wall. And so it happened that, as he drew his last breath, he was leaning against a post that buttressed the wall on the outside. He passed away on the last day of August, in the seventeenth year of his episcopate, and his body was soon taken across to Lindisfarne Island and buried in the monks' cemetery. When a larger church, dedicated to the most blessed Prince of the Apostles, was built there some while later, his bones were transferred to it and buried at the right side of the altar in accordance with the honours due to so great a prelate.

Finan, who had also come from the Scottish island and monastery of Iona, succeeded him as bishop and held the office for a considerable time. Some years later, Penda, King of the Mercians, came into these parts with an invading army and destroyed everything that he found with fire and sword; and he burned down the village and the church where Aidan had died. But, in a wonderful manner, the beam against which he was leaning at his death was the only object untouched by the flames which devoured everything around it. This miracle was noticed and a church was soon rebuilt on the same site, with the beam supporting the structure from the outside as before. Sometime later in another fire, caused this time by carelessness, the village and church were again destroyed;

but even on this occasion the beam remained undamaged. For, although in a most extraordinary way the flames licked through the very holes of the pins that secured it to the building, they were not permitted to destroy the beam. When the church was rebuilt for the third time, the beam was not employed as an outside support again, but was set up inside the church as a memorial of this miracle, so that those who entered might kneel there and ask God's mercy. Since that day many are known to have obtained the grace of healing at this spot, and many have cut chips of wood from the beam and put them in water, by which means many have been cured of their diseases.

I have dealt at length with the character and life of Aidan, although one cannot commend or approve his inadequate knowledge of the proper observance of Easter; indeed, as I have made clear in my book on the seasons, I strongly disapprove of these practices. None the less, as a truthful historian, I have given an accurate account of his life, commending all that was excellent and preserving his memory for the benefit of my readers. He cultivated peace and love, purity and humility; he was above anger and greed, and despised pride and conceit; he set himself to keep as well as to teach the laws of God, and was diligent in study and prayer. He used his priestly authority to check the proud and powerful; he tenderly comforted the sick; he relieved and protected the poor. To sum up in brief what I have learned from those who knew him, he took pains never to neglect anything that he had learned from the writings of the evangelists, apostles and prophets, and he set himself to carry them out with all his powers.

I greatly admire and love all these things about Aidan, because I have no doubt that they are pleasing to God; but I cannot approve or commend his failure to observe Easter at the proper time, whether he did it through ignorance of the canonical times or in deference to the customs of his own nation. But this in him I do approve, that in keeping his Easter he believed, worshipped, and taught exactly what we do, namely the redemption of the human race through the Passion, Resurrection, and Ascension into heaven of the Man Jesus Christ, the Mediator between God and man. He always kept Easter, not as some mistakenly suppose, on the fourteenth moon whatever the day was, as the Jews do, but on the Lord's Day falling between the fourteenth and twentieth days of the moon. He did so because he held that the Resurrection of our Lord took place on the day following the Sabbath and because, like the rest of Holy Church, he rightly expected our own resurrection to take place on the same day after the Sabbath, which we now call the Lord's Day.

CHAPTER 18: *The life and death of the devout King Sigbert*
[A.D. 635]

ABOUT this time, after the death of Earpwald, successor to Redwald, the kingdom of the East Angles was ruled by his brother Sigbert, a good and religious man who had been baptized long previously in Gaul while he had been living in exile to escape the hostility of Redwald. When he returned home and became king, he wished to copy what he had seen well contrived in Gaul, and he was quick to found a school for the education of boys in the study of letters.★ In this project he was assisted by Bishop Felix, who had come to him from Kent and provided him with teachers and masters according to the practice of Canterbury.

King Sigbert became so ardent in his love for the kingdom of heaven that he abandoned the affairs of his earthly kingdom, and entrusted them to his kinsman Egric, who had already governed part of the kingdom. He then entered a monastery★ that he had founded and, after receiving the tonsure, devoted his energies to winning an everlasting kingdom. A considerable while later, the Mercians led by King Penda attacked the East Angles who, finding themselves

less experienced in warfare than their enemies, asked Sigbert
to go into battle with them and foster the morale of the
fighting men. When he refused, they dragged him out of the
monastery regardless of his protests, and took him into battle
with them in the hope that their men would be less likely to
panic or think of flight if they were under the eye of one who
had once been a gallant and distinguished commander. But,
mindful of his monastic vows, Sigbert, surrounded by a
well-armed host, refused to carry anything more than a stick,
and when the heathen charged, both he and King Egric were
killed and the army scattered.

These kings were succeeded by Anna son of Eni, an
excellent man of royal stock, and father of a distinguished
family, of whom I shall give an account in due course. Anna
also was later killed by the same pagan king of the Mercians
who had slain his predecessors.

CHAPTER 19: *Fursey establishes a monastery among the
East Angles: the incorruption of his body after death attests
to his visions and holiness* [A.D. 633]

DURING Sigbert's reign there came from Ireland a
holy man named Fursey, renowned for his words and
doings and outstanding in virtue. His purpose was to spend
his life as a pilgrim for love of our Lord, and to go wherever
he found an opening. On his arrival in the province of the
East Angles, he was honourably received by the king and
preached the Gospel as he always did. Inspired by the example
of his goodness and the effectiveness of his teaching, many
unbelievers were converted to Christ, and many who already
believed were drawn to greater love and faith in him.

Once when he was ill, God granted Fursey to enjoy a
vision, in which he was directed to continue his diligent
preaching of the word and to maintain his accustomed vigils
and prayers with indefatigable zeal; for although death is

certain, its coming is unpredictable, as our Lord says: '*Watch therefore, for ye know neither the day nor the hour.*' Stimulated by this vision, Fursey set himself with all speed to build a monastery on a site given him by King Sigbert, and to establish a regular observance in it. This monastery was pleasantly situated in some woods close to the sea, within the area of a fortification that the English call Cnobheresburg,* meaning Cnobhere's Town. Subsequently, Anna, king of the province, and his nobles endowed the house with finer buildings and gifts.

Fursey was of noble Irish blood and even more noble in mind than in birth; for from his boyhood he had not only read sacred books and observed monastic discipline but, as is fitting in saints, had also diligently practised all that he learned.

In course of time he had built himself a monastery in which he might devote himself more freely to sacred studies. There, as the book on his life informs us, he fell ill and entered a trance; and quitting his body from sunset to cockcrow, was privileged to see the choirs of angels, and to hear the songs of the blessed. He used to say that, among other things, he clearly heard them sing: '*The saints shall go from strength to strength*', and '*The God of gods shall be seen in Sion*'. Then he returned to bodily consciousness; but three days later he was again withdrawn from it, and saw not only the greater joys of the blessed, but the amazing struggles of evil spirits, who fought to prevent his approach to heaven by constant wicked accusations: nevertheless, under the protection of the angels, he reached his goal. And if any one wishes to learn about these experiences in greater detail, let him read the above-mentioned little book on his life, and I think that he will reap great benefit from it. It describes the deceitful cunning with which the devils threw back at him his actions, his idle words, and even his thoughts, as though they were recorded in a book; and it tells of the joyful and sorrowful things that he learned both from the angels and from the saints who appeared among the angels.

I have, however, thought it proper to record in this history one happening which may be helpful to many. When Fursey had been carried up to a great height, he was told by his angel guides to look back at the world. As he looked down, he saw what appeared to be a gloomy valley beneath him, and four fires in the air, not far from one another. Asking what these were, the angels told him that they were the fires which were to burn and consume the world. 'One of them is Falsehood, when we do not renounce Satan and all his works as we promised at our Baptism. The next is Covetousness, when we put the love of worldly wealth before the love of God. The third is Discord, when we needlessly offend our neighbours, even in small matters. The fourth is Cruelty, when we think it no crime to rob and defraud the weak.' These fires gradually grew together and merged into one vast conflagration, so that Fursey in alarm cried to the angel: 'Master, the fire is coming near me!' To which the angel replied: 'It will not burn you, because you did not kindle it; for although it appears as a great and terrible fire, it tests everyone according to his deserts, and will burn away his sinful desires. For as every man's body is set on fire by unlawful desire, so when death frees him from the body, he must make due atonement for his sins by fire.' Then he saw one of the three angels who had been his guides in both his visions go forward and divide the flames, while the other two flew on each side of him to protect him from harm. He also saw devils, who flew through the flames stirring up the fires of war against the just. These evil spirits made accusations against him, while the good spirits spoke in his defence. Fursey also saw a greater vision of the heavenly hosts and of the saints of his own nation who had once worthily adorned the dignity of priesthood, and from them he learned many things of spiritual benefit both to himself and to those who were ready to listen. And when they had ended speaking and returned to heaven with the other angelic spirits, there remained with Fursey the three angels who were to restore him to his body. As they approached

the great fire, the angel divided the flames as before for him
to pass. But when the man of God came to the passage
opened among the flames, wicked spirits seized one of those
whom they had been tormenting in the fire, and thrust him
against Fursey, so that he was burned on his shoulder and
jaw. He recognized this man, and remembered that he had
received some of his clothing when he died. And when the
holy angel quickly took the man and cast him back into the
flames, the malicious devil said: 'Don't reject one of your
own friends; for since you accepted the property of this
sinner, you must share his punishment.' But the angel de-
fended Fursey, saying: 'He did not accept them out of greed,
but in order to save the man's soul.' The fire then died down,
and the angel turned to Fursey, saying: 'You lit this fire, so
you were burned: had you not accepted property from one
who died in his sins, you would not have shared his punishment.' And he went on to instruct Fursey in salutary words
what should be done for the salvation of those who repented
on their death-bed. And when Fursey had been restored to
his body, he found that the burn that he had received in his
soul had left a permanent and visible scar on his shoulder and
jaw; and in this strange way his body afforded visible evidence of the inward sufferings of his soul. He continued to set
an example of virtue to others in his life and teaching as
before, but he would relate his visions only to those who were
moved by penitence to ask him. An old brother of our monastery, who is still living, testifies that he once knew a truthful
and devout man who had met Fursey in the province of the
East Angles, and heard of these visions from his own mouth.
He added that it was a frosty and bitter winter's day when
Fursey told his story; and yet, though he wore only a thin
garment, he was sweating profusely as though it had been
summer, either because of the consolation or the terror of his
recollections.

To return to my original narrative, when Fursey had
preached the word of God among the Irish for many years,

he could no longer endure the crowds that thronged him. So he abandoned everything he seemed to possess and, leaving his native island with a few companions, crossed into Britain to the province of the Angles, where he preached the word of God and built the above-mentioned noble monastery. Having done this with success, he began to long to be rid of all worldly business, even of the affairs of the monastery; and having entrusted the care of souls to his brother Fullan and the priests Gobban and Dicul, he freed himself of all worldly responsibilities and resolved to end his life as a hermit. Now Fursey had another brother named Ultan, who after many years in a monastery had adopted the life of a hermit. So Fursey sought him out alone and for a year shared his life of prayer and austerity, supporting himself by daily manual labour.

At this period, the province was again distressed by the attacks of the heathen, and Fursey, foreseeing that even monasteries would be endangered, set his affairs in order and sailed over to Gaul, where he was honourably received by King Clovis [II] and his chamberlain Earconwald, and built a monastery at Latiniacum.* Not long afterwards, when he fell sick and died, the noble Earconwald took his body and placed it in the porch of a church he was building in his estate called Péronne, until the church itself should be consecrated. This took place twenty-seven days later, and when the body was taken from the porch to be buried near the altar, it was found to be as free from decay as on the day of his death. Four years later a more suitable chapel was built for his resting-place to the east of the altar, and his still uncorrupt body was transferred to it with great honour. In this chapel God has granted many miracles as evidence of the saint's merits. I have briefly recorded these events and the incorruption of his body, so that the reader may understand more clearly how great a man Fursey was. But he will find a fuller account of Fursey and his companions in the book on his life which I have mentioned.

CHAPTER 20: *On the death of Honorius* [A.D. 653], *Deusdedit succeeds him as Archbishop of Canterbury. The succession of the bishops of the East Angles and of Rochester*

MEANWHILE Felix, Bishop of the East Angles, died after an episcopate of seventeen years, and Archbishop Honorius consecrated Thomas his deacon from the province of the Gyrwas★ to succeed him. He died after five years in the bishopric, and was followed by Bertgils, a man of Kent known as Boniface. Archbishop Honorius himself, having run his course, died on the thirtieth of September 653, and after a vacancy of eighteen months Deusdedit, a West Saxon, was elected to the archiepiscopal see and so became the sixth Archbishop. He was consecrated by Ithamar, Bishop of Rochester, on the twenty-sixth of March (655), and ruled the see until his death nine years, four months, and two days later. And on the death of Ithamar, Deusdedit himself con-consecrated Damian, a South Saxon, in his place.

CHAPTER 21: *The Province of the Middle Angles, under its king Peada, becomes Christian* [A.D. 653]

ABOUT this time the Middle Angles, ruled by their king Peada, son of Penda, accepted the true Faith and its sacraments. Peada, who was a noble young man, well deserving the title and dignity of a king, whom his father had appointed to the kingship of this people, went to Oswy king of the Northumbrians and requested the hand of his daughter Alchfled in marriage. Oswy, however, would not agree to this unless the king and his people accepted the Christian Faith and were baptized. So when Peada had received instruction in the true Faith, and had learned of the promises of the kingdom of heaven and of man's hope of resurrection and eternal life to come, he said that he would gladly become a Christian, even if he were refused the princess. He was chiefly influenced to accept the Faith by King Oswy's son Alchfrid, who was his kinsman and friend, and had married his sister Cyniburg, daughter of King Penda.

Accordingly, Peada was baptized by Bishop Finan, together with his companions and thanes and all their servants, at a well-known village belonging to the king known as At-Wall.* Then, taking with him four priests, chosen for their learning and holy life, to instruct and baptize his people, he returned home full of joy. These priests were Cedd, Adda, Betti, and Diuma, all of whom were English except Diuma, who was a Scot. As I have said, Adda was brother of Utta, a well-known priest and Abbot of Gateshead. On their arrival in the province with the king, these priests preached the word of God and found a ready hearing, both noble and common folk alike coming in great numbers daily to renounce their idols and receive Baptism.

King Penda himself did not forbid the preaching of the Faith to any even of his own Mercians who wished to listen; but he hated and despised any whom he knew to be insincere in their practice of Christianity once they had accepted it, and said that any who despised the commandments of the God in whom they professed to believe were themselves despicable wretches. This Christian mission was begun two years before Penda's death. And when Penda was killed, and was succeeded by the Christian King Oswy, as I shall tell later, Diuma, one of these four priests, was consecrated Bishop of the Middle Angles and Mercians by Bishop Finan, since a shortage of priests made it necessary for one bishop to preside over two peoples.* During his short episcopate, Diuma converted many to the Faith, and died among the Middle Angles in the district known as In-Feppingum. He was succeeded by Ceol-lach, a Scot who relinquished the see after a short time and returned to the Isle of Iona, the chief and mother-house of many Scots monasteries. His successor was Bishop Trumhere, a devout man trained as a monk, English by race but conse-crated bishop by the Scots. This took place during the reign of King Wulfhere, of whom I shall speak later.

About this time also, the East Saxons, who had once rejected the Faith and driven out Bishop Mellitus, again accepted it under the influence of King Oswy. For Sigbert their king, successor to Sigbert the Small, was a friend of Oswy and often used to visit him in the province of the Northumbrians. Oswy used to reason with him how gods made by man's handiwork could not be gods, and how a god could not be made from a log or block of stone, the rest of which might be burned or made into articles of everyday use or possibly thrown away as rubbish to be trampled underfoot and reduced to dust. He showed him how God is rather to be understood as a being of boundless majesty, invisible to human eyes, almighty, everlasting, Creator of heaven and earth and of the human race. He told him that he rules and will judge the world in justice, abiding in eternity, not in base and perishable metal; and that it should be rightly understood that all who know and do the will of their Creator will receive an eternal reward from him. King Oswy advanced these and other arguments during friendly and brotherly talks with Sigbert, who, encouraged by the agreement of his friends, was at length convinced. So he talked it over with his advisers, and with one accord they accepted the Faith and were baptized with him by Bishop Finan in the king's village of At-Wall, so named because it stands close to the wall which the Romans once built to protect Britain, about twelve miles from the eastern coast.

Having now become a citizen of the kingdom of heaven, Sigbert returned to the capital of his earthly kingdom after asking Oswy to send him teachers to convert his people to the Faith of Christ and baptize them. Accordingly Oswy sent to the province of the Middle Angles and summoned the man of God, Cedd, whom he dispatched with another priest as companion to evangelize the East Saxons. When these priests had visited the entire province and established a strong Christian community, Cedd returned home to Lindisfarne for consultations with Bishop Finan. When the latter learned the great success of his preaching, he invited two other bishops to assist him, and consecrated Cedd Bishop of the East Saxons. And when Cedd had been raised to the dignity of bishop, he returned to his province and used his increased authority to promote the work already begun. He built churches in several places and ordained priests and deacons to assist in teaching the Faith and baptizing the people, especially in the city which the Saxons call Ythan-caestir* and that called Tilaburg.[1] The former place stands on the bank of the River Pant, the latter on the River Thames. Here Cedd established communities of the servants of Christ and taught them to maintain the discipline of the regular life so far as these untutored folk were then capable of doing.

To the great joy of the king and all his people, the Gospel of eternal life made daily headway throughout the province for a considerable time until, at the instigation of the Enemy of all good men, the king was murdered by his own kinsmen. This horrid crime was committed by two brothers who, on being asked their motive, had no answer to make except that they hated the king because he was too lenient towards his enemies and too readily forgave injuries when offenders asked pardon. This then was the fault for which the king was killed, that he sincerely observed the teachings of the Gospel. Yet in this undeserved fate he was overtaken by punishment for his real fault, as the man of God had once foretold. For one of the nobles who murdered him had contracted an illicit marriage, and the bishop, being unable to prevent or correct this, had therefore excommunicated him, forbidding anyone to enter his house or eat at his table. But the king had disregarded this ban and had accepted the noble's

1. Tilbury.

invitation to a feast. As he was leaving the house, the bishop met him, and the king immediately dismounted from his horse and fell trembling at his feet, begging pardon for his fault. The bishop, for he too had been on horseback, also dismounted in great anger and, touching the prostrate king with the staff in his hand, exercised his pontifical authority and said: 'I tell you that, since you have refused to avoid the house of a man who is lost and damned, this very house will be the place of your death.' However, since the death of this religious king was due to his loyal obedience to Christ's commandments, we may believe that it atoned for his earlier offence and increased his merits.

Sigbert was succeeded as king by Swidhelm, son of Sexbald, who had been baptized by Cedd in the province of the East Angles at the king's country-seat of Rendlesham, that is, Rendil's House: his godfather was Ethelwald, King of the East Angles, brother of king Anna.

CHAPTER 23: *Cedd receives the site for a monastery from King Ethelwald, and hallows it to our Lord with prayer and fasting: his death* [A.D. 659]

DURING his episcopate among the East Saxons, God's servant Cedd often visited his own province, that is the province of the Northumbrians, to preach. Ethelwald, son of King Oswald, who ruled in the region of Deira, knowing Cedd to be a wise, holy, and virtuous man, asked him to accept a grant of land to found a monastery, to which he himself might often come to pray and hear the word of God and where he might be buried: for he firmly believed that the daily prayers of those who would serve God there would be of great help to him. The king's chaplain had been Cedd's brother, a priest named Caelin, a man equally devoted to God, who had ministered the Word and Sacraments to himself and his family, and it was mainly through him that

the king came to know and love the bishop. In accordance
with the king's wishes, Cedd chose a site for the monastery
among some high and remote hills, which seemed more
suitable for the dens of robbers and haunts of wild beasts
than for human habitation. His purpose in this was to fulfil
the prophecy of Isaiah: '*in the habitation of dragons, where each
lay, shall be grass, with reeds and rushes*', so that the fruits of
good works might spring up where formerly lived only wild
beasts, or men who lived like the beasts.

The man of God wished first of all to purify the site of the
monastery from the taint of earlier crimes by prayer and
fasting and make it acceptable to God before laying the foundations. He therefore asked the king's permission to remain
there throughout the approaching season of Lent, and during
this time he fasted until evening every day except Sunday
according to custom. Even then, he took no food but a
morsel of bread, a hen's egg and a little watered milk. He
explained that it was the custom of those who had trained
him in the rule of regular discipline to dedicate the site of any
monastery or church to God with prayer and fasting. But
ten days before the end of Lent a messenger arrived to
summon him to the king. So in order that the king's business
should not interrupt the work of dedication, Cedd asked his
brother the priest Cynibil to complete this holy task. The
latter readily consented, and when the period of prayer, and
fasting came to an end, he built the monastery now called
Laestingaeu,[1] and established there the observance of the
usages of Lindisfarne where he had been trained.

When Cedd had been bishop of the province and administered the affairs of this monastery for many years through
his chosen representatives, he happened to visit the monastery
during a time of plague, and there fell sick and died. He was
first buried in the open, but in the course of time a stone
church was built, dedicated to the blessed Mother of God,
and in it his body was reinterred on the right side of the altar.

1. Lastingham, near Whitby.

The bishop bequeathed the abbacy of the monastery to his brother Chad, who subsequently became a bishop as I shall record later. The four brothers I have mentioned – Cedd, Cynibil, Caelin, and Chad – all became famous priests of our Lord, and two became bishops, which is a rare occurrence in one family. When the brethren of Cedd's monastery in the province of the East Saxons heard that their founder had died and been buried in the province of the Northumbrians, about thirty of them came there wishing either, God willing, to live near the body of their Father, or else to die and be laid to rest at his side. They were kindly welcomed by their brothers and fellow-soldiers of Christ, and all of them died there of the plague with the exception of one little boy who must surely have been preserved from death by the prayers of his Father Chad. For many years afterwards, when this boy was still alive and applying himself to the study of the Scriptures, he suddenly learned that he had never been baptized; so he at once sought salvation in the waters of the font, and was subsequently admitted to the priesthood and proved himself a support to many in the Church. So I have no doubt that, when the boy visited the tomb of his beloved Father, he was saved from imminent death by his prayers, in order that he might escape eternal death and by his witness exercise a ministry of life and salvation to the other brethren.

CHAPTER 24: *On the death of Penda, the Province of the Mercians accepts the Faith of Christ: in gratitude for his victory, Oswy gives endowments and lands to God for the building of monasteries* [A.D. 655]

A T this period King Oswy was subjected to savage and intolerable attacks by Penda, the above-mentioned King of the Mercians who had slain his brother. At length dire need compelled him to offer Penda an incalculable quantity of regalia and presents as the price of peace, on condition that he returned home and ceased his ruinous devastation of the provinces of his kingdom. But the treacherous king refused to consider his offer, and declared his intention of wiping out the entire nation from the highest to the humblest in the land. Accordingly Oswy turned for help to the mercy of God, who alone could save the land from its barbarous and godless enemy; and he bound himself with an oath, saying: 'If the heathen refuses to accept our gifts, let us offer them to the Lord our God.' So he vowed that, if he were victorious, he would offer his daughter to God as a consecrated virgin and give twelve estates to build monasteries. This done, he gave battle with an insignificant force to the pagan armies, which are said to have been thirty times greater than his own and comprised thirty battle-hardened legions under famous commanders. Oswy and his son Alchfrid, trusting in Christ as their leader, met them, as I have said, with very small forces. His other son Egfrid was at the time held hostage at the court of Queen Cynwise in the province of the Mercians. But Oswald's son Ethelwald, who should have helped them, had gone over to the enemy and had acted as guide to Penda's army against his own kin and country, although during the actual battle he withdrew and awaited the outcome in a place of safety. When battle had been joined, the pagans suffered defeat. Almost all the thirty commanders who had come to Penda's aid were killed. Among them Ethelhere, brother and successor of King Anna of the East Angles, who had been responsible for the war, fell with all his men. This battle was fought close by the River Winwaed, which at the time was swollen by heavy rains and had flooded the surrounding country: as a result, many more were drowned while attempting to escape than perished by the sword.

In fulfilment of his vow to the Lord, King Oswy gave thanks to God for his victory and dedicated his daughter Aelffled, who was scarcely a year old, to his service in perpetual virginity. He also gave twelve small grants of land,

where heavenly warfare was to take the place of earthly, and
to provide for the needs of monks to make constant intercession for the perpetual peace of his nation. Six of these lay
in the province of Deira, and six in Bernicia, each of ten
hides in extent, making one hundred and twenty in all. The
daughter whom King Oswy had in this way dedicated to
God entered the monastery of Heruteu[1] or Hart's Island, at
that time ruled by Abbess Hilda. Two years later, the Abbess
acquired a property of ten hides at a place called Streanaeshalch,[2]★ where she founded a monastery. In this the king's
daughter became first a novice and later a mistress of the
monastic life, until at fifty-nine years of age this holy virgin
departed to the wedding-feast and embrace of her heavenly
Bridegroom. In the church of this monastery, dedicated to
the holy Apostle Peter, she herself, her father Oswy, her
mother Eanfled, her mother's father Edwin, and many other
noble folk are buried. This battle was won by King Oswy in
the region of Loidis[3] on the fifteenth of November in the
thirteenth year of his reign, to the great benefit of both
nations. For not only did he deliver his own people from
the hostile attacks of the heathen, but after cutting off their
infidel head he converted the Mercians and their neighbours
to the Christian Faith.

The first Bishop in the province of the Mercians, together
with the people of Lindsey and the Middle Angles, was the
above-mentioned Diuma, who died and was buried among
the Middle Angles. The second was Ceollach, who resigned
the bishopric and returned to the land of the Scots; for both
he and Diuma were of Scottish race. The third was Trumhere,
an Englishman trained and ordained by the Scots, who was
abbot of the monastery of In-Getlingum.[4] As I have said, this
was the place where King Oswin had been killed and where
his kinswoman Queen Eanfled, in expiation for his unjust
death, petitioned King Oswy to grant God's servant Trum-

1. Hartlepool.   2. Whitby.   3. Leeds.
            4. Gilling, near Richmond.

here, who was also a near relative of the king, land on which
to build a monastery; in this way, prayer could be offered
for the eternal salvation of both kings, slayer and slain alike.
For three years after the death of Penda, King Oswy ruled
both the Mercians and the other peoples of the southern
provinces; he also subjected most of the Picts to English rule.

At this time he granted Peada, son of Penda, because he
was his kinsman, the Kingdom of the South Mercians, which
consists of five thousand hides of land and is divided by the
River Trent from the land of the North Mercians, which
consists of seven thousand hides. In the following spring,
however, during the Festival of Easter, Peada was foully
assassinated through the treachery, it is said, of his own wife.
And three years after Penda's death the Mercian leaders
Immin, Eafa, and Eadbert rebelled against Oswy and proclaimed as king Wulfhere, son of Penda, a youth whom they
had kept hidden; and having driven out the representatives
of a king whom they refused to acknowledge, they boldly
recovered their liberty and lands. Free under their own king,
they gave willing allegiance to Christ their true King, so that
they might win his eternal kingdom in heaven. King Wulfhere ruled the Mercians for seventeen years and, as I have said,
had Trumhere as his first bishop. The second bishop was
Jaruman; the third, Chad; the fourth, Wynfrid. All these in
turn held the bishopric of the Mercians under King Wulfhere.

CHAPTER 25: *Controversy arises with the Scots over the
date of Easter* [A.D. 664]

WHEN Bishop Aidan departed this life, he was succeeded in the Bishopric by Finan, who had been consecrated and sent by the Scots. He built a church in the Isle
of Lindisfarne suitable for an episcopal see, constructing it,
however, not of stone, but of hewn oak thatched with reeds
after the Scots manner. It was later dedicated by the most

reverend Archbishop Theodore in honour of the blessed
Apostle Peter. But Eadbert, a later Bishop of Lindisfarne,
removed the thatch, and covered both roof and walls with
sheets of lead.

About this time there arose a great and recurrent controversy on the observance of Easter, those trained in Kent and
Gaul maintaining that the Scottish observance was contrary
to that of the universal Church. The most zealous champion
of the true Easter was a Scot named Ronan, who had been
instructed in Gaul and Italy in the authentic practice of the
Church. He disputed against Finan and convinced many, or
at least persuaded them to make more careful enquiry into
the truth. But he entirely failed to move Finan, a hot-tem-
pered man whom reproof made more obstinate and openly
hostile to the truth. James, formerly the deacon of the venerable Archbishop Paulinus, of whom I have spoken, kept the
true and Catholic Easter with all whom he could persuade
to adopt the right observance. Also Queen Eanfled and her
court, having a Kentish priest named Romanus who followed
the Catholic practice, observed the customs she had seen in
Kent. It is said that the confusion in those days was such that
Easter was sometimes kept twice in one year, so that when the
King had ended Lent and was keeping Easter, the Queen and
her attendants were still fasting and keeping Palm Sunday.
During Aidan's lifetime these differences of Easter observance were patiently tolerated by everyone; for it was realized that, although he was in loyalty bound to retain the
customs of those who sent him, he nevertheless laboured
diligently to cultivate the faith, piety, and love that marks out
God's saints. He was therefore rightly loved by all, even by
those who differed from his opinion on Easter, and was held
in high respect not only by ordinary folk, but by Honorius
of Canterbury and Felix of the East Angles.

When Finan, who followed Aidan as bishop, died, he was
succeeded by another Irishman, Colman, under whom an
even more serious controversy arose about Easter and also

about other rules of Church discipline. This dispute rightly
began to trouble the minds and consciences of many people,
who feared that they might have received the name of Christian in vain. Eventually the matter came to the notice of King
Oswy and his son Alchfrid. Oswy thought nothing could be
better than the Scots teaching, having been instructed and
baptized by the Scots and having a complete grasp of their
language. But Alchfrid, who had been instructed in the
Faith by Wilfrid – a very learned man who had gone to Rome
to study the doctrine of the Church, and spent a long time at
Lyons under Dalfin, Archbishop of Gaul, from whom he had
received the tonsure – knew that Wilfrid's doctrine was in
fact preferable to all the traditions of the Scots. He had therefore given him a monastery with forty hides of land at
In-Hrypum.[1] Actually, he had given this not long previously
to the adherents of the Scottish customs; but since, when
offered the alternative, these preferred to give up the place
rather than alter their customs, he then offered it to Wilfrid,
whose life and teaching made him a worthy recipient. About
this time, Agilbert, Bishop of the West Saxons, whom I have
mentioned, had come to visit the province of the Northumbrians. He was a friend both of King Alchfrid and of Abbot
Wilfrid and stayed with them for some time, and at the
king's request he made Wilfrid a priest in his monastery. He
also had with him a priest named Agatho. So when discussion arose there on the questions of Easter, the tonsure,
and various other church matters, it was decided to hold a
synod to put an end to this dispute at the monastery of
Streanaeshalch, which means The Bay of the Beacon, then
ruled by the Abbess Hilda, a woman devoted to God. Both
kings, father and son, came to this synod, and so did Bishop
Colman with his Scots clergy, and Bishop Agilbert with the
priests Agatho and Wilfrid. James and Romanus supported
the latter, while Abbess Hilda and her community, together
with the venerable bishop Cedd, supported the Scots. Cedd,

1. Ripon.

who as already mentioned had long ago been ordained by
the Scots, acted as a most careful interpreter for both parties
at the council.

King Oswy opened by observing that all who served the
One God should observe one rule of life, and since they all
hoped for one kingdom in heaven, they should not differ in
celebrating the sacraments of heaven. The synod now had
the task of determining which was the truer tradition, and
this should be loyally accepted by all. He then directed his
own bishop Colman to speak first, and to explain his own
rite and its origin. Then Colman said: 'The Easter customs
which I observe were taught me by my superiors, who sent
me here as a bishop; and all our forefathers, men beloved of
God, are known to have observed these customs. And lest
anyone condemn or reject them as wrong, it is recorded that
they owe their origin to the blessed evangelist Saint John,
the disciple especially loved by our Lord, and all the churches
over which he presided.' When he had concluded these and
similar arguments, the king directed Agilbert to explain the
origin and authority of his own customs. Agilbert replied:
'May I request that my disciple the priest Wilfrid be allowed
to speak in my place? For we are both in full agreement with
all those here present who support the traditions of our
Church, and he can explain our view in the English language
more competently and clearly than I can do through an
interpreter.' When Wilfrid had received the king's command
to speak, he said: 'Our Easter customs are those that we have
seen universally observed in Rome, where the blessed Apostles
Peter and Paul lived, taught, suffered, and are buried. We have
also seen the same customs generally observed throughout
Italy and Gaul when we travelled through these countries
for study and prayer. Furthermore, we have learnt that Easter
is observed by men of different nations and languages at one
and the same time, in Africa, Asia, Egypt, Greece, and
throughout the world wherever the Church of Christ has
spread. The only people who stupidly contend against the

whole world are these Scots and their partners in obstinacy the Picts and Britons, who inhabit only a portion of these the two uttermost islands of the ocean.' In reply to this statement, Colman answered: 'It is strange that you call us stupid when we uphold customs that rest on the authority of so great an Apostle, who was considered worthy to lean on our Lord's breast, and whose great wisdom is acknowledged throughout the world.' Wilfrid replied: 'Far be it from us to charge John with stupidity, because he literally observed the Law of Moses at a time when the Church followed many Jewish practices, and the Apostles were not able immediately to abrogate the observances of the Law once given by God, lest they gave offence to believers who were Jews (whereas idols, on the other hand, being inventions of the Devil, must be renounced by all converts). For this reason Paul circumcised Timothy, offered sacrifice in the Temple, and shaved his head at Corinth with Aquila and Priscilla, for no other reason than that of avoiding offence to the Jews. For James said to Paul: "*Thou seest, brother, how many thousands of Jews there are which believe; and they are all zealous of the law.*" But today, as the Gospel spreads throughout the world, it is unnecessary and indeed unlawful for the faithful to be circumcised or to offer animals to God in sacrifice. John, following the custom of the Law, used to begin the Feast of Easter on the evening of the fourteenth day of the first month, not caring whether it fell on the Sabbath or on any other day. But Peter, when he preached in Rome, remembering that it was on the day after the Sabbath that our Lord rose from the dead and gave the world the hope of resurrection, realized that Easter should be kept as follows: like John, in accordance with the Law, he waited for moonrise on the evening of the fourteenth day of the first month. And if the Lord's Day, then called the morrow of the Sabbath, fell on the following day, he began to observe Easter the same evening, as we all do today. But, if the Lord's Day did not fall on the day following the fourteenth day of the moon, but on the sixteenth, seventeenth, or any other day up to the twenty-first, he waited until that day, and on the Sabbath evening preceding it he began the observance of the Easter Festival. This evangelical and apostolical tradition does not abrogate but fulfil the Law, which ordained that the Passover be kept between the eve of the fourteenth and twenty-first days of the moon of that month. And this is the custom of all the successors of blessed John in Asia since his death, and is also that of the world-wide Church. This is the true and only Easter to be observed by the faithful. It was not newly decreed by the Council of Nicaea, but reaffirmed by it, as Church history records. It is quite apparent, Colman, that you follow neither the example of John, as you imagine, nor that of Peter, whose tradition you deliberately contradict. Your keeping of Easter agrees neither with the Law nor with the Gospel. For John, who kept Easter in accordance with the decrees of Moses, did not keep to the first day after the Sabbath; but this is not your practice, for you keep Easter only on the first day after the Sabbath. Peter kept Easter between the fifteenth and twenty-first days of the moon; you do not, for you keep it between the fourteenth and twentieth days of the moon. As a result, you often begin Easter on the evening of the thirteenth day, which is not mentioned in the Law. Nor did our Lord, the Author and Giver of the Gospel, eat the old Passover or institute the Sacrament of the New Testament to be celebrated by the Church in memory of His Passion on that day, but on the fourteenth. Furthermore, when you keep Easter, you totally exclude the twenty-first day, which the Law of Moses particularly ordered to be observed. Therefore, I repeat, you follow neither John nor Peter, the Law nor the Gospel, in your keeping of our greatest Festival.'

Colman in reply said: 'Do you maintain that Anatolius, a holy man highly spoken of in Church history, taught contrary to the Law and the Gospel, when he wrote that Easter should be kept between the fourteenth and twentieth days

of the moon? Are we to believe that our most revered Father
Columba and his successors, men so dear to God, thought or
acted contrary to Holy Scripture when they followed this
custom? The holiness of many of them is confirmed by
heavenly signs, and their virtues by miracles; and having no
doubt that they are Saints, I shall never cease to emulate their
lives, customs, and discipline.'

'It is well established that Anatolius was a most holy,
learned, and praiseworthy man,' answered Wilfrid; 'but how
can you claim his authority when you do not follow his directions? For he followed the correct rule about Easter, and
observed a cycle of nineteen years; but either you do not
know of this general custom of the Christian Church, or else
you ignore it. He calculated the fourteenth day of the moon
at Easter according to the Egyptian method, counting it in
the evening as the fifteenth day; similarly, he assigned the
twentieth to Easter Sunday, regarding it after sunset as the
twenty-first day. But it appears that you do not realize this
distinction, since you sometimes keep Easter before full
moon, that is, on the thirteenth day. And with regard to your
Father Columba and his followers, whose holiness you claim
to imitate and whose rules and customs you claim to have
been supported by heavenly signs, I can only say that when
many shall say to our Lord at the day of judgement: "*Have
we not prophesied in Thy name, and cast out devils, and done many
wonderful works?*" the Lord will reply, "*I never knew you.*"
Far be it from me to apply these words to your fathers; for it
is more just to believe good rather than evil of those whom
one does not know. So I do not deny that they were true
servants of God and dear to Him, and that they loved Him
in primitive simplicity but in devout sincerity. Nor do I
think that their ways of keeping Easter were seriously harmful,
so long as no one came to show them a more perfect way to
follow. Indeed, I feel certain that, if any Catholic reckoner
had come to them, they would readily have accepted his
guidance, as we know that they readily observed such of

God's ordinances as they already knew. But you and your colleagues are most certainly guilty of sin if you reject the decrees of the Apostolic See, indeed of the universal Church, which are confirmed by Holy Writ. For, although your Fathers were holy men, do you imagine that they, a few men in a corner of a remote island, are to be preferred before the universal Church of Christ throughout the world? And even if your Columba – or, may I say, ours also if he was the servant of Christ – was a Saint potent in miracles, can he take precedence before the most blessed Prince of the Apostles, to whom our Lord said: "*Thou art Peter, and upon this rock I will build my Church, and the gates of hell shall not prevail against it, and I will give unto thee the keys of the kingdom of heaven*"?'

When Wilfrid had ended, the king asked: 'Is it true, Colman, that these words were spoken to that Peter by our Lord?' He answered: 'It is true, Your Majesty.' Then the king said: 'Can you show that a similar authority was given to your Columba?' 'No,' replied Colman. 'Do you both agree', the king continued, 'that these words were indisputably addressed to Peter in the first place, and that our Lord gave him the keys of the kingdom of heaven?' Both answered: 'We do.' At this, the king concluded: 'Then, I tell you, Peter is guardian of the gates of heaven, and I shall not contradict him. I shall obey his commands in everything to the best of my knowledge and ability; otherwise, when I come to the gates of heaven, there may be no one to open them, because he who holds the keys has turned away.'*

When the king said this, all present, both high and low, signified their agreement and, abandoning their imperfect customs, hastened to adopt those which they had learned to be better.

CHAPTER 26: *After his defeat Colman returns home and Tuda succeeds to his bishopric* [A.D. 664]: *the condition of the Church under these teachers*

IN this way the controversy was terminated, the company dispersed, and Agilbert returned home. Colman, seeing his teachings rejected and his following discounted, took away with him all who wished to follow him, that is, all who still dissented from the Catholic Easter and tonsure* – for there was no small argument about this as well – and returned to the land of the Scots in order to consult his compatriots on their future course of action. Cedd, on the other hand, having abandoned the Scots' customs and accepted the Catholic, returned to his own bishopric. This Synod took place in the year of our Lord 664, which was the twenty-second year of King Oswy's reign, and the thirtieth anniversary of the coming of the Scots bishops to England, Aidan having held his bishopric for seventeen years, Finan for ten, and Colman for three.

On Colman's return to his own land, the servant of God, Tuda, became bishop of the Northumbrians in his place. He had been trained and consecrated bishop by the southern Scots, and had worn the ecclesiastical tonsure according to the customs of the province, and observed the Catholic Easter customs. He was a good devout man, but ruled the diocese only for a short time. He had arrived from the land of the Scots during Colman's episcopate, and taught the truths of the Faith diligently in word and deed. Then Eata, abbot of the monastery of Mailros,¹ a gentle man and greatly revered, was appointed Abbot of Lindisfarne to rule the brethren who elected to remain there when the Scots withdrew. It is said that before Colman left, he asked and obtained this favour from King Oswy, because Eata had been one of the twelve English boys whom Aidan received to be taught the Christian Faith when he first became bishop; for the king had high

1. Melrose.

regard for Bishop Colman's inherent good sense. This is the same Eata who not long afterwards was raised to the bishopric of the church of Lindisfarne. On his return home, Colman took with him a portion of the bones of the most reverend Father Aidan; but he left some of them in the church over which he had ruled, directing that they be enshrined in the sacristy.

So frugal and austere were Colman and his predecessors that when they left the seat of their authority there were very few buildings except the church; indeed, no more than met the bare requirements of a seemly way of life. They had no property except cattle, and whenever they received any money from rich folk, they immediately gave it to the poor; for they had no need to amass money or provide lodging for important people, since such visited the church only in order to pray or hear the word of God. Whenever opportunity offered, the king himself used to come with only five or six attendants; and when he had completed his prayer in the church, he used to leave. But if they happened to remain for a meal, they were content with the plain daily food of the brothers and asked nothing more. For in those days the sole concern of these teachers was to serve God, not the world; to satisfy the soul, not the belly. Accordingly the religious habit at that time was held in high esteem. Wherever any priest or monk paid a visit, he was joyfully welcomed by all as the servant of God. And if people met him on the road, they ran to him and bowed, eager to be signed by his hand or receive a blessing from his lips. Whenever he spoke a word of encouragement, he was given an attentive hearing. On Sundays the people flocked to the churches and monasteries, not to obtain food, but to hear the word of God. When a priest visited a village, the people were quick to gather together to receive the word of life; for priests and clerics always came to a village solely to preach, baptize, visit the sick, and, in short, to care for the souls of its people. They were so free from the sin of avarice that none of them would accept lands or gifts for the building of monasteries unless expressly directed to do so by the secular authorities. This continued to be the general practice for some years among the churches of the Northumbrians. But enough has been said on such matters.

CHAPTER 27: *Egbert, an Englishman of holy life, becomes a monk in Ireland*

IN the same year of our Lord 664 an eclipse of the sun occurred about ten o'clock in the morning on the third of May; and a sudden plague, which first decimated the southern parts of Britain and later spread into the province of the Northumbrians, raged for a long time and brought widespread death to many people. Bishop Tuda fell a victim to this plague, and was buried with honour in the monastery of Paegnalaech. The plague was equally destructive in Ireland. At this period there were many English nobles and lesser folk in Ireland who had left their own land during the episcopates of Bishops Finan and Colman, either to pursue religious studies or to lead a life of stricter discipline. Some of these soon devoted themselves to the monastic life, while others preferred to travel, studying under various teachers in turn. The Scots welcomed them all kindly, and, without asking for any payment, provided them with daily food, books, and instruction.

Among these English nobles were Ethelhun and Egbert, two young men of outstanding ability. The former was brother of Ethelwin, a man no less dear to God, who at a later date also travelled to study in Ireland and, after a full course of instruction, returned home and was made Bishop of Lindsey, where he enjoyed a long and illustrious episcopate. These two young men, who were studying in the monastery which the Scots call Rathmelsigi, having lost all their companions either through the plague or through their dispersal to other places, were themselves stricken by the same disease and fell dangerously ill. And I am told by a most dependable priest of venerable age, who says that he learnt the story at first hand, that Egbert,* believing himself about to die, went out one morning from the room where the sick were lying and, sitting down in a place by himself, began seriously to examine his past life. Tears fell from his eyes as he sorrowfully recalled his sins, and he begged God from the bottom of his heart not to let him die until he could atone for the offences of his boyhood and youth, and exert himself to better purpose in good deeds. He also made a vow that he would remain an exile and never return to his native island of Britain; and that, unless prevented by sickness, in addition to the canonical hours of prayer, he would recite the entire Psalter daily to the praise of God and would fast once a week for a day and a night. When he had ended his tears, vows and prayers, he returned to the house where he found his companion asleep; and lying down on his pallet, he composed himself to rest. When he had lain there a short while, his companion awoke, and looking at him, said: 'O brother Egbert, what have you done? I was hoping that we should enter eternal life together; but now you may be sure that what you have prayed for will be granted.' For he had learned in a vision what his friend had prayed for, and that his prayer was heard. The rest is soon told. Ethelhun died the following night; but Egbert threw off the disease, recovered, and lived for many years. He became a worthy ornament of the priestly order, and, as he had prayed, lived a life of great merit, entering the kingdom of heaven at the age of ninety in the year of our Lord 729. Egbert led a life of great humility, gentleness, purity, simplicity, and uprightness. He brought great blessings both to his own nation, and to the Picts and Scots among whom he exiled himself, setting them an example of holy life. He was indefatigable in teaching, firm in administering reproof, and generous in distributing whatever he received from the rich. In addition to his earlier vows, he ate only one meal a day during Lent, allowing himself a scanty ration of bread and skim milk;

for he used to keep the previous day's fresh milk in a flask, and having skimmed off the cream next day, he drank what was left with a little bread. He practised a similar abstinence for forty days before Christmas, and as many after the Feast of Pentecost.

CHAPTER 28: *On Tuda's death, Wilfrid is consecrated bishop in Gaul and Chad among the West Saxons, to be bishops in the Province of the Northumbrians* [A.D. 665]

MEANWHILE King Alchfrid sent Wilfrid, then a priest, to the King of the Gauls* to be consecrated bishop for himself and his people. He sent him for consecration to Agilbert, who, as I have said, had been made Bishop of Paris after his return from Britain. Summoning several other bishops to the royal country-seat at Compiègne, he consecrated Wilfrid with great splendour. But since Wilfrid remained overseas for a considerable time on account of his consecration, King Oswy meanwhile, following his son's example, sent to Canterbury to be consecrated Bishop of York, a holy man, modest in his ways, learned in the Scriptures, and careful to practise all that he found in them. This was a priest named Chad, a brother of the above-mentioned most reverend Bishop Cedd, and at that time Abbot of Lastingham. With Chad the king sent a priest named Eadhaed, who later, during the reign of Egfrid, became Bishop of Ripon. On arriving in Kent, they found that Archbishop Deusdedit had died and that no successor had yet been appointed. They therefore went on to the province of the West Saxons, consecrated Chad as bishop with the assistance of two bishops of the British,* who, as I have often observed, keep Easter contrary to canonical practice between the fourteenth and twentieth days of the moon. For at that time Wini was the only bishop in all Britain who had been canonically consecrated.

When he became bishop, Chad immediately devoted
himself to maintaining the truth and purity of the Church,
and set himself to practise humility and continence and to
study. After the example of the Apostles, he travelled on foot
and not on horseback when he went to preach the Gospel,
whether in towns or country, in cottages, villages, or strongholds; for he was one of Aidan's disciples and always sought
to instruct his people by the same methods as Aidan and his
own brother Cedd. And Wilfred too, when he returned to
Britain as a bishop, introduced into the English churches
many Catholic customs, with the result that the Catholic
Rite daily gained support and all the Scots then living among
the English either conformed to it or returned to their own
land.

CHAPTER 29: *The priest Wighard is sent from Britain to
Rome to be made archbishop: letters from the apostolic Pope
tell of his death there* [A.D. 655]

AT this time, the most noble English kings Oswy of
the Northumbrians and Egbert of the Kentish folk
conferred together on the state of the Church of the English;
for Oswy, although educated by the Scots, was fully aware
that the Roman Church was the Catholic and Apostolic
Church. With the choice and approval of the holy Church
of the English, the two kings accepted the priest Wighard,
one of Archbishop Deusdedit's clergy, a good man well
fitted to be a bishop, and sent him to Rome to be consecrated
bishop, so that, when he had received the rank of Archbishop,
he could consecrate Catholic bishops for the churches of the
English throughout Britain. Wighard arrived in Rome, but
died before he could be consecrated; and the following letter
was sent to Oswy in Britain:

'To our son, the most excellent Lord Oswy, King of the
Saxons, from Bishop Vitalian, servant of the servants of God.

'We have read Your Excellency's welcome letter, in which we recognize your very sincere devotion and fervent desire for eternal life. And we know how you have been converted to the true and apostolic Faith by the guiding hand of God, and trust that, as you now reign over your own nation, so you will one day reign with Christ. Your nation is fortunate to have a king so wise and devoted to the worship of God, who not only adores God himself, but labours day and night to lead all his people to the Catholic Apostolic Faith, and to save his own soul. Who can help being glad to hear such encouraging news? And who will not be delighted at such works of devotion? For your nation has come to believe in Christ our mighty God in fulfilment of the words of God's prophets, as Isaiah says: "*In that day there shall be a root of Jesse, which shall stand as an ensign of the people; to it shall the Gentiles seek.*" And again: "*Listen, O isles, unto Me; and hearken, ye people, from far.*" And a little later he says: "*It is a light thing that thou shouldest be My servant, to raise up the tribes of Jacob, and to restore the preserved of Israel. I will also give thee for a light to the Gentiles, that thou mayest be My salvation unto the end of the earth.*" And again: "*Kings shall see, princes also shall arise and worship.*" And later: "*I have given thee for a covenant of the people, to establish the earth and possess the desolate heritages; that thou mayest say to the prisoners, Go forth; to them that are in darkness, Show yourselves.*" And again: "*I, the Lord, have called thee in righteousness, and will hold thine hand, and will keep thee, and give thee for a covenant of the people, for a light of the Gentiles; to open the blind eyes, to bring out the prisoners from prison, and them that sit in darkness out of the prison-house.*"

'Here you may see, most excellent son, how clearly it is prophesied, not only of you but of all nations, that they shall believe in Christ the Maker of all things. It must therefore be the task of Your Majesty, as a living member of Christ, always to observe the holy precepts of the Prince of the Apostles, both in keeping Easter, and in everything transmitted to us by the holy Apostles Peter and Paul, who, as the two heavenly bodies light the world, give daily light by their teaching to the hearts of all believers.'

And after some observations on the keeping of one true Easter throughout the world, the Pope continues:

'In view of the lengthy journey involved, we have not yet been able to discover a man wholly suitable to be your bishop, as you request in your letters. But as soon as such a man can be found, we will give him instructions and send him to your country, so that under God's guidance, through his own witness and the teachings of God, he may uproot the tares sown by the Enemy throughout your island. We gratefully acknowledge the gifts sent by Your Highness to the blessed Prince of the Apostles in tribute to his immortal memory, and pray for your safety together with the Christian clergy. But the bearer of your gifts has departed this life, and is buried in the Church of the Apostles. We are deeply distressed that he should have died here. We have directed, however, that blessings of the Saints – that is, relics of the blessed Apostles Peter and Paul, and of the holy martyrs Laurence, John, and Paul, Gregory and Pancras – be given to the bearers of this letter for delivery to Your Excellency. By the same bearers we send to our spiritual daughter, your queen, a cross made from the fetters of the blessed Apostles Peter and Paul with a golden key. Learning of her pious zeal, the entire apostolic see rejoices with us as greatly as her holy deeds shine and blossom in the sight of God. We trust that Your Highness will soon fulfil our hope, and dedicate your whole island to Christ our God. For assuredly you have as your protector the Redeemer of the human race, our Lord Jesus Christ, who will support all your efforts to draw together a new people in Christ, and establish there the Catholic and Apostolic Faith. For Scripture says: " *Seek first the kingdom of God and His righteousness, and all these things shall be added unto you*"; and you assuredly seek, and will obtain what we too desire, that is, the conversion of all your islands. We greet Your Excellency with fatherly affection, constantly praying that God of His mercy will assist you and yours in all good works, so that you may reign with Christ in the world to come. May Heaven's grace preserve Your Excellency in health.'

The next book will provide a more suitable place to tell who was actually discovered and consecrated in place of Wighard.

CHAPTER 30: *During a plague the East Saxons lapse into idolatry, but are quickly recalled from their errors by Bishop Jaruman* [A.D. 665]

A T the same time, the kings Sighere and Sebbi succeeded Swidhelm, of whom I have spoken, as rulers of the East Saxons under Wulfhere, King of the Mercians. While the plague was causing a heavy death-roll in the province, Sighere and his people abandoned the mysteries of the Christian Faith and relapsed into paganism. For the king himself, together with many of the nobles and common folk, loved this life and sought no other, or even disbelieved in its existence. Hoping for protection against the plague by this means, they therefore began to rebuild the ruined temples and restore the worship of idols. But Sebbi his fellow-king and colleague held with all his people loyally to the Faith they had accepted, and, as will appear later, remained faithful and ended his days happily.

As soon as King Wulfhere learned that part of the province had apostatized from the Faith, he sent Bishop Jaruman, Trumhere's successor, to correct their error and recall the province to the true Faith. I am told by a priest who accompanied him on his journey and shared his preaching that Jaruman proceeded with great energy, for he was a good devout man, who travelled far and wide and succeeded in bringing back both king and people to the path of righteousness. As a result, they abandoned or destroyed the temples and

altars they had erected, and opened the churches, glad to
confess the name of Christ whom they had denied, and more
ready to die with him believing in the Resurrection than to
continue living among their idols in the degradation of
apostasy. Their task accomplished, these priests and teachers
then returned home full of joy.

BOOK FOUR

CHAPTER I: *On the death of Archbishop Deusdedit, Wighard is sent to Rome to be consecrated in his stead: on the latter's death there, Theodore is consecrated Archbishop and sent to Britain with Abbot Hadrian* [A.D. 664]

On the fourteenth of July in the above-mentioned year, when an eclipse was quickly followed by plague, and during which Bishop Colman was refuted by the unanimous decision of the Catholics and returned to his own country, Deusdedit the sixth Archbishop of Canterbury died. Earconbert, King of the Kentish folk, died on the same day, and was succeeded by his son Egbert, who reigned for nine years. The See of Canterbury was then vacant for a considerable time, until Wighard, an English priest with great experience in church administration, was sent to Rome by the common consent of Egbert and King Oswy of the Northumbrians, with the request that he be consecrated Archbishop of the Church of the English. This I have already briefly noted in the preceding book. At the same time the two kings sent presents to the apostolic Pope, including many gold and silver vessels. On his arrival in Rome, where Vitalian was ruling the apostolic see, Wighard explained to the Pope the reason for his journey; but shortly afterwards he and nearly all his companions fell victim to a plague that broke out at the time.

The apostolic Pope therefore took advice on the situation, and made careful enquiry as to whom he could send as Archbishop of the churches of the English. Not far from Naples

in Campania is the monastery of Niridano,* whose Abbot
Hadrian, a native of Africa, was very learned in the Scriptures,
experienced in ecclesiastical and monastic administration,
and a great scholar in Greek and Latin. So the Pope summoned
Hadrian, and directed him to accept the bishopric and go to
Britain. Hadrian excused himself on the grounds that he was
not fitted for such high dignity, but said that he could recom-
mend another, whose learning and age were more suited to
the office of bishop. He proposed to the Pope a monk named
Andrew, who was chaplain to a neighbouring convent of
women, and was considered as worthy of a bishopric by all
who knew him; but Andrew excused himself on the grounds
of ill health. Then Hadrian was again pressed to accept the
bishopric; but he asked for a delay in order to make a fresh
attempt to find a more suitable man.

At this time there was in Rome a monk named Theodore,
a native of Tarsus in Cilicia, who was well known to Hadrian.
He was learned both in sacred and in secular literature, in
Greek and in Latin, of proved integrity, and of the venerable
age of sixty-six. Hadrian, therefore, suggested the name of
Theodore to the Pope, who agreed to consecrate him, but
made it a condition that Hadrian himself should accompany
him to Britain, since he had already travelled through Gaul
twice on various missions and had both a better knowledge
of the road and sufficient men of his own available. The Pope
also ordered Hadrian to give full support to Theodore in his
teaching, and to ensure that he did not introduce into the
Church which he was to rule any Greek customs which
conflicted with the teachings of the true Faith. On receiving
the subdiaconate, Theodore waited four months for his hair
to grow so that he could receive the circular tonsure; for
hitherto he had worn the tonsure of the holy Apostle Paul in
conformity to Eastern custom. He was then consecrated
bishop by Pope Vitalian on Sunday the 26th of March 668,
and on the 27th of May he set out for Britain, accompanied
by Hadrian.

The travellers crossed by sea to Massilia,[1] and thence over-land to Arles, where they delivered Pope Vitalian's letters of commendation to John, Archbishop of that city, who gave them hospitality until Ebroin, Mayor of the king's palace, gave them a permit to travel wherever they wished. Armed with this Theodore then went on to Agilbert, Bishop of Paris, of whom I have already spoken, who welcomed him kindly and entertained him for a considerable time. Hadrian meanwhile went first to Emme, Bishop of Sens, and then to Faro, Bishop of Meaux, and made lengthy stays with them, since the approach of winter obliged travellers to remain quietly wherever they could. When messengers informed King Egbert that the bishop whom they had requested from the Pope was now in the kingdom of the Franks, he at once sent his High Reeve Raedfrid to escort him; and when the Reeve arrived, he obtained Ebroin's permission to escort Theodore to the port of Quentavic.[2] Here exhaustion com-pelled Theodore to rest for a while; but as soon as he began to recover, he took ship for Britain. But Hadrian was de-tained by Ebroin, who suspected that he bore some message from the Emperor to the kings of Britain, which might be to the disadvantage of the kingdom for whose interests he was largely responsible. But when he ascertained that Hadrian had in fact no such mission, he released him and allowed him to follow Theodore. And as soon as Hadrian arrived, Theodore appointed him abbot of the monastery of blessed Peter the Apostle, where, as I have said, the Archbishops of Canterbury are buried. For when he left Rome the apostolic Pope had instructed Theodore to provide for him in his diocese, and give him a suitable place to live with his followers.

1. Marseilles.   2. Étaples.

CHAPTER 2: *Theodore makes a general visitation: the English churches begin to receive instruction in Catholic truth, and sacred study is fostered. Putta succeeds Damian as Bishop of Rochester* [A.D. 669]

THEODORE arrived in his see on Sunday May 27th in the second year after his consecration, and held it for twenty-one years, three months, and twenty-six days. Soon after his arrival, he visited every part of the island occupied by the English peoples, and received a ready welcome and hearing everywhere. He was accompanied and assisted throughout his journey by Hadrian, and he taught the Christian way of life and the canonical method of keeping Easter. Theodore was the first archbishop whom the entire Church of the English obeyed, and since, as I have observed, both he and Hadrian were men of learning both in sacred and in secular literature, they attracted a large number of students, into whose minds they poured the waters of wholesome knowledge day by day. In addition to instructing them in the holy Scriptures, they also taught their pupils poetry, astronomy, and the calculation of the church calendar. In proof of this, some of their students still alive today are as proficient in Latin and Greek as in their native tongue. Never had there been such happy times as these since the English settled in Britain; for the Christian kings were so strong that they daunted all the barbarous tribes. The people eagerly sought the new-found joys of the kingdom of heaven, and all who wished for instruction in the reading of the Scriptures found teachers ready at hand.

The knowledge of sacred music, hitherto limited to Kent, now began to spread to all the churches of the English. With the exception of the deacon James, already mentioned, the first singing-master in the Northumbrian churches was Eddi, known as Stephen, who was invited from Kent by the most reverend Wilfrid, the first bishop of English blood★ to teach the churches of the English the Catholic way of life.

During his visitation, Theodore consecrated bishops in suitable places, and with their assistance he corrected abuses wherever he found them. When he informed Bishop Chad that his consecration was irregular,* the latter replied with the greatest humility: 'If you know that my consecration as bishop was irregular, I willingly resign the office; for I have never thought myself worthy of it. Although unworthy, I accepted it solely under obedience.' At this humble reply, Theodore assured him that there was no need for him to give up his office, and himself completed his consecration according to Catholic rites. About the time that Deusdedit died and a successor for the See of Canterbury was sought for, consecrated, and sent, Wilfrid also was sent from Britain to Gaul for consecration. Returning before Theodore, he ordained certain priests and deacons in Kent, pending the archbishop's arrival in his own see. Shortly afterwards Theodore himself came to Rochester, where the see had been vacant ever since the death of Damian, and there consecrated Putta as its bishop. He was a man of simple life, who was well acquainted with church affairs, but had little experience in worldly matters. He was a most skilled exponent of the Roman chant, which he had learnt from pupils of blessed Pope Gregory.

CHAPTER 3: *Chad is appointed Bishop of the Mercians* [c. A.D. 667]: *his life, death* [A.D. 672], *and burial*

THE Mercians at this time were ruled by King Wulfhere, who on the death of Jaruman asked Theodore to provide him and his people with a bishop. Theodore, however, did not wish to consecrate a new bishop for them, but asked King Oswy to give them Chad as their bishop. Chad was then living quietly in his monastery at Lastingham, while Wilfrid ruled the Bishopric of York, and indeed of all the lands of the Northumbrians and Picts to the borders of Oswy's realms. The most reverend Bishop Chad always preferred to undertake his preaching missions on foot rather than on horseback; but Theodore ordered him to ride whenever he undertook a long journey. He was most reluctant to forgo this pious exercise which he loved, but the archbishop, who recognized his outstanding holiness and considered it more proper for him to ride, himself insisted on helping him to mount his horse. So Chad received the Bishopric of the Mercians and the people of Lindsey, and administered the diocese in great holiness of life after the example of the early Fathers. King Wulfhere gave him fifty hides of land to build a monastery at a place called At-Barwe – that is, At the Wood – in the province of Lindsey, and evidences of the regular observance that he established remain to this day.

Chad established his episcopal seat in the town of Lyccid-felth,[1] where he also died and was buried, and where the succeeding bishops of the province have their see to this day. There he built himself a house near the church, where he used to retire privately with seven or eight brethren in order to pray or study whenever his work and preaching permitted. When he had ruled the church of the province with great success for two and a half years, divine providence ordained a time such as is spoken of in Ecclesiastes: '*There is a time to cast away stones, and a time to gather stones together.*' For heaven sent a plague which, bringing bodily death, bore away the living stones of the Church from their earthly stations to the temple in heaven. And when death had freed many members of the revered bishop's church from the burden of the flesh, the hour drew near when Chad himself was to pass out of this world to our Lord. One day he was alone in his house with a brother whose name was Owini, his other companions having had occasion to return to the church. This Owini was a monk of great merit, who had renounced the world with the pure intention of winning a heavenly reward, so that he was altogether a fit person to receive a revelation of God's secrets, and one whose word everyone could trust. He had

1. Lichfield.

accompanied Queen Etheldreda from the province of the East Angles, and had been her chief thane and steward of her household. Growing in devotion to the Faith, he decided to renounce the world, which he did in no half-hearted fashion; for he rid himself so completely of worldly ties that he abandoned all his possessions, put on a simple garment, and carrying in his hand an axe and an adze, set off for the reverend father Chad's monastery at Lastingham. This he did to show that he was entering the monastery not for the sake of an idle life, as some do, but in order to work, and he demonstrated this in practice; for since he found himself less able to meditate on the Scriptures with profit, he undertook a larger amount of manual labour. In short, recognizing his reverence and devotion, the bishop admitted him to his house among the brethren; and whenever they were engaged in study, he used to busy himself in essential tasks out of doors. One day, while Owini was working outside and the other brethren had departed to the church, the bishop was reading and praying alone in his oratory. Suddenly, as he used afterwards to relate, he heard the sound of sweet and joyful singing coming down from heaven to earth. The sound seemed at first to emanate from the south-east, gradually coming closer to him until it centred over the roof of the oratory where the bishop was at prayer. It then entered the oratory, and seemed to fill both it and the surrounding air. He listened with rapt attention to what he heard, and after about half an hour he heard the song of joy rise from the roof of the oratory, and return to heaven as it had come with inexpressible sweetness. Owini stood astonished for a while, turning over in his mind what this might portend, when the bishop threw open the oratory window and, clapping his hands, as he often used to do if someone was outside, summoned him indoors. When he hurried in, the bishop said: 'Go at once to the church, and fetch these seven brethren here, and come back with them yourself.' On their arrival, he first urged them to live in love and peace with each other and with all the faithful, and to be constant and tireless in keeping the rules of monastic discipline that he had taught them and they knew him to observe, and those that they had learned from the lives and teachings of former abbots. He then announced that his own death was drawing near, saying: 'The welcome guest who has visited many of our brethren has come to me today, and has deigned to summon me out of this world. Therefore return to the church, and ask the brethren to commend my passing to our Lord in their prayers. And let each prepare for his own passing by vigils, prayers, and good deeds; for no man knows the hour of his death.' Having said this and much besides, he gave them his blessing, and they left him sadly; but the brother who had heard the heavenly music came back alone and flung himself to the ground, saying: 'Father, I beg you to let me ask you a question.' 'Ask what you wish,' Chad replied. 'Tell me, I pray,' he asked, 'what was the glad song that I heard of singers coming down from heaven upon this oratory and later returning to heaven?' 'Since you heard the singing and were aware of the coming of the heavenly company,' Chad answered, 'I command you in the name of our Lord not to tell anyone of this before my death. The truth is that they were angelic spirits, who came to summon me to the heavenly reward that I have always hoped and longed for, and they promised to return in seven days and take me with them.' All took place as he had been told: for Chad was quickly attacked by a disease which steadily grew worse until the seventh day. Then he prepared for death by receiving the Body and Blood of our Lord, his holy soul was released from the prison-house of the body and, one may rightly believe, was taken by the angels to the joys of heaven. Nor is it strange that he regarded death with joy as the Day of the Lord; for he had always been careful to prepare for his coming.

In addition to Chad's many virtues of continence, humility, right preaching, prayer, voluntary poverty, and many others, he was so filled with the fear of God and so mindful of his last end in all that he did, that I was told by one of his monks named Trumbert – who was one of my tutors in the Scriptures and had been trained in the monastery under Chad's direction – that, if a gale arose while he was reading or doing anything else, he would at once call upon God for mercy and pray him to show mercy on mankind. And if the wind increased in violence, he would close his book and prostrate himself on the ground, praying even more earnestly. But if there was a violent storm of wind and rain, or thunder and lightning startled earth and air, he would go to the church and devote all his thoughts to prayers and psalms continuously until the tempest had passed. When his monks asked him why he did this, Chad replied: 'Have you not read, " *The Lord thundered in the heavens, and the Highest gave His voice. He sent out His arrows and scattered them; He shot out lightnings and discomfited them* "? For God stirs the air and raises the winds; He makes the lightning flash and thunders out of heaven, to move the inhabitants of the earth to fear Him, and to remind them of judgement to come. He shatters their conceit and subdues their presumption by recalling to their minds that awful Day when heaven and earth will flame as He comes in the clouds with great power and majesty to judge the living and the dead. Therefore we should respond to His heavenly warnings with the fear and love we owe Him,' said Chad. 'And whenever He raises His hand in the trembling air as if to strike, yet spares us still, we should hasten to implore His mercy, examining our inmost hearts and purging the vileness of our sins, watchful over our lives lest we incur His just displeasure.'

This brother's account of the bishop's death is supported by the evidence of the above-mentioned most reverend Father Egbert, who lived the monastic life in Ireland with Chad when they were both youths, constantly occupied in prayer, fasting, and meditation on the sacred scriptures. But when Chad returned to his own country, Egbert remained an exile for God's sake until the end of his life. A long time afterwards, Hygbald, a very holy and austere man who was an abbot in the province of Lindsey, came from Britain to visit him. And while they were discussing the lives of the early Fathers and delighting to imitate them as was fitting in holy men, the name of the most holy Bishop Chad was mentioned. Whereupon Egbert said: 'I know a man still living in this island who, when the bishop died, saw the soul of his brother Cedd descend from heaven accompanied by angels, and carry away his soul to the heavenly kingdom.' Whether he was speaking of himself or another is uncertain; but the truth of a statement by so great a man cannot be doubted.

Chad died on the second of March [672], and was first buried close by Saint Mary's church; but when a church of the most blessed Peter, Prince of the Apostles, was built there later, his body was transferred to it.* In both of these places, frequent miracles of healing attested to his virtues. More recently, a madman wandering at large arrived there one evening, and passed the night in church unnoticed and unheeded by the watchmen. And in the morning, to the amazement and delight of all, he left the place in his right mind, showing clearly what healing he had been granted there by the goodness of God. Chad's burial place is covered by a wooden tomb made in the form of a little house with an aperture in the wall through which those who visit it out of devotion may insert their hand and take out some of the dust. They mix this in water and give it to sick men or beasts to drink, by which means their ailment is quickly relieved and they are restored to the longed for joys of health.

In Chad's place Theodore consecrated Wynfrid, a good and modest man, who like his predecessors, presided over the provinces of the Mercians, Middle Angles, and Lindsey folk, all of which were subject to King Wulfhere, who was still living. Wynfrid was one of his predecessor's clergy, and had been his deacon for a considerable time.

MEANWHILE the Scots bishop Colman left Britain, taking with him all the Scots he had collected at Lindisfarne, together with about thirty English whom he had likewise trained in the monastic life. Leaving some brethren in his own church, he first visited the isle of Hii,[1] from which he had originally been sent to preach the word to the English. He subsequently retired to a small island at some distance from the west coast of Ireland, known in the Scots tongue as Inisboufinde,[2] meaning the Isle of the White Heifer. On his arrival, he founded a monastery, and established there the monks of both races whom he had gathered. But a dispute arose among them because in summer the Scots went off to wander on their own around places they knew instead of assisting at harvest, and then, as winter approached, came back and wanted to share whatever the English monks had gathered. Colman sought a remedy for this dispute, and after searching near and far, discovered a site suitable for a monastery on the Irish mainland, a place which the Scots call Mageo.* Here he bought a small tract of land from the nobleman who owned the land, who made it a condition of sale that the monks who settled there should pray for him. So a monastery was promptly built with the help of the nobleman and all the neighbours, and Colman established the English monks there, leaving the Scots on the original island. This monastery is still occupied by English monks. For this is the place, grown large from small beginnings, that is now usually known as Muigeo and, under an improved constitution* houses a distinguished community of monks drawn from the English provinces. After the example of the venerable Fathers, they live devoutly and austerely by the labour

1. Iona.   2. Inishboffin.

213

of their own hands and observe a Rule under a canonically
elected abbot.

CHAPTER 5: *The death of King Oswy and King Egbert.
Archbishop Theodore presides over a Synod held at Hertford*
[A.D. 673]

IN the year of our Lord 670, the second year after Archbishop
Theodore's arrival in Britain, King Oswy of the Northumbrians was stricken with an illness, of which he died at the age
of fifty-eight. At this time the King held the apostolic Roman
see in such high esteem that, had he recovered from his illness, it was his intention to travel to Rome and end his life
among its holy places, and he had persuaded Bishop Wilfrid to
conduct him on the journey with the promise of a considerable gift. He died on February 15th, leaving his son Egfrid
to succeed him as king. In the third year of the latter's reign,
Theodore summoned a council of bishops and the many other
teachers of the Church who both understood and loved the
canonical statutes of the Fathers. As befitted his authority as
archbishop, when they were assembled, he began by charging
them to observe whatsoever things were conducive to the
peace and unity of the Church. The decisions of the Council
are in the following form:

'In the name of the Lord God and our Saviour Jesus Christ,
and under the everlasting governance and guidance of His
Church by the same Lord Jesus Christ, it was thought right
that we should assemble in accordance with the custom of
venerable canons to deliberate concerning the necessary
affairs of the Church. We therefore assembled on the 24th
day of September, the first indiction, at the place called Hertford; that is, myself, Theodore, though unworthy, Bishop of
the See of Canterbury by the authority of the apostolic see;
our fellow-bishop and brother the most reverend Bisi,
Bishop of the East Angles; also our brother the Bishop

Wilfrid, Bishop of the Northumbrian people, who is represented by his own proxies. Also present were our brothers and fellow-bishops Putta, Bishop of the Kentish fortress of Rochester; Leutherius, Bishop of the West Saxons, and Wynfrid, Bishop of the province of the Mercians. When all the above had assembled and taken their places in due order, I said: "My dearest brothers, for the love and reverence you bear our Redeemer, I beg that we may all deliberate in harmony for our Faith, preserving inviolate the decrees and definitions of our holy and respected Fathers." I dealt with these and many other matters relating to charity and the preservation of the Church's unity. And having concluded this introductory address, I asked each in turn whether they agreed to observe all the canonical decrees of the ancient Fathers. To which all our fellow-priests replied: "We are all resolved that we will cheerfully and willingly obey whatever is laid down in the canons of the holy Fathers." I then produced the said book of canons, and publicly showed them ten chapters which I had marked in certain places, because I knew them to be of the greatest importance to us, and I asked that all should devote special attention to them.

'*Chapter* 1. "That we all unite in observing the holy day of Easter on the Sunday after the fourteenth day of the moon of the first month."

'*Chapter* 2. "That no bishop intrude into the diocese of another, but confine himself to the guidance of the people committed to his charge."

'*Chapter* 3. "That no bishop shall interfere in any way with monasteries dedicated to God, nor take anything from them forcibly."

'*Chapter* 4. "That monks shall not wander from place to place, that is, from monastery to monastery, except with letters dimissory from their own abbot; and that they keep the promise of obedience which they made at the time of their profession."

'*Chapter* 5. "That no clergy shall leave their own bishop

and wander about at will, nor be received anywhere without letters of commendation from their own bishop. And should such a person, once received, refuse to return when so directed, both receiver and received shall incur excommunication.'

'*Chapter* 6. "That bishops and clergy when travelling shall be content with whatever hospitality is offered them; and that it shall be unlawful for any of them to exercise any priestly function without permission from the bishop in whose diocese they are known to be."

'*Chapter* 7. "That a synod be held twice a year." In view of various obstacles, however, it was unanimously agreed that we should meet once a year on the first of August at the place called Clofeshoch.[1]

'*Chapter* 8. "That no bishop claim precedence over another out of ambition: seniority of consecration shall alone determine precedence."

'*Chapter* 9. It was generally discussed, "That more bishops shall be consecrated as the number of the faithful increases." But we have announced no decision in the matter for the present.

'*Chapter* 10. On marriages: "That lawful wedlock alone is permissible; incest is forbidden; and no man may leave his lawful wife except, as the gospel provides, for fornication. And if a man puts away his own wife who is joined to him in lawful marriage, he may not take another if he wishes to be a good Christian. He must either remain as he is, or else be reconciled to his wife."

'After discussing these chapters and reaching decisions by our common consent, in order that no occasion for unedifying controversy or differences between ourselves may arise, it has been thought right that each of us should ratify our decisions by his own signature. I have dictated this expression of our decisions to Titillus our secretary to be written down, and this has been done in the month and indiction mentioned

1. Clovesho (probably near London).

216

above. Therefore, if anyone shall presume in any way to contravene or disobey these decisions confirmed by our agreement and ratified by our signatures, according to canonical decrees, let him take notice that he incurs suspension from every priestly function and exclusion from our fellowship.

'May divine grace preserve us all in safety, who live in the unity of His Holy Church.'

This synod took place in the year of our Lord 673, in July of which year King Egbert died and was succeeded by his brother Hlothere, who reigned eleven years and seven months. Bisi, Bishop of the East Angles, who is said to have attended this synod, was successor to Boniface, of whom I have spoken, and was a man of great holiness and devotion; for when Boniface died in the eighteenth year of his episcopate, Theodore consecrated Bisi in his place. And when severe illness prevented him from administering his diocese, two bishops,* Aecci and Badwin, were chosen and consecrated to carry out his duties, and from then until the present day this province has had two bishops.

CHAPTER 6: *Wynfrid is deposed, and Sexwulf appointed to his see: Earconwald is made Bishop of the East Saxons*

NOT long afterwards Archbishop Theodore, displeased at some disobedience on the part of Bishop Wynfrid of the Mercians, deposed him from the bishopric which he had held only a few years, and appointed in his place Sexwulf, founder and abbot of the monastery of Medeshamstedi[1] in the Gyrwas' country. On his deposition, Wynfrid retired to his own monastery of At-Barwe, and lived a most holy life there until his death.

Theodore also made Earconwald Bishop of the East Saxons, whose kings were the above-mentioned Sebbi and Sighere, with the city of London as his see. Both before and after his

1. Now Peterborough.

consecration as bishop, Earconwald is said to have lived so
holy a life that heaven still affords proofs of his virtues. To this
day, the horse-litter in which he travelled when ill is preserved
by his disciples, and continues to cure many folk troubled by
fever and other complaints. Sick people are cured when
placed under or against the litter, and even chips cut from it
bring speedy relief when taken to the sick.

Before he became bishop, Earconwald had built two well-
known monasteries, one for himself and the other for his
sister Ethelburga, and had established an excellent regular
discipline in both houses. His own monastery stood by the
river Thames at Cerotaesei[1] – meaning Cerot's island – in
the district of Surrey. The convent where his sister was to
rule as mother and instructress of women devoted to God was
at a place called In-Berecingum[2] in the province of the East
Saxons. Entrusted with the affairs of this convent, she always
bore herself in a manner worthy of her brother the bishop,
upright of life and constantly planning for the needs of her
community, as heavenly miracles attest.

CHAPTER 7: *A heavenly light indicates where the bodies of the nuns of Barking should be buried*

IN this convent many proofs of holiness were effected,
which many people have recorded from the testimony of
eyewitnesses in order that the memory of them might edify
future generations; I have therefore been careful to include
some in this history of the Church. When the plague that I
have often mentioned was at its height, it attacked the men's
part of the monastery, and daily carried off some to meet their
God. The watchful Mother of the Community therefore
began to ask the sisters of the convent where they wished
their bodies to be buried, and where the cemetery should be
made when the plague should enter the enclosure where these

1. Chertsey.   2. Barking.

handmaids of God lived separately from the men, and snatch
them out of this world by the same deadly stroke. But when
her frequent enquiries of the sisters had elicited no definite
reply, both she and the whole Community received a very
clear indication of the wishes of heaven. For one night when
they had finished singing the morning psalms* of praise to
God, these servants of Christ left the oratory to visit the graves
of the brothers who had departed this life before them.
And as they were singing their customary praises to our Lord,
a light from heaven like a great sheet suddenly appeared and
shone over them all, so alarming them that they even broke
off their singing in consternation. After a short while, this
brilliant light, compared to which the noonday sun would
appear dark, rose and travelled to the south side of the convent
westward of the oratory and, having remained over that area
for a time, withdrew heavenwards in the sight of them all.
This occurrence left no doubt in their minds that the light,
which was to guide or receive the souls of Christ's servants
into heaven, had also indicated the spot where their bodies
were to rest and await the day of resurrection. So brilliant
was this light that one of the older brothers, who was in the
oratory at the time with another younger brother, reported
next morning that the rays of light penetrating the chinks of
doors and windows seemed brighter than the brightest
daylight.

CHAPTER 8: *A little boy, dying in the convent, announces
the approaching death of one of the sisters. A nun, about to
depart this life, sees a glimpse of future glory*

IN this convent lived a little boy named Aesica, not more
than three years old, who, being so young, was being
brought up and taught his lessons in the cell of these virgins
vowed to God. Attacked by the plague and about to die, he
three times called the name of one of Christ's virgins as

though she were present, saying: 'Edith! Edith! Edith!' Then he left this present world, and passed to eternal life. The nun whose name he had called with his dying breath was at once stricken where she was by the same disease, and departed this life, following the child who had called her to the kingdom of heaven.

Again, one of the handmaids of God was brought to her last hour by this disease, and in the middle of the night she began to call to those who attended her to put out the lamp that burned by her bed. But in spite of her repeated requests, none of them paid any attention. At length she said: 'I know that you think that my mind is wandering, but I assure you that it is not so. I tell you truthfully that I see the house filled with such brilliant light that your lamp appears to me only as darkness.' And when they still disregarded her request and made no reply, she said again: 'Let the lamp burn as long as you wish; but I assure you that it gives me no light. My light will come to me when dawn draws near.' She then told them how a man of God, who had died the same year, had appeared to her and informed her that at daybreak she would depart to eternal light. The reality of this vision was quickly confirmed; for the nun died at dawn.

CHAPTER 9: *Signs from heaven appear when the Mother of the Community departs this life*

WHEN Ethelburga, the devout Mother of this God-fearing Community, was herself about to be taken out of this world, one of the sisters whose name was Tortgyth saw a wonderful vision. This nun had lived for many years in the convent, humbly and sincerely striving to serve God, and had helped the Mother to maintain the regular observances by instructing and correcting the younger sisters. In order that her strength might be '*made perfect in weakness*' as the Apostle says, she was suddenly attacked by a serious disease. Under the good providence of our Redeemer, this caused her great distress for nine years, in order that any traces of sin that remained among her virtues through ignorance or neglect might be burned away in the fires of prolonged suffering. Leaving her cell one night at first light of dawn, this sister saw distinctly what appeared to be a human body wrapped in a shroud and shining more brightly than the sun. This was raised up and carried out of the house where the sisters used to sleep. She observed closely to see how this appearance of a shining body was being raised, and saw what appeared to be cords brighter than gold which drew it upwards until it entered the open heavens and she could see it no longer. When she thought about this vision, there remained no doubt in her mind that some member of the Community was shortly to die, and that her soul would be drawn up to heaven by her good deeds as though by golden cords. And so it proved not many days later, when God's beloved Ethelburga, the Mother of the Community, was set free from her bodily prison. And none who knew her holy life can doubt that when she departed this life the gates of our heavenly home opened at her coming.

In the same convent there was also a nun of noble family in the world, who was yet more noble in her love for the world to come. For many years she had been so crippled that she could not move a single limb; and hearing that the venerable abbess' body had been carried into the church until its burial, she asked to be carried there, and to be bowed towards it in an attitude of prayer. Then she spoke to Ethelburga as though she were still alive, and begged her to pray to God on her behalf, and ask him of his mercy to release her from her continual pain. Her request received a swift reply; for twelve days later she was set free from the body, and exchanged her earthly troubles for a heavenly reward.

Three years after the death of the abbess, Christ's servant Tortgyth was so wasted away by the disease that I mentioned earlier that her bones scarcely held together, until finally, as death drew near, she lost the use of her limbs and even of her tongue. After three days and nights in this condition, she was suddenly refreshed by a vision from heaven, opened her eyes, and spoke. Looking up to heaven, she began to address the vision that she saw: 'I am so glad that you have come; you are most welcome.' She then remained silent for awhile, as if awaiting an answer from the person whom she saw and spoke to; then, seeming a little displeased, she said: 'This is not happy news.' After another interval of silence, she spoke a third time: 'If it cannot be today, I beg that it may not be long delayed.' Then she kept silent a little while as before, and ended: 'If this decision is final and unalterable, I implore that it may not be delayed beyond the coming night.' When she had finished, those around her asked her to whom she had spoken. 'To my dearest Mother Ethelburga', she replied; and from this they understood that she had come to announce that the hour of her passing was near. So after a day and a night her prayers were answered, and she was delivered from the burden of the body and entered the joys of eternal salvation.

CHAPTER 10: *A blind woman regains her sight while praying in the convent burial-ground*

ETHELBURGA was succeeded in the office of abbess by a devout servant of God named Hildilid, who ruled the convent with great energy until extreme old age, promoting observance of the regular discipline and making provision for the needs of the Community. Owing to the restricted space on which the convent was built, she decided that the bones of Christ's servants buried there, both men and women, should be exhumed and transferred to a single tomb within the church of the blessed Mother of God. And whoever wishes to read about the wonderful things that happened there will find in the book which is the source of my information how a bright, heavenly light was often seen there, and how a wonderfully fragrant scent was often evident.

It would not be right to omit mention of a miraculous cure which this same book records as having taken place in the cemetery of this God-serving Community. In the neighbourhood there lived a nobleman whose wife was afflicted by a gradual loss of sight, which daily grew worse until she could no longer see the faintest glimmer of light. When she had been totally blind for some while, it suddenly occurred to her that if she were taken to the convent of these holy nuns and prayed before the relics of the saint, she might recover her lost sight. She lost no time in putting this inspiration into effect. Professing a firm belief that she would be healed, she was taken by her maids to the near-by convent and guided to the burial ground, where she remained a long while on her knees in prayer. Her petition was quickly granted; for as she rose from prayer and before she left the place, her sight was restored. And whereas she had been led there by the hands of her maids, she walked home unaided and full of delight. It might almost seem that she had lost her bodily sight solely in order that its restoration might show how great a light is enjoyed by the saints in heaven, and how great a power their virtues possess.

CHAPTER 11 : *Sebbi, King of the East Saxons, ends his days as a monk*

THE same little book informs us that Sebbi, a man who dearly loved God and of whom I have already spoken, ruled the kingdom of the East Saxons at this time. He devoted himself to religious exercises, frequent prayer, and acts of mercy, and he preferred a retired, monastic life to all the riches and honours of a kingdom. In fact, had not his wife absolutely refused to be separated from him, he would long before have abdicated and entered a monastery. For this reason many people thought and often said that a man of such disposition should have been a bishop rather than a

king. When this soldier of the heavenly kingdom had ruled
his earthly kingdom for thirty years, he was attacked by the
serious disease that was to cause his death. He therefore urged
his wife that, since they could no longer enjoy or serve the
world, they should both devote themselves to the service of
God. Having obtained her reluctant consent, the king went
to Waldhere, Bishop of London, successor to Earconwald,
and with his blessing received the monastic habit that he had
so long desired. He brought the bishop a considerable sum of
money to be distributed among the poor, and kept nothing at
all for himself, wishing to be *poor in spirit* for the sake of the
kingdom of heaven.

As his malady gained ground and he felt the day of his
death approaching, Sebbi, who was a man of kingly spirit,
became apprehensive that the sufferings of a painful death
might wring from him some word or gesture unbecoming
to his dignity. He therefore summoned the Bishop of London,
in which city he was living, and asked that none but the
bishop himself and two attendants might be present at his
death. The bishop readily promised this, and not long afterwards this godly man saw in his sleep a comforting vision,
which removed his anxiety on this score, and also revealed to
him on what day he was to depart this life. As he subsequently
related, he saw three men in bright robes come to him, one
of whom sat down in front of his pallet while his companions
remained standing and enquired about the condition of the
sick man they had come to visit. The first man replied that
his soul would leave his body without pain in a splendour of
light, and that he would die in three days' time. Both of these
things happened as he had learned in the vision; for on the
third day, at the hour of None, he seemed suddenly to fall
into a light sleep and breathed out his spirit without any
feeling of pain.

A stone sarcophagus had been made ready for the burial;
but when they came to lay his body in it, they found it a
hand's breadth too long for the sarcophagus. So they chiselled

out sufficient stone to add a further two fingers in length to it; but it still proved too short to receive the body. In this quandary, they wondered whether to look for another coffin, or whether, if possible, to shorten the body by bending the knees until it fitted the sarcophagus. But an amazing thing happened, undoubtedly caused by providence, that rendered both these alternatives unnecessary; for in the presence of the bishop and of Sighard, son of the monk-king – who succeeded him as king jointly with his brother Swefred – and a considerable number of men, the sarcophagus was suddenly found to be the correct length for the body, so much so that a pillow could be placed at the head, while the feet rested four fingers short of the end of the sarcophagus. Sebbi was buried in the church of the blessed Apostle of the Gentiles,* through whose teachings he had learned to aspire to heavenly things.

CHAPTER 12: *Haeddi succeeds Leutherius as Bishop of the West Saxons: Cuichelm succeeds Putta in the See of Rochester, and is himself succeeded by Gebmund. The succession of the Northumbrian bishops*

LEUTHERIUS was the fourth Bishop of the West Saxons, Birinus being the first, Agilbert the second, and Wini the third. On the death of Coenwalh, during whose reign Leutherius was made bishop, under-kings took over the government of the realm, which they divided amongst them and ruled for about ten years. During this period Leutherius died and was succeeded in the bishopric by Haeddi, who had been consecrated by Theodore in the city of London. During Haeddi's episcopate, Cadwalla defeated and deposed these under-kings and assumed control himself; but after a reign of two years, while the same bishop remained in authority, desire for the kingdom of heaven moved the king to resign his powers, and, as I shall record more fully later, he went away to end his days in Rome.

In the year of our Lord's incarnation 676, Ethelred, King of the Mercians, ravaged Kent with his wicked soldiery, profaning churches and monasteries without fear of God or respect to religion, and among the rest he destroyed the city of Rochester, Putta's see, the bishop being absent at the time. When he learned that his church was looted and destroyed, Putta went to Sexwulf, Bishop of the Mercians, who granted him a church and a small plot of land, where he ended his days quietly, making no attempt to re-establish his see. As I have said, he was more at home in religious than in worldly matters, and therefore served God only in his own church, travelling about wherever invited to teach church music. In his place Theodore consecrated Cuichelm as Bishop of Rochester, but after a short time he resigned this see because of its poverty and withdrew elsewhere; Theodore appointed Gebmund in his place.

In the month of August 678, in the eighth year of Egfrid's reign, there appeared a star known as a comet, which remained visible for three months, rising in the morning and emitting what seemed to be a tall column of bright flame. In the same year a dispute arose between King Egfrid and the most reverend Bishop Wilfrid, who was driven from his diocese, and two bishops were appointed to preside over the Northumbrian people in his place. These were Bosa, Bishop of Deira, and Eata, Bishop of Bernicia; the former had the city of York as his see, and the latter had Hexham or Lindisfarne. Both of them were monks before their elevation to the episcopate. At the same time Eadhaed was made bishop of the province of Lindsey, which King Egfrid had recently annexed after defeating and driving out Wulfhere. So for the first time this province had its own bishop; the second was Ethelwin, the third, Edgar, and the fourth, Cynibert, the present bishop. Before Eadhaed, Sexwulf had been bishop not only of Lindsey, but also of the Mercians and Middle Angles; when he was expelled from Lindsey, he continued to preside over the other two provinces. Eadhaed, Bosa, and Eata were consecrated at York by Archbishop Theodore, who, three years after Wilfrid's departure, consecrated two others, Tunbert to the see of Hexham – Eata remaining at Lindisfarne – and Trumwine to be bishop of those Picts* who were then subject to English rule. When Ethelred recovered the province of Lindsey, Eadhaed returned and was appointed by Theodore as Bishop of Ripon.

CHAPTER 13: *Wilfrid converts the Province of the South Saxons to Christ*

DRIVEN out of his see, Wilfrid spent a considerable time travelling in various parts and also went to Rome. When he returned to Britain, the hostility of King Egfrid made it impossible for him to return to his own province or diocese, but nothing could deter him from preaching the Gospel. He therefore made his way to the province of the South Saxons, which stretches west and south from Kent as far as the land of the West Saxons, and covers an area of seven thousand hides. As the province was still pagan, Wilfrid preached the Christian Faith there, and administered the baptism of salvation. Ethelwalh its king had been baptized in the province of the Mercians not long previously under the influence of King Wulfhere, who was present at his baptism and became his godfather at the font. In token of their relationship, Wulfhere gave him two provinces, the Isle of Wight and the province of the Meanwaras* in the territory of the West Saxons. With the king's approval and greatly to his satisfaction, the bishop baptized the leading thanes and soldiers of the province. The remainder of the people were baptized either then or subsequently by the priests Eappa, Padda, Burghelm, and Oiddi. Queen Eabae, who had already received baptism in her own province of the Hwiccas, was the daughter of Eanfrid, brother of Aenheri, both of whom were Christians, as were their people. Otherwise the whole

South Saxon province was ignorant of the Name and Faith of Christ. There was, however, a Scots monk named Dicul, who had a very small monastery at a place called Bosanham,[1] surrounded by woods and the sea, where five or six brothers served the Lord in a life of humility and poverty: but none of the natives was willing to follow their way of life or listen to their teaching.

By preaching to these folk, Bishop Wilfrid not only delivered them from the penalty of eternal damnation, but also saved them from a cruel and horrible extinction in this life. For no rain had fallen in the province for three years prior to his arrival, and a terrible famine had ensued, which reduced many to an awful death. It is said that frequently forty or fifty emaciated and starving people would go to a precipice, or to the edge of the sea, where they would join hands and leap over, to die by the fall or by drowning. But on the very day that the nation received the baptism of faith a soft but ample rainfall refreshed the earth, restoring greenness to the cornfields and giving a happy and fruitful season. Having once abandoned their earlier superstition and rejected idolatry, *'the heart and flesh of all cried out for the living God'*, and they came to understand how He who is true God, had of his divine mercy granted them both spiritual and material blessings. For when Wilfrid had first arrived in the province and found so much misery from famine, he taught the people to obtain food by fishing; for although fish were plentiful in the sea and rivers, the people had no knowledge of fishing and caught only eels. So the bishop's men collected eel-nets from all sides and cast them into the sea, where, by the aid of God's grace, they quickly caught three hundred fishes of various kinds. These they divided into three portions, giving a hundred to the poor, a hundred to those who had lent their nets, and retaining a hundred for their own needs. By this good turn the bishop won the hearts of all, and the people began to listen more readily to his teaching, hoping to obtain heav-

1. Bosham, near Chichester.

enly blessings through the ministry of one to whom they already owed these material benefits.

At this time, King Ethelwalh granted the most reverend Bishop Wilfrid eighty-seven hides of land so that he could maintain his exiled companions. This land lay at Selsey, which means the seal's island, a place surrounded by the sea on all sides except to the west, where there is an approach about a sling's cast in width. A place of this description is known as a *peninsula* by the Latins, and as a *chersonese* by the Greeks. Bishop Wilfrid accepted this land, and having built a monastery there, established the regular life, most of the monks being his own companions: his successors are known to occupy the place to this day. Until the death of King Egfrid five years later, Wilfrid performed the duties of a bishop in word and deed in these parts, and was held in high esteem by all. And since the king had given him not only the land but all the property and inhabitants on it, Wilfrid instructed and baptized them all in the Faith of Christ. Among them were two hundred and fifty male and female slaves, all of whom he released from the slavery of Satan by baptism and by granting them their freedom released them from the yoke of human slavery as well.

CHAPTER 14: *A fatal epidemic is halted by the intercession of King Oswald*

CERTAIN proofs of heaven's especial favour are said to have been shown to this monastery; for once the tyranny of the Devil had been overthrown, the rule of Christ began. I have thought it fitting to preserve the memory of one of these stories, often told me by the very reverend Bishop Acca, who said that it was vouched for by some very reliable brethren of the monastery.

About the time that this province accepted the Faith of Christ, a dangerous epidemic struck many provinces of

Britain. When, by God's dispensation, it reached the monastery, ruled at the time by the most religious priest of Christ, Eappa, it swept from this life many of the brethren, some of whom had come with the bishop, while others were South Saxons recently converted to the Faith. The brethren therefore decided to observe a three-day fast and implore God in his mercy to show pity on them, that he would preserve those who were in danger of death by disease, and deliver the souls of those already departed this life from eternal damnation.

In the monastery at this time lived a little Saxon boy, who had recently been converted to the Faith; this child had caught the disease, and for a long time had been confined to bed. About the second hour on the second day of prayer and fasting, he was alone in the place where he lay sick, when, under divine providence, the most blessed Princes of the Apostles deigned to appear to him; for he was a boy of innocent and gentle disposition, who sincerely believed the truths of the Faith that he had accepted. The Apostles greeted him very lovingly, and said: 'Son, put aside the fear of death that is troubling you; for today we are going to take you with us to the kingdom of heaven. But first of all you must wait until the Masses are said, and you have received the Viaticum of the Body and Blood of our Lord. Then you shall be set free from sickness and death, and carried up to the endless joys of heaven. So call the priest Eappa, and tell him that our Lord has heard the prayers of the brethren and regarded their fasting and devotion with favour. No one else in this monastery and its possessions is to die of this disease, and all who are now suffering from it will recover and be restored to their former health. You alone are to be set free by death today, and shall be taken to heaven to see the Lord Christ whom you have served so faithfully. God in his mercy has granted you this favour at the intercession of the devout King Oswald, so beloved by God, who once ruled the people of the Northumbrians with outstanding devotion as their earthly king

and whose Christian piety has won him an everlasting kingdom. For today is the anniversary of the king's death in battle
at the hands of the heathen, when he was taken up to the joys
of the souls in heaven and enrolled among the company of
the Saints. If the brethren will consult the annals that record the
burials of the dead, they will find that this is the day on which
he departed this life, as we have said. So let them say Masses
in all the oratories of the monastery, either in thanksgiving
for God's answer to their prayers, or in commemoration of
King Oswald the former ruler of their nation, who has prayed
for them as newcomers of his nation. Let all the brethren
assemble in church, and join in offering the heavenly Sacrifice; and let them end their fast and take food to restore their
strength.'

When the boy had called Eappa and told him all that the
Apostles had said, the priest particularly asked him to describe the clothes and appearance of these men who had
appeared to him. 'They wore wonderful robes,' the boy
replied, 'and their faces were very kindly and handsome, such
as I have never seen before. I did not believe that there could
be men so distinguished and wonderful. One of them was
tonsured like a priest and the other had a long beard; and they
said that one of them was Peter and the other Paul, and that
they were servants of our Lord and Saviour Jesus Christ, sent
by Him to protect our monastery.' The priest then believed
the boy's statement, and went off at once to consult his
annals, where he found that King Oswald had indeed been
killed on that very day. So he summoned the brethren,
ordered a meal to be prepared, Masses to be said, and all the
brethren to communicate as usual. He also directed that a
particle of the Lord's Offering should be taken to the sick
boy at the time of the holy Sacrifice.

A little while later the same day the boy died, and his death
proved the truth of what Christ's Apostles had told him. In
further confirmation of his statement, no one except himself
died in the monastery at that time. Many who heard about

this vision were wonderfully inspired to implore God's mercy in every trouble, and to adopt the wholesome remedy of fasting. And from that time the heavenly birthday of Christ's warrior King Oswald was commemorated each year by the offering of Masses, not only in this monastery but in many other places as well.

CHAPTER 15: *King Cadwalla of the Gewissae kills King Ethelwalh and devastates his province with plundering and slaughter*

MEANWHILE Cadwalla, a daring young man of the royal house of the Gewissae, exiled from his own country, came with an army and killed King Ethelwalh, wasting the province with slaughtering and plunder. But the last king's ealdormen Berthun and Andhun soon drove him out, and administered the country from then on. The former was subsequently killed by Cadwalla when he had become king of the Gewissae, and the province was reduced to a worse state of subjection. Similarly Ini, who succeeded Cadwalla, held the province in subjection for several years. For this reason, it had no bishop of its own during all this period; for when Wilfrid its first bishop had been recalled home, it became dependent on the Bishop of the Gewissae, that is, the West Saxons, whose see was at Winchester.

CHAPTER 16: *The Isle of Wight receives Christian settlers. Two young princes of the island are killed immediately after Baptism* [A.D. 686]

AFTER Cadwalla became king of the Gewissae, he captured the Isle of Wight, which was still entirely devoted to idolatry and strove to exterminate all the natives and

replace them by settlers from his own province. Although
not yet baptized, he is said to have bound himself by an oath
to dedicate a quarter of the land and spoils to the Lord if he
conquered the island; and he fulfilled this oath by offering it
for God's use to Bishop Wilfrid, who chanced at this time to
have left his own people in order to visit the island. By English
reckoning, the island has an area of twelve hundred hides,
so that the bishop was given three hundred hides of land.
This share he entrusted to Bernwini, one of his clerks who
was his own sister's son, and he appointed a priest named
Hiddila to preach and administer Baptism to all who sought
salvation.

It would not be right to omit mention of two young
princes, brothers of Arwald, king of the island, who were
especially favoured by God's grace, and became the first
natives of the island to believe and be saved. On the approach
of the invaders, these princes had escaped from the island and
crossed to the adjoining province of the Jutes. Here they were
guided to a place called At-the-Stone,[1] where they hoped to
remain hidden from the victorious king; but they were
betrayed and ordered to be put to death. This was reported
to the priest Cynibert, Abbot of a not far distant monastery at
a place called Hreutford, that is, the Ford of Reeds;[2] so he
sought out the king, who was living in seclusion in the district
while he recovered from wounds received while fighting in
the Isle of Wight, and begged him that, if it was necessary
for these lads to die, he might first be allowed to instruct them
in the mysteries of the Christian Faith. The king consented to
this, and when Cynibert had taught them the word of truth,
he baptized them in the fount of salvation, and assured their
entry into the kingdom of heaven. So when the executioner
arrived, they met bodily death gladly, in the firm faith that
through it their souls would pass to eternal life. So last of all
the provinces of Britain, the Isle of Wight accepted the Faith
of Christ; but owing to its subjection to an alien rule, it had

1. Stoneham, Hants.   2. Redbridge.

no bishop or see of its own until the time of Daniel, who is now Bishop of the West Saxons.

The Isle of Wight lies opposite the boundary between the South Saxons and the Gewissae, and is separated from it by three miles of sea, known as the Solent. In this strait, two ocean tides that flow round Britain from the boundless northern seas meet in daily opposition off the mouth of the River Homelea.[1] This enters the sea after flowing through the lands of the Jutes who lived in the Gewissae country; and when the turbulence ceases, they flow back into the ocean whence they spring.

CHAPTER 17: *Theodore presides over a Synod held in the Plain of Haethfeld (Hatfield)* [A.D. 680]

ABOUT this time, Theodore learned that the faith of the Church at Constantinople was greatly disturbed by the heresy of Eutyches.* Wishing to preserve the churches of the English that he ruled untainted by this error, he summoned a large number of venerable bishops and teachers to a conference; and when he had carefully ascertained their individual beliefs, he found them all united in support of the Catholic Faith. He therefore took pains to record this fact in a synodical letter, to serve as a reminder and guide to future generations. This letter opens as follows:

'In the Name of our Lord and Saviour Jesus Christ. On the seventeenth of September in the eighth indiction; in the tenth year of the reign of our most devout lord Egfrid, King of the Northumbrians; in the sixth year of King Ethelfrid of the Mercians; in the seventeenth year of King Aldwulf of the East Angles; and in the seventh year of King Hlothere of the Kentish people. Under the presidency of Theodore, by the grace of God Archbishop of the island of Britain and the City of Canterbury, we the venerable bishops of the

1. The Hamble.

island of Britain assembled in conclave at the place which is called in the Saxon language Haethfeld, having the most holy Gospels before us, hereby unite to proclaim the true and orthodox faith. This same faith our Lord Jesus Christ delivered in the flesh to His disciples, who saw Him in person and heard His teaching. This is now set forth in the Creed of the holy fathers, and by all the sacred General Councils, and by the united voice of the accredited doctors of the Catholic Church. We follow them in devotion and right faith, professing our belief in their divinely inspired teachings; and we unite with the holy fathers in acknowledging the Father, the Son, and the Holy Spirit, the Trinity consubstantial in Unity, and Unity in Trinity, that is, One God subsisting in three consubstantial Persons of equal glory and honour.'

And after a great deal more to this effect, in which they affirm their confession of the true Faith, the letter of this holy synod continues: 'We accept the decisions of the five holy General Councils of the blessed fathers who were acceptable to God; that is, the Council of three hundred and eighteen bishops assembled at Nicaea, which condemned the impious Arius and his teachings; the Council of one hundred and fifty bishops at Constantinople, which condemned the madness of Macedonius and Eudoxius and their teachings; the first Council of two hundred bishops at Ephesus, which condemned the wicked Nestorius and his teachings; the Council of six hundred and thirty bishops at Chalcedon, which condemned Eutyches and Nestorius and their teachings; and the fifth Council at Constantinople in the reign of Justinian the younger, which condemned Theodorus, Theodoret, the epistles of Ibas, and their teachings against Cyril.'

Shortly after this, the letter continues: 'We also accept the decisions of the Council held in Rome* under the blessed Pope Martin in the eighth indiction and ninth year of the reign of the most pious Emperor Constantine [IV]. We glorify our Lord Jesus Christ as they glorified Him, neither adding nor withdrawing anything; we anathematize with heart and voice those whom they anathematized, and accept those whom they accepted. And we glorify God the Father, who is without beginning, and His only-begotten Son, begotten of the Father before all worlds, and the Holy Spirit ineffably proceeding from the Father and the Son, as proclaimed by all the holy Apostles, prophets, and teachers whom we have already mentioned. And we who have all joined with Archbishop Theodore in proclaiming the Catholic Faith affix our signatures hereto.'

CHAPTER 18: *John, Arch-cantor of the apostolic see, comes to teach in Britain* [A.D. 680]

AMONG those who signed the affirmation of the Catholic Faith at this Synod was the venerable John, Arch-cantor of the church of the holy Apostle Peter and Abbot of the monastery of Saint Martin, who had recently come from Rome under instructions from Pope Agatho with the most reverend Abbot Benedict, of whom I have spoken. For when Benedict had built a monastery in Britain near the mouth of the River Wear[1] in honour of the blessed Prince of the Apostles, he travelled to Rome with his colleague and partner in the work, Ceolfrid, who later succeeded him as abbot of the monastery. As he had made several earlier visits to Rome, he was received with honour by Pope Agatho of blessed memory. From him he asked and obtained a letter of privilege, granted with his apostolic authority, which confirmed the independence of the monastery that he had founded; for he knew this to accord with the wishes of King Egfrid, with whose approval and grant he had built the monastery.

Benedict received Abbot John and conducted him to Britain, where he was to teach his monks the chant for the liturgical year as it was sung at Saint Peter's, Rome. In accordance

1. Monkwearmouth.

with the Pope's instructions, Abbot John taught the cantors of the monastery the theory and practice of singing and reading aloud, and he put into writing all that was necessary for the proper observance of festivals throughout the year. This document is still preserved in this monastery, and many copies have been made for other places. John's instruction was not limited to the brethren of this monastery alone; for men who were proficient singers came from nearly all the monasteries of the province to hear him, and he received many invitations to teach elsewhere.

In addition to his task of teaching the arts of singing and reading, John had also been directed by the apostolic Pope to make careful enquiries about the faith of the Church of the English, and report on it when he returned to Rome. He had brought with him the decisions of the Council recently held in Rome by blessed Pope Martin and one hundred and five bishops, which particularly condemned those who taught that only one will operated in Christ, and he handed this over for a transcript to be made in the monastery of the most religious Abbot Benedict. Those who supported such views had caused great confusion in the Church of Constantinople at the time, but by God's help they were exposed and refuted. For this reason, Pope Agatho wished to be informed on the state of the Church in Britain as well as in other provinces, and whether it was free from contamination by heretics; so he entrusted this mission to the most reverend Abbot John, who had already been ordered to visit Britain. After the above-mentioned Synod had been summoned for the purpose in Britain, the Catholic Faith was shown to be held untainted by all, and a copy of its decisions was given to John to take back to Rome.

Not long after crossing the sea, on his return journey to his own country, John fell sick and died; and out of devotion to Saint Martin, of whose monastery he was abbot, his friends carried his body to Tours, where he was buried with great honour. For on his journey to Britain he had been courteously welcomed there by the brethren, who begged him to travel by the same route on his return to Rome and pay another visit to their house. They also provided him with assistants to accompany him on his journey and help him in his appointed task. And although he died on his journey, John's testimony to the Catholic Faith of the English was taken on to Rome, where it was received with great satisfaction by the apostolic Pope and by all who heard or read it.

CHAPTER 19: *Queen Etheldreda preserves her virginity, and her body remains incorrupt in the grave* [A.D. 660]

KING EGFRID married Etheldreda,* a daughter of Anna, King of the East Angles, of whom I have often spoken; he was a very devout man, noble in mind and deed. Before her marriage to Egfrid, Etheldreda had been married to Tondbert, a prince of the South Gyrwas; but he died shortly after the wedding, and she was given to King Egfrid. Although she lived with him for twelve years, she preserved the glory of perpetual virginity. This fact is absolutely vouched for by Bishop Wilfrid of blessed memory, of whom I made enquiry when some people doubted it. He said that Egfrid promised to give estates and much wealth to him if he could persuade the queen to consummate the marriage, knowing that there was no man for whom she had a higher regard. And there is no reason to doubt that such a thing could happen in our own day, since reliable histories record it as having happened on several occasions in the past through the grace of the same Lord who has promised to remain with us until the end of the world. For the miraculous preservation of her body from corruption in the tomb is evidence that she had remained untainted by bodily intercourse.

For a long time Etheldreda begged the king to allow her to retire from worldly affairs and serve Christ the only true

King in a convent. And having at length obtained his reluctant consent, she entered the convent of the Abbess Ebba, King Egfrid's aunt, at Coludesbyrig,[1] where she received the veil and clothing of a nun from the hands of Bishop Wilfrid. A year later she was herself made Abbess in the district called Ely, where she built a convent and became the virgin mother of many virgins vowed to God and displayed the pattern of a heavenly life in word and deed. It is said that from the time of her entry into the convent she never wore linen but only woollen garments, and that she would seldom wash in hot water except on the eve of the greater festivals such as Easter, Pentecost, and the Epiphany, and then only after she and her assistants had helped the other handmaids of Christ to wash. She seldom had more than one meal a day except at the greater festivals or under urgent necessity, and she always remained at prayer in the church from the hour of Matins until dawn unless prevented by serious illness. Some say that she possessed the spirit of prophecy, and that in the presence of all the community, she not only foretold the plague that was to cause her death, but also the number who would die of it in the convent. She was taken to Christ in the presence of her nuns seven years after her appointment as abbess, and in accordance with her instructions she was buried among them in the wooden coffin in which she died.

Etheldreda was succeeded in the office of abbess by her sister Sexburg,* who had been wife of King Earconbert of Kent. Sixteen years after Etheldreda's burial, this abbess decided to have her bones exhumed, placed in a new coffin, and transferred into the church. She therefore directed some of the brethren to search for stone to make this coffin. And since the district of Ely was surrounded on all sides by sea and fens and had no large stones, they took a boat and came to a small ruined city not far distant which the English call Grantchester. After a short while they discovered near the

1. Coldingham.

city walls a white marble sarcophagus of very beautiful workmanship* with a close-fitting lid of similar stone; and realizing that God had prospered their journey, they returned thanks to him and brought it back to the convent.

When the tomb of the holy and virginal spouse of Christ was opened and her body brought to light, it was found as free from decay as if she had died and been buried that very day; this is vouched for by Bishop Wilfrid and many others of their own knowledge. But even fuller proof is given by the physician Cynifrid, who was present at both her death and her exhumation. Cynifrid used to relate that during her last illness she had a large tumour under the jaw. 'I was asked,' he said, 'to open the tumour and drain away the poisonous matter in it. I did this, and for two days she seemed somewhat easier, so that many thought that she would recover from her illness. But on the third day her earlier pain returned, and she was taken from this world, and exchanged all pain and death for everlasting life and health. When her bones were to be taken up out of the grave so many years later, a pavilion was raised over it, and the whole community stood around it chanting, the brothers on one side, and the sisters on the other. The abbess herself, with a few others, went in to take up and wash the bones, when we suddenly heard her cry out in a loud voice, "Glory to the Name of the Lord!" Shortly afterwards they opened the door of the pavilion and called me in. There I saw the body of the holy virgin taken from its grave and laid on a bed as though asleep; and when they had uncovered her face, they showed me that the incision which I had made had healed. This astounded me; for in place of the open gaping wound with which she was buried, there remained only the faint mark of a scar. All the linen cloths in which the body had been enfolded appeared so fresh and new that they looked as if they had been wrapped that very day around her pure body.'

It is said that when she was affected by this tumour and pain in her jaw and neck, she welcomed pain of this kind,

and used to say: 'I realize very well that I deserve this wearisome disease in my neck, on which, as I well remember, when
I was a girl, I used to wear the needless burden of jewellery.
And I believe that God in His goodness wishes me to endure
this pain in my neck so that I may be absolved from the guilt
of my needless vanity. So now I wear a burning red tumour
on my neck instead of gold and pearls.' At the touch of these
robes devils were expelled from the bodies of those whom
they possessed, and other complaints were sometimes cured.
And the coffin in which she was first buried is said to have
cured diseases of the eye, relieving pain and failing sight in
those who placed their heads on the coffin as they prayed.
When the sisters had washed the virgin's body and clothed it
in new robes, they carried it into the church and laid it in the
sarcophagus which had been brought, where it is held in
great veneration to this day. This same sarcophagus was found
to fit the virgin's body in a marvellous way, as though it
had been especially made for her, and the special place cut
out for the head exactly fitted the measurements of her
own.

Ely lies in the province of the East Angles, an area of about
six hundred hides. As I have said, it resembles an island surrounded by water and marshes, and it derives its name from
the vast quantity of eels that are caught in the marshes. And
the servant of Christ wished to have her monastery in this
place because, as already mentioned, her forbears came from
the province of the East Angles.

CHAPTER 20: *A hymn in honour of Etheldreda*

IT seems appropriate to insert in this History an elegiac hymn
in praise of virginity which I composed many years ago
in honour of this same queen and bride of Christ – all the more
a queen because a bride of Christ. In this I am following the
example of Holy Scripture, in which the narrative is fre-

quently interspersed with songs which are known to have
been composed in verse.[1]

> All-guiding Trinity, guide my design.
> Battles were Virgil's theme; let peace be mine,
> Chanting in lieu of Helen's wantonness
> Divine compassion, to redeem and bless,
> Entering a virgin's womb, God's gate to earth.
> Fair maid, who gav'st the whole world's Parent birth,
> God gave thee grace. And by that grace empowered
> How many virgin blossoms since have flowered!
> In fiery torment stood chaste Agatha
> Joyful to death; so stood Eulalia.
> Kindled with love, Thecla with virgin breast
> Laughed at wild beasts; so was Euphemia blest.
> More strong than steel, Agnes disdained its thrust;
> Nor did Cecilia's strength betray her trust.
> Our age at length in triumphs such as these
> Partakes through ETHELDREDA'S victories.
> Queenly by birth, an earthly crown she wore
> Right nobly; but a heavenly pleased her more.
> Scorning the marriage bed, a virgin wife
> Twelve years she reigned, then sought a cloistered life.
> Unspotted to her heavenly spouse she came,
> Virgin in soul, her virgin robe and frame,
> When sixteen winters they had lain entombed,
> Xrist willing it, still fresh and unconsumed.
> Yea, from their touch Eve's Tempter flees dismayed,
> Zealous for evil, vanquished by a maid.
>
> Ah bride of Christ, bright fame on earth is thine.
> More bright in Heaven thy bridal torches shine.
> Exultant hymns proclaim in glad accord:
> No power henceforth may part thee from thy Lord.

1. The following version reproduces the alphabetic acrostic with which
Bede adorns his tale, including his spelling of *Christ* with initial *X* (the Greek
letter *chi*) as in the familiar abbreviation *Xmas*. It does not attempt to imitate
his elaborate device of repetitive half-lines, which makes the hymn remarkable rather for ingenuity than for any claim to poetic excellence.

CHAPTER 21: *Archbishop Theodore makes peace between King Egfrid and King Ethelred* [A.D. 679]

I N the ninth year of his reign, King Egfrid fought a great battle near the river Trent against King Ethelred of the Mercians, in which Egfrid's brother Elfwin was killed. The latter was a young man of about eighteen, who was much loved in both provinces since Ethelred had married his sister Osthryd. This gave every indication of causing fiercer strife and more lasting hatred between the two warlike kings and peoples, until Archbishop Theodore, the beloved of God, enlisting God's help, smothered the flames of this awful peril by his wholesome advice. As a result, peace was restored between the kings and peoples, and in lieu of further bloodshed the customary compensation* was paid to King Egfrid for his brother's death. The peace thus made was maintained between these kings and their peoples for many years.

CHAPTER 22: *A prisoner's chains fall off when Masses are sung on his behalf* [A.D. 679]

I N the above battle in which King Elfwin was killed, a remarkable thing occurred, which I should not fail to mention, since it will further the salvation of many. During the battle, a young thane named Imma belonging to Elfwin's forces was struck down, and lay apparently dead all that day and the following night among the bodies of the slain. At length he recovered consciousness, sat up, and bandaged his wounds as well as he could; then when he had rested awhile, he got up and tried to find some friends to help him. While so engaged he was found and captured by men of the enemy forces, and taken before their leader, who was a nobleman of King Ethelred. When asked his identity, he was afraid to reveal that he was a soldier, and answered that he was a poor married peasant who had come with others of his kind to bring provisions to the army. The nobleman ordered him to be given shelter and treatment for his wounds; and when he began to recover, he ordered him to be chained at night to prevent his escape. But this proved impossible, for no sooner had those who chained him left than the fetters fell off.*

Now this young man had a brother named Tunna, who was a priest and abbot of a monastery that is still called Tunnacaestir after him. And when he heard that his brother had been killed in battle, he went to see whether he could find his body. Finding another very similar to him, he concluded that it was his; so he took the body back to his monastery, gave it honourable burial, and offered many Masses for the repose of his brother's soul. And it was on account of these Masses that, as I have said, when anyone tried to chain him, he was immediately set free. The nobleman, whose prisoner he was, was astonished, and asked why he could not be bound, and whether he possessed any written charms to protect him from binding like those mentioned in fables. He replied: 'I know nothing about such things. But I have a brother who is a priest in my own province, and I am sure that, thinking me killed, he is saying many Masses for me; and were I now in another life, my soul would be freed from its pains by his prayers.' After he had been held some time in the nobleman's custody, those who observed the young man closely realized from his appearance, clothing, and speech that he was no common peasant as he said, but of noble birth. The nobleman then sent for him privately, and pressed him to disclose his identity, promising that he would do him no harm if he told him the truth about who he was. On this assurance, the young man revealed that he was a king's thane. At this the nobleman said: 'I realized by all your answers that you were no peasant. You deserve to die, because all my brothers and kinsmen were killed in that battle: but I will not put you to death, because I have given you my promise.'

As soon as Imma recovered, the nobleman sold him to a

Frisian in London, who took him away, but found that he was unable to fetter him. When one kind of fetter after another had been put on him and none could hold him, his buyer gave him permission to ransom himself if he could. It was at the hour of Terce, the customary time of saying Mass, that his chains were most frequently loosed. Promising either to return or to send his ransom money, Imma went to King Hlothere of Kent, who was nephew to the above Queen Etheldreda, because he had once been one of the queen's thanes. From him he obtained the money for his ransom, and sent it to his master as he had promised.

When Imma returned to his own country, he visited his brother and gave him a full account of all his troubles and how he had been helped in them; and from him he learned that his chains had been loosed at the times when Mass was being said on his behalf. He also realized how he had received comfort and strength from heaven in many other dangers through the prayers of his brother and his offering of Christ's saving Sacrifice. He related his experiences to many people, who were thereby inspired to greater faith and devotion and gave themselves to prayer, almsgiving, and offering the Holy Sacrifice to God for the deliverance of their friends who had departed this life; for they understood how this saving Sacrifice availed for the eternal redemption of soul and body.

Among those who told me this story were some who had actually heard it from the mouth of the man to whom these things had happened, so that I have no hesitation about including it in this history of the Church as it was related.

CHAPTER 23: *The life and death of Abbess Hilda* [A.D. 680]

IN the following year, that is the year of our Lord 680, Hilda, abbess of the monastery of Streanaeshalch, of which I have already spoken, a most religious servant of Christ, after an earthly life devoted to the work of heaven passed

away to receive the reward of a heavenly life on the seventeenth of November at the age of sixty-six. Her life on earth
fell into two equal parts: for she spent thirty-three years
most nobly in secular occupations, and dedicated the ensuing
thirty-three even more nobly to our Lord in the monastic
life. She was nobly born, the daughter of Hereric, nephew to
King Edwin. With Edwin she received the Faith and sacraments of Christ through the preaching of Paulinus of blessed
memory, first bishop of the Northumbrians, and she preserved this Faith inviolate until she was found worthy to see
her Master in heaven.

When she decided to abandon the secular life and serve
God alone, she went to the province of the East Angles,
whose king was her kinsman; for having renounced her
home and all that she possessed, she wished if possible to
travel on from there into Gaul, and to live an exile for our
Lord's sake in the monastery of Cale,[1] so that she might the
more easily attain her eternal heavenly home. For her sister
Hereswith, mother of Aldwulf, King of the East Angles,
was already living there as a professed nun and awaiting her
eternal crown. Inspired by her example, Hilda remained in
the province a full year, intending to join her overseas; but
she was recalled home by Bishop Aidan and was granted one
hide of land on the north bank of the River Wear, where she
observed the monastic rule with a handful of companions
for another year.

After this, Hilda was made abbess of the monastery of
Heruteu,[2] founded not long previously by Heiu, a devout
servant of Christ, said to have been the first woman in the
province of the Northumbrians to take vows and be clothed as
a nun, which she did with the blessing of Bishop Aidan. But
soon after establishing the monastery she left for the town of
Calcaria, which the English call Kaelcacaestir,[3] and settled
there. Then Christ's servant Hilda was appointed to rule this
monastery, and quickly set herself to establish a regular

1. Chelles, near Paris.   2. Hartlepool.   3. Possibly Tadcaster.

246

observance, following the instructions of learned men; for Bishop Aidan and other devout men, who knew her and admired her innate wisdom and love of God's service, often used to visit her, to express their affection and offer thoughtful guidance.

When she had ruled this monastery for some years, constantly occupied in establishing the regular life, she further undertook to found or organize a monastery at a place known as Streanaeshalch, and carried out this appointed task with great energy. She established the same regular life as in her former monastery, and taught the observance of righteousness, mercy, purity, and other virtues, but especially of peace and charity. After the example of the primitive Church, no one there was rich, no one was needy, for everything was held in common, and nothing was considered to be anyone's personal property. So great was her prudence that not only ordinary folk, but kings and princes used to come and ask her advice in their difficulties and take it. Those under her direction were required to make a thorough study of the Scriptures and occupy themselves in good works, to such good effect that many were found fitted for Holy Orders and the service of God's altar.

Five men from this monastery later became bishops – Bosa, Aetla, Oftfor, John, and Wilfrid – all of them men of outstanding merit and holiness. As already mentioned, Bosa was consecrated Bishop of York; of Aetla let it suffice to note that he became Bishop of Dorchester; and I shall tell in due course how John became Bishop of Hexham, and Wilfrid Bishop of York. Meanwhile I wish to speak of Oftfor, who having devoted himself to reading and applying the Scriptures in both Hilda's monasteries, wished to win greater perfection, and travelled to Kent in order to visit Archbishop Theodore, of blessed memory. When he had continued his studies under him for some while, he decided to visit Rome, which in those days was considered an act of great merit. On his return to Britain he visited the province of the Hwiccas, then ruled by King Osric, where he remained a long time, preaching the word of faith and setting an example of holy life to all who met and heard him. At this time Bosel, bishop of the province, was in such ill health that he was unable to carry out his duties in person, and Oftfor was therefore unanimously elected bishop in his place. At the request of King Ethelred, he was consecrated by Bishop Wilfrid of blessed memory, who was acting as Bishop of the Middle Angles, since Theodore had died and as yet no bishop had been appointed to succeed him. A little earlier, before the man of God Bosel, an energetic and very learned man of great ability named Tatfrid had been elected bishop while a monk in Hilda's monastery, but met an untimely death before he could be consecrated.

Christ's servant Abbess Hilda, whom all her acquaintances called Mother because of her wonderful devotion and grace, was not only an example of holy life to members of her own community; for she also brought about the amendment and salvation of many living at a distance, who heard the inspiring story of her industry and goodness. Her life was the fulfilment of a dream which her mother Breguswith had when Hilda was an infant, during the time that her husband Hereric was living in banishment under the protection of the British king Cerdic, where he died of poison. In this dream she fancied that he was suddenly taken away, and although she searched everywhere, she could find no trace of him. When all her efforts had failed, she discovered a most valuable jewel under her garments; and as she looked closely, it emitted such a brilliant light that all Britain was lit by its splendour. This dream was fulfilled in her daughter, whose life afforded a shining example not only to herself but to all who wished to live a good life.

When Hilda had ruled this monastery for many years, it pleased the Author of our salvation to try her holy soul by a long sickness, in order that, as with the Apostle, her strength might be *made perfect in weakness*. She was attacked by a burning fever that racked her continually for six years; but during all this time she never ceased to give thanks to her Maker or to instruct the flock committed to her, both privately and publicly. For her own example taught them all to serve God obediently when in health, and to render thanks to him faithfully when in trouble or bodily weakness. In the seventh year of her illness the pain passed into her innermost parts, and her last day came. About cockcrow she received the Viaticum of the holy Communion, and when she had summoned all the handmaids of Christ in the monastery, she urged them to maintain the gospel peace among themselves and with others. And while she was still speaking, she joyfully welcomed death, or rather, in the words of our Lord, passed from death to life.

That same night it pleased Almighty God to make her death known by means of a vision in a monastery some considerable distance away, which she had founded that same year at Hackness. In this place there was a devout nun named Begu, who had vowed herself to God in virginity in the monastic life over thirty years previously. As she was resting in the sisters' dormitory, she suddenly heard in the air the well-known note of the bell that used to wake and call them to prayer when any of the sisters had died. Opening her eyes, as she thought, she saw the roof open, and a great light pour in from above and flood the room. While she gazed into this light, she saw the soul of God's servant Hilda borne up to heaven in the midst of the light accompanied and guided by angels. Then she awoke, and seeing the other sisters lying around her, realized that what she had seen was either a dream or a vision. Rising at once in alarm, she ran to Frigyth, who was Prioress at the time, and with many sighs and tears told her that their Mother the Abbess Hilda had departed this life, and that she had seen her surrounded by angels in a great light, and ascending to the abode of eternal light to join the company of the saints in heaven. When she had heard the nun's story Frigyth roused all the sisters, and when she had gathered them into the church, she enjoined them to pray and recite the psalter for the soul of their Mother. They did this for the remainder of the night, and at daybreak some brothers arrived from the monastery where she had died with news of her passing. The sisters replied that they already knew, and when they explained how and when they had heard it, it was evident that her death had been revealed to them by means of the vision at the very hour that the brothers said she had died. Thus with fitting harmony the mercy of heaven ordained that while some of her Community attended her death-bed, the others were made aware of her soul's entry into eternal life, although these monasteries are about thirteen miles apart.

It is said that Hilda's death was revealed also on the same night in a vision to one of the sisters in the actual monastery where the servant of God passed away. This sister, who loved her dearly, saw her soul ascend to heaven in the company of angels, and immediately awoke the servants of Christ with her and told them to pray for her soul. This was at the very hour of her death, even before the rest of the Community knew of it; for it was only made known to them early in the morning. At this time the nun was with certain other handmaids of Christ in a remote part of the monastery, where novices were admitted to test their vocation until they were fully instructed and admitted to membership of the Community.

CHAPTER 24: *A brother of the monastery is found to possess God's gift of poetry* [A.D. 680]

IN this monastery of Streanaeshalch lived a brother singularly gifted by God's grace. So skilful was he in composing religious and devotional songs that, when any passage of Scripture was explained to him by interpreters, he could quickly turn it into delightful and moving poetry in his own English tongue. These verses of his have stirred the hearts of many folk to despise the world and aspire to heavenly things.

Others after him tried to compose religious poems in English, but none could compare with him; for he did not acquire the art of poetry from men or through any human teacher but received it as a free gift from God. For this reason he could never compose any frivolous or profane verses; but only such as had a religious theme fell fittingly from his devout lips. He had followed a secular occupation until well advanced in years without ever learning anything about poetry. Indeed it sometimes happened at a feast that all the guests in turn would be invited to sing and entertain the company; then, when he saw the harp coming his way, he would get up from table and go home.

On one such occasion he had left the house in which the entertainment was being held and went out to the stable. where it was his duty that night to look after the beasts. There when the time came he settled down to sleep. Suddenly in a dream he saw a man standing beside him who called him by name. 'Caedmon,' he said, 'sing me a song.' 'I don't know how to sing,' he replied. 'It is because I cannot sing that I left the feast and came here.' The man who addressed him then said: 'But you shall sing to me.' 'What should I sing about?' he replied. 'Sing about the Creation of all things,' the other answered. And Caedmon immediately began to sing verses in praise of God the Creator that he had never heard before, and their theme ran thus:

> Praise we the Fashioner now of Heaven's fabric,
> The majesty of his might and his mind's wisdom,
> Work of the world-warden, worker of all wonders,
> How he the Lord of Glory everlasting,
> Wrought first for the race of men Heaven as a rooftree,
> Then made he Middle Earth to be their mansion.

This is the general sense, but not the actual words that Caedmon sang in his dream; for verses, however masterly, cannot be translated literally from one language into another without losing much of their beauty and dignity. When Caedmon awoke, he remembered everything that he had sung in his dream, and soon added more verses in the same style to a song truly worthy of God.

Early in the morning he went to his superior the reeve, and told him about this gift that he had received. The reeve took him before the abbess, who ordered him to give an account of his dream and repeat the verses in the presence of many learned men, so that a decision might be reached by common consent as to their quality and origin. All of them agreed that Caedmon's gift had been given him by our Lord. And they explained to him a passage of scriptural history or doctrine and asked him to render it into verse if he could. He promised to do this, and returned next morning with excellent verses as they had ordered him. The abbess was delighted that God had given such grace to the man, and advised him to abandon secular life and adopt the monastic state. And when she had admitted him into the Community as a brother, she ordered him to be instructed in the events of sacred history. So Caedmon stored up in his memory all that he learned, and like one of the clean animals chewing the cud, turned it into such melodious verse that his delightful renderings turned his instructors into auditors. He sang of the creation of the world, the origin of the human race, and the whole story of Genesis. He sang of Israel's exodus from Egypt, the entry into the Promised Land, and many other events of scriptural history. He sang of the Lord's Incarnation, Passion, Resurrection, and Ascension into heaven, the coming of the Holy Spirit, and the teaching of the Apostles. He also made many poems on the terrors of the Last Judgement, the horrible pains of Hell, and the joys of the Kingdom of Heaven. In addition to these, he composed several others on the blessings and judgements of God, by which he sought to turn his hearers from delight in wickedness and to inspire them to love and do good. For Caedmon was a deeply religious man, who humbly submitted to regular discipline and hotly rebuked all who tried to follow another course. And so he crowned his life with a happy end.

For, when the time of his death drew near, he felt the onset of physical weakness for fourteen days, but not seriously enough to prevent his walking or talking the whole time. Close by there was a house to which all who were sick or likely to die were taken. Towards nightfall on the day when he was to depart this life, Caedmon asked his attendant to prepare a resting-place for him in this house. The attendant was surprised at this request from a man who did not appear likely to die yet; nevertheless, he did as he was asked. So Caedmon went to the house, and conversed and jested cheerfully with those who were already there; and when it was past midnight, he asked: 'Is the Eucharist in the house?'* 'Why do you want the Eucharist?' they enquired; 'you are not likely to die yet, when you are talking so cheerfully to us and seem to be in perfect health.' 'Nevertheless,' he said, 'bring me the Eucharist.' And taking It in his hands, Caedmon asked whether they were all charitably disposed towards him, and whether they had any complaint or ill-feeling against him. They replied that they were all most kindly disposed towards him, and free from all bitterness. Then in turn they asked him to clear his heart of bitterness towards them. At once he answered: 'Dear sons, my heart is at peace with all the servants of God.' Then, when he had fortified himself with the heavenly Viaticum, he prepared to enter the other life, and asked how long it would be before the brothers were roused to sing God's praises in the Night Office. 'Not long,' they replied. 'Good, then let us wait until then,' he answered; and signing himself with the holy Cross, he laid his head on the pillow and passed away quietly in his sleep. So, having served God with a simple and pure mind, and with tranquil devotion, he left the world and departed to his presence by a tranquil death. His tongue, which had sung so many inspiring verses in praise of his Maker, uttered its last words in his praise as he signed himself with the Cross and commended his soul into his hands. For, as I have already said, Caedmon seems to have had a premonition of his death.

A т this time, the monastery of nuns called Coludesbyrig, which I have already mentioned, was burned down through carelessness. However, all who knew the facts could readily perceive that it happened because of the wickedness of its members, and in particular of those who were supposed to be in authority. But God's mercy gave them a warning of punishment, and if they had followed the example of the Ninevites in fasting, prayers, and tears, they could have averted the anger of the just Judge.

In this monastery lived a Scot named Adamnan, who led a life so devoted to God in prayer and austerity that he took no food or drink except on Sundays and Thursdays, and often spent the entire night in vigil and prayer. He had originally adopted this severe life from necessity, to overcome his evil inclinations; but as time went on, this necessity became his custom. During his youth he had committed some crime for which, when he came to his senses, he was thoroughly ashamed, and dreaded punishment by the strict Judge. So he visited a priest from whom he hoped to learn a way of salvation, confessed his sins to him, and asked for advice how he might escape the wrath to come. When he had heard his confession, the priest said: 'A severe wound calls for an ever more severe remedy. Therefore spend your time as far as possible in fasting, reciting the psalter, and prayer, so that you may avert God's anger in confession, and deserve to find His mercy.' Already deeply smitten in conscience and longing for speedy release from the inward fetters of the sin that burdened him, he replied: 'I am still young and strong in body, and I will readily undergo whatever penance you impose on me, if only I may be saved at Judgement Day. Even if you order me to remain standing in prayer all night, or to remain the whole week fasting, I will do it.' But the priest answered: 'To remain the whole week without food is too severe a penance: it will be sufficient if you fast for two or three days. Do this until I return shortly, when I will explain more fully what you should do, and how long you should continue this penance.' So, having prescribed the extent of his penance, the priest went away; but he was suddenly called by an urgent need to Ireland, which was his native land, and never returned to him as he had arranged. But Adamnan bore in mind his directions and his own promise, and earnestly applied himself to penitent tears, holy vigils, and fasting. He took food only on Sundays and Thursdays, as I have said, and ate nothing on the other days of the week. And when he heard that his priest had left for Ireland and died there, he continued to observe the austerity that he had imposed; what he had undertaken through fear of God in remorse for his sin he continued without flagging through love of God in enjoyment of his reward.

When he had followed this way of life for a considerable time, it happened one day that he had travelled some distance from the monastery accompanied by one of the brothers. On the return journey, as they were approaching the monastery and saw its buildings towering up, the man of God burst into tears, and his face betrayed the sorrow of his heart. Seeing this, his companion enquired the reason, and he replied: 'The time is near when all the public and private buildings that you see in front of you will be burned to ashes.' When his companion heard this, he went and informed Ebba, the Mother of the Community, as soon as he reached the monastery. She was naturally alarmed, and summoning Adamnan, pressed him to tell her how he knew such a thing. He answered: 'One night recently I was occupied in keeping vigil and reciting the psalter, when a stranger suddenly appeared beside me, and I was greatly startled. He told me not to be afraid, and spoke kindly to me, saying, "You do well to employ these night hours of rest in vigil and prayer instead of indulging in sleep." I answered, "I am aware that I have great need of wholesome vigils and earnest prayer to God to pardon my sins." He said, "You are right; and many besides yourself need to atone for their sins by good works, and employ the time of their release from worldly occupations in seeking their eternal welfare. But there are very few who do this. For I have visited every room and every bed of this monastery, and entered every building and dormitory. Nowhere have I found anyone except yourself concerned with the health of his own soul. All of them, men and women alike, are either sunk in unprofitable sleep, or else awake only to sin. Even the cells, which were built for prayer and study, are now converted into places for eating, drinking, gossip, or other amusements. When they have leisure, even the nuns vowed to God abandon the propriety of their calling and spend their time weaving fine clothes, which they employ to the peril of their calling, either to adorn themselves like brides or to attract attention from strange men. For this reason a heavy and well-deserved punishment is about to fall on this place and its people in the form of a terrible fire." ' The abbess asked: 'Why did you not reveal this to me earlier?' Adamnan replied: 'I hesitated to do so out of regard for you, lest it should cause you grave distress: but let it be some comfort to you that this calamity will not happen in your own time.' Once the vision became known, the Community was somewhat alarmed for a few days, and began to refrain from wrong-doing and undergo penance. But after the death of the abbess they relapsed into their earlier sins and became even more wicked. And when they said 'Peace and safety', then sudden destruction came upon them.

My informant in all these events was my fellow-priest, Edgils, who was living in the monastery at the time. And when the majority of the inhabitants had left the ruined building, he lived a long while in our own monastery, and died there. I have thought it desirable to include this in my history to warn the reader of the workings of God, and how terrible He is in his doings toward the children of men. Let us beware lest at some time we should indulge in the pleasures of the flesh, and pay such scant heed to the judgements of God that we incur his sudden anger. For we shall either be justly and severely punished by losses in this world, or else be even more strictly judged and carried away to eternal perdition.

CHAPTER 26: *On the death of King Egfrid and King Hlothere* [A.D. 685]

IN the year of our Lord 684, King Egfrid of the Northumbrians sent an army into Ireland under the command of Bert, which brutally harassed an inoffensive people who had always been friendly to the English, sparing neither churches nor monasteries from the ravages of war. The islanders resisted force by force as well as they could, and implored the merciful aid of God, praying Heaven long and earnestly to avenge them. And although those who curse may not inherit the kingdom of God, one may well believe that those who were justly cursed for their wickedness quickly suffered the penalty of their guilt at the hands of God their Judge. For in the following year King Egfrid, ignoring the advice of his friends and in particular of Cuthbert, of blessed memory, who had recently been made bishop, rashly led an army to ravage the province of the Picts. The enemy pretended to retreat, and lured the king into narrow mountain passes, where he was killed with the greater part of his forces on the twentieth of May in his fortieth year and the fifteenth of his reign.* As I have said, his friends had warned him against this campaign; but in the previous year he had refused to listen to the reverend Father Egbert, who begged him not to attack the Scots who had done him no harm; and this was his punishment, that he now refused to listen to those who tried to save him from destruction.

Henceforward the hopes and strength of the English realm began:

> 'to waver and slip backward ever lower.'[1]

The Picts recovered their own lands that had been occupied by the English, while the Scots living in Britain and a proportion of the Britons themselves regained their freedom, which they have now preserved for about forty-six years. Many of the English at this time were killed, enslaved, or forced to flee from Pictish territory. Among them, the most reverend man of God Trumwine, who had been appointed their bishop, withdrew with his people from the monastery of Abercurnig, which was situated in English territory but stood close to the firth that divides the lands of the English from those of the Picts. Wherever he could, he recommended his own people to friends in various monasteries. He himself chose to live in the often-mentioned monastery of Streanaeshalch. There, for several years, he lived an austere life with a few of his own folk, to the benefit of many besides himself. On his death, he was buried in the church of blessed Peter the Apostle with the honours due to his life and dignity. The royal nun Aelffled, with her mother Eanfled whom I mentioned earlier, ruled the monastery at this period: and when Bishop Trumwine came, she found him a great help in the administration of the monastery and a great comfort in her own life. Egfrid's successor on the throne was Aldfrid, a man well-read in the Scriptures, who was said to be brother of Egfrid and son of King Oswy. He ably restored the shattered fortunes of the kingdom, though within smaller boundaries.

On the sixth of February in the same year of our Lord 685, King Hlothere of Kent died after a reign of twelve years, his brother Egbert having reigned nine years. He was wounded in battle against the South Saxons, whom Edric, son of Egbert, had raised against him, and he died as his wound was being dressed. This Edric succeeded him and reigned a year

1. Virgil: *Aeneid* II, 169.

and a half; on his death, various alien kings and usurpers plundered the kingdom for a while, until Wictred, son of Egbert, its rightful king, established himself on the throne, and freed the nation from foreign invasion by his devotion and diligence.

CHAPTER 27: *Cuthbert, a man of God, is made bishop* [A.D. 685]: *his life and teaching as a monk*

IN the year of his death, King Egfrid appointed as Bishop of Lindisfarne the holy and venerable Cuthbert, who for many years had lived a solitary life in great self-mastery of mind and body on a tiny island known as Farne, which lies in the ocean about nine miles from the church. From his earliest boyhood he had always longed to enter the religious life, and as soon as he became a youth was clothed and professed as a monk. He first entered the monastery of Melrose on the banks of the River Tweed, then ruled by Abbot Eata, the gentlest and simplest of men, who later became Bishop of the church of Hexham or Lindisfarne, as already noted. The prior of Melrose was Boisil, a priest of great virtues and prophetic spirit. Cuthbert humbly submitted himself to the direction of Boisil, who gave him instruction in the Scriptures and showed him an example of holy life.

When Boisil departed to our Lord, Cuthbert was made prior in his place and trained many men in the monastic life with masterly authority and by his personal example. He did not restrict his teaching and influence to the monastery, but worked to rouse the ordinary folk far and near to exchange their foolish customs for a love of heavenly joys. For many profaned the Faith that they professed by a wicked life, and at a time of plague some had even abandoned the Christian sacraments and had recourse to the delusive remedies of idolatry, as though they could expect to halt a plague ordained of God by spells, amulets, and other devilish secret arts.

Following Boisil's example, in order to correct such errors he often used to leave the monastery, sometimes on horseback but more frequently on foot, and visit the neighbouring towns, where he preached the way of truth to those who had gone astray. In those days, whenever a clerk or priest visited a town, English folk always used to gather at his call to hear the Word, eager to hear his message and even more eager to carry out whatever they had heard and understood. But Cuthbert was so skilful a speaker, and had such a light in his angelic face, and such a love for proclaiming his message, that none presumed to hide his inmost secrets, but all openly confessed their wrong-doing; for they felt it impossible to conceal their guilt from him, and at his direction they blotted out by works of penance the sins that they had confessed. He used mainly to visit and preach in the villages that lay far distant among high and inaccessible mountains, which others feared to visit and whose barbarity and squalor daunted other teachers. Cuthbert, however, gladly undertook this pious task, and taught with such patience and skill that when he left the monastery it would sometimes be a week, sometimes two or three, and occasionally an entire month, before he returned home, after staying in the mountains to guide the peasants heavenward by his teachings and virtuous example.

When this venerable servant of our Lord had spent many years in the monastery of Melrose and become renowned for his wonderful acts of virtue, the most reverend Abbot Eata transferred him to Lindisfarne to instruct the brethren there in the observance of regular discipline, both in his official capacity as prior and by his personal example. For the most reverend Father Eata was then Abbot of Lindisfarne as well. And in ancient times, the bishop used to reside at Lindisfarne with his clergy and the abbot with his monks, the latter being regarded as part of the bishop's household. For Aidan, first Bishop of Lindisfarne, himself a monk, brought monks with him and established the regular life there. The blessed Father

Augustine is known to have done the same earlier in Kent, which is shown in the letter addressed to him by the most reverend Pope Gregory, which I included earlier: 'In your case, my brother, having been trained under monastic rule, you should not live apart from your clergy in the Church of the English, which by God's help has lately been brought to the Faith. You are to follow the way of life practised by our forefathers of the primitive Church, among whom none said that anything which he possessed was his own, but they had all things common.'

CHAPTER 28: *Cuthbert becomes a hermit: his prayers obtain a spring from dry ground, and a crop from seed sown out of season*

THEN Cuthbert with a growing sense of his religious vocation entered, as I have said, upon a life of solitary contemplation and silence. But, as I wrote a full account of his life and virtues both in heroic verse and prose a few years ago, it may suffice to record here a single incident. When he was about to leave for the island, he assured the brethren: 'If God's grace will enable me to live in this place by the labour of my own hands, I shall gladly remain there; but if it proves otherwise, then, God willing, I will soon return to you.' Now the island had no water, corn, or trees, and being the haunt of evil spirits was very ill-suited to human habitation. But when the man of God came, he ordered the evil spirits to withdraw, and the island became quite habitable. And when he had expelled these hostile forces, the brethren helped him to build a tiny dwelling surrounded with a ditch, and such essential buildings as an oratory and a communal shelter. He then directed the brethren to dig a well in the floor of the shelter, although the ground was hard and stony and there seemed no hope whatever of finding a spring. But they did so, and through the faith and prayers of God's servant it was found full of water next day; and this spring still provides an ample supply of its heaven-sent bounty for those who come here. Cuthbert also asked for farming implements and wheat to be brought him; but although he prepared the ground and sowed at the right season, when summer came, not a single ear of corn had come up, not even so much as a blade. So when the brethren paid their accustomed visit, he asked them to bring some barley, in case the nature of the soil and the laws of the divine Giver required that a crop of this grain rather than wheat should be sown. This he planted in the same soil as soon as it was brought, but after the proper season, when there was no hope of its maturing; nevertheless, a rich crop quickly sprang up, and gave the man of God the much desired opportunity to support himself by his own labour.

Thus Cuthbert served God in solitude for many years in a hut surrounded by an embankment so high that he could see nothing but the heavens for which he longed so ardently. Then it came about that a great Synod was held under the presidency of Archbishop Theodore of blessed memory, and in the presence of King Egfrid. This assembled near the river Alne at a place called Twyford, or the Two Fords; and the whole company unanimously elected Cuthbert as bishop of the church of Lindisfarne. But although many messengers and letters were sent to him, nothing would induce him to abandon his hermitage. At length the king in person, accompanied by the most holy Bishop Trumwine and other devout and distinguished men, took boat to the island. There they were joined by many of the Lindisfarne brethren, and the whole company knelt before him and adjured him in God's name and begged him with tears to consent, until eventually they drew him, also in tears, from his dearly loved retreat, and brought him to the Synod. Still profoundly reluctant, he at length bowed to the unanimous decision of the whole assembly, and was persuaded to assume the burden of episcopal dignity. He was chiefly influenced to do so by the prophetic words of God's servant Boisil, who had foretold all that was to happen to him, and how he would become a bishop. His consecration did not take place at once; but after the winter, which was then approaching, it was performed at York on Easter Day in the presence of King Egfrid by the Primate Theodore of blessed memory, assisted by six other bishops. In the first instance, Cuthbert was appointed to the Bishopric of Hexham in place of Tunbert, who had been deposed: but since he much preferred to rule the church of Lindisfarne, where he had been trained, it was arranged that Eata should return to the See of Hexham, to which he had originally been appointed, and that Cuthbert should assume the direction of the church of Lindisfarne.

As bishop he followed the example of the blessed Apostles and enhanced his dignity by his holy actions, protecting the people entrusted to him by his constant prayer and inspiring them to heavenly things by his salutary teachings. Like a good teacher, he taught others to do only what he first practised himself. Above all else, he was afire with heavenly love, unassumingly patient, devoted to unceasing prayer, and kindly to all who came to him for comfort. He regarded as equivalent to prayer the labour of helping the weaker brethren with advice, remembering that he who said, '*Thou shalt love the Lord thy God*', also said, '*Love thy neighbour*'. His self-discipline and fasting were exceptional, and through the grace of contrition he was always intent on the things of heaven. Lastly, whenever he offered the sacrifice of the Saving Victim to God, he offered his prayers to God not in a loud voice but with tears welling up from the depths of his heart.

CHAPTER 29: *Cuthbert foretells his own death to the hermit Herebert* [A.D. 687]

WHEN he had spent two years in his bishopric, Cuthbert returned to his island hermitage, God having made known to him that the day of his death was drawing near, or rather, the day of his entry into that life which alone may be called life. In his usual simple way, he mentioned this fact to some people at the time in somewhat veiled terms, though such that they could be clearly understood later; but to others he spoke openly.

There was a priest of praiseworthy life named Herebert, who had for a long time been linked in a spiritual friendship with the man of God. He lived the life of a hermit on an island in the great lake which is the source of the river Derwent, and used to visit Cuthbert each year to seek his advice on matters of eternal salvation. Hearing that Cuthbert had come to the city of Lugubalia,[1] he went to visit him as usual, wishing to be ever more fervently inspired to heavenly desires by his salutary guidance. As each in turn regaled the other with exhilarating draughts of heavenly life, Cuthbert said among other things: 'Brother Herebert, remember that, whatever you wish to ask or tell me, you must do before we part, because we shall not see one another again in this world. For I know that the day of my death is approaching, and I shall soon put off this earthly tabernacle.' At these words, the other fell at his feet with sighs and tears, saying: 'In the Name of our Lord, I beg you not to leave me! Remember that I am your most devoted friend, and ask God of His mercy to grant that, as we have served Him together on earth, we may pass away together to the vision of heavenly grace. You know how I have always tried to live as you directed; and whenever I have sinned out of ignorance or frailty, I have at once tried to make amends in any way you enjoined.' So the bishop prostrated himself in prayer, and soon received inward intimation that God had granted his request. 'Rise, my brother, and do not weep. Be glad. For God in His mercy has heard our prayer.'

Subsequent events proved the truth of this prophecy; for when they parted, they never saw one another again in this life and on the twentieth of March, their souls left their

1. Carlisle.

bodies on the same day and were together borne by angels to see the beatific vision in the kingdom of heaven. But Herebert was first tried by a long illness. And one may believe that God's mercy decreed this in order that, if his merits were inferior to those of blessed Cuthbert, the chastening of a long illness might supply whatever was lacking: in this way, he would be made equal in grace with his intercessor and in departing this life at the same time would merit to enter into the same state of eternal blessedness.

The most reverend Father Cuthbert died on Farne Island, earnestly requesting the brethren to bury him in this place where he had served God so long. But at length he yielded to their entreaties and consented that his body should be taken back to Lindisfarne and buried within the church. This was accordingly done; and the venerable Bishop Wilfrid held the see for a year until a successor could be appointed. Subsequently Eadbert was consecrated, a man who was well known for his knowledge of the Scriptures, his obedience to God's Commandments, and especially for his generosity in almsgiving. For each year, in accordance with the Law, he used to give a tenth not only of all his beasts but also of all his grain, fruit and clothing to the poor.

CHAPTER 30: *After eleven years in the grave, Cuthbert's body is found incorrupt. His successor departs this life soon afterwards* [A.D. 698]

IN order to make more widely known the height of glory attained after death by God's servant Cuthbert, whose illustrious life on earth had been marked by so many miracles even before his death, Divine Providence guided the brethren to exhume his bones. After eleven years, they expected to find his flesh reduced to dust and the remains withered, as is usual in dead bodies; and they proposed to place them in a new coffin on the same site but above ground level, so that he might receive the honours due to him. When they informed Bishop Eadbert of their wish, he gave approval and directed that it should be carried out on the anniversary of his burial. This was done; and when they opened the grave, they found the body whole and incorrupt as though still living and the limbs flexible, so that he looked as if he were asleep rather than dead. Furthermore, all the vestments in which he was clothed appeared not only spotless but wonderfully fresh and fair. At this sight the brothers were awestruck, and hastened to inform the bishop of their discovery. At that time he was living alone at some distance from the church in a place surrounded by the sea, where he always used to spend Lent and the forty days before the Nativity of our Lord in fasting, prayer, and penitence. It was here that his venerable predecessor Cuthbert had served God in solitude for a period before he went to Farne Island.

The brothers brought with them some of the garments in which the holy body had been clothed. The bishop received these gifts with gratitude, and as he listened with joy to their account of the miracle, he lovingly kissed the garments as though they were still on the father's body. 'Clothe the body in new garments,' he said, 'in place of those that you have removed, and place it in the coffin you have prepared. I have certain knowledge that the grave hallowed by so great and heavenly a miracle will not remain empty for long. And blessed is the man to whom our Lord, the Author and Giver of all bliss, shall grant the privilege of resting in it.' When the bishop had said this and more to the same effect in a trembling voice with tears and deep feeling, the brethren carried out his instructions: having clothed the body in fresh garments, they laid it in a new coffin, which they placed on the pavement of the sanctuary.

Not long afterwards, God's beloved Bishop Eadbert was attacked by an illness that rapidly grew more serious, and in a short time he departed to our Lord on the sixth of May. Whereupon the brethren laid his body in the tomb of the blessed Father Cuthbert, and above it they placed the coffin containing the uncorrupt body of the Father. The miracles of healing that take place from time to time at the tomb bear witness to the holiness of them both. I have recorded some instances in my book on his life. And in this present history I have included further examples that have recently come to my knowledge.

CHAPTER 31: *A brother is cured of paralysis at Cuthbert's tomb*

IN the monastery was a brother named Baduthegn, who served for a considerable time in the guest-house and is still alive. All the brethren and visitors testify that he was a very devout and religious man, who did his appointed task solely for the sake of a heavenly reward. One day he had washed the cloaks used in the guest-house in the sea. As he was returning homewards, he had a sudden seizure and fell to the ground, where he lay prostrate for some while before he could rise. When at last he got up, he found that one side of his body was paralysed from head to foot, and made his way home with the greatest difficulty leaning on a stick. The disease gradually increased and at nightfall became even more serious, so that next day he could hardly rise or walk without help. Crippled as he was, he conceived the excellent plan of making his way to the church as best he could to visit the tomb of the most reverend Father Cuthbert. There on bended knee he would implore God's mercy either to heal his disease, if this were to his good, or else to give him grace to bear his affliction calmly and with patience should Divine Providence decree that he be afflicted with it longer. Acting on this resolve and supporting his feeble limbs with a staff, he entered the church and prostrated himself before the body of the man of God, earnestly praying that at Cuthbert's intercession our Lord would show mercy. As he prayed, he fell into a deep sleep and, as he used afterwards to relate, seemed to feel a great, broad hand rest on the seat of the pain in his head. At this touch, the entire area of his body affected by the disease was gradually eased of its pain, and health was restored right down to the feet. He soon awoke and rose completely cured and after giving thanks to God for his recovery, told the brethren what had happened to him. And to the joy of all he returned to the duties that he had always carried out so faithfully, as though chastened by the scourge of suffering.

The garments that had clothed Cuthbert's hallowed body both before and after his death continued to possess healing virtues, as anyone may read in the book of his life and miracles.

CHAPTER 32: *The relics of Saint Cuthbert heal another brother's diseased eye*

I CANNOT omit mention of a cure that took place through his relics three years ago and was told me by the very brother to whom it happened. It occurred in a monastery which was in course of construction near the river Dacore,[1] from which it took its name, and whose head was the devout Abbot Swidbert. In this house lived a young man who developed a tumour on his eyelid, which daily increased in size and threatened to destroy the eye. Although the physicians applied poultices to reduce it, they had no success: some advised cutting it out, while others opposed this, fearing graver complications. So the brother suffered great pain for a long time, and it seemed that no human skill could prevent the loss of his eye, whose condition was deteriorating daily, till he was suddenly cured by the goodness of God and by means of the relics of the most holy father Cuthbert. This came about because, when the brethren found his body uncorrupt after many years in the grave, they had taken some

1. Dacre, near Penrith.

of his hair to provide relics for their friends and to show as evidence of this miracle.

At that time a small portion of these relics was in the possession of Thruidred, then one of the priests of the monastery and now its abbot. And one day, when he went into the church and opened the casket of relics in order to give a portion to a friend who had requested it, the young man with the diseased eye happened to be present. Having given the required portion to his friend, Thruidred handed the remainder to the young man to replace in their casket. Moved by a beneficent impulse, the youth took the hairs of holy Cuthbert's head in his hand and applied them to his eyelid, and tried by holding them there for a while to soften and reduce the swelling. He then replaced the relics in their casket as he had been directed, confident that, now that his eye had been touched by the hair of the man of God, it would soon be cured. Nor was his faith in vain. For, as he tells, it was then about Terce, and thenceforward he was busy about the day's duties until nearly Sext, when he suddenly felt his eye and found both it and the lid sound, as though there had never been any deformity or swelling on it.

BOOK FIVE

CHAPTER 1: *The hermit Ethelwald, Cuthbert's successor, calms a storm by his prayer when some brethren are in danger at sea*

CUTHBERT, the man of God, had a successor in the solitary life that he had lived on Farne Island before he became a bishop. This was a venerable man named Ethelwald who had received the priesthood many years previously in the monastery of Ripon and adorned the office by conduct worthy of it. To illustrate more clearly his virtue and the kind of life that he led, I will relate a miracle of his that was told me by one of the brethren among whom and for whose benefit it was performed; this was the venerable priest and servant of Christ Guthfrid, who afterwards presided as abbot over the brethren of the church of Lindisfarne where he had been brought up.

'I came with two other brothers to Farne Island,' he said, 'wishing to speak with the most reverend Father Ethelwald. We were greatly inspired by his discourse and, having asked his blessing, were returning homewards. Then, while we were in the middle of the sea, the calm weather that was favouring our crossing suddenly changed. There followed a storm of such ferocity and violence that sail and oars were useless and we expected nothing but death. Having struggled unavailingly against the wind and waves for a long time, we looked back to see whether it were practicable to fight our way back to the island we had left, but found the storm equally violent on all sides, so that in ourselves there was no hope for us of escape. But, as we looked into the distance, we saw that Father Ethelwald, the beloved of God, had come out of his cell on Farne and was watching our progress; for he had heard the roar of

270

the gale and raging of the sea and had come out to discover how we were faring. When he saw us in distress and despair, he fell on his knees to the Father of our Lord Jesus Christ and prayed for our safety. Directly his prayer was ended, the raging sea grew calm, the severity of the storm lessened on all sides, and a following wind bore us over calm water towards the land. As soon as we had reached the shore and were lifting our little boat out of the surf, the wind that had dropped awhile for our sakes at once began to blow again and continued strongly all that day. So we realized that the short interval of calm had been granted by the mercy of heaven at the prayer of the man of God so that we might escape.'

The man of God remained on Farne Island for twelve years and died there; but he was buried on the island of Lindisfarne in the church of the blessed Apostle Peter next to the bodies of the above-mentioned bishops. These events took place in the time of King Aldfrid, who succeeded his brother Egfrid as King of the Northumbrians and reigned for nineteen years.

CHAPTER 2: *The blessing of Bishop John cures a dumb man*

AT the beginning of King Aldfrid's reign Bishop Eata died, and was succeeded as Bishop of Hexham by a holy man named John.* Many miracles are told of him by those who knew him well, and in particular by Berthun, a most reverend and truthful man, formerly John's deacon and now abbot of the monastery known as In-Derawuda, which means 'In the wood of the Deiri'.[1] I have thought it fitting to preserve the memory of some of these miracles for posterity.

Whenever opportunity offered and especially during Lent, this man of God used to retire with a few companions to read and pray quietly in an isolated house surrounded by open woodland and a dyke. It stood about a mile and a half from the church at Hexham across the river Tyne, and had a

1. Now Beverley.

burial-ground dedicated to Saint Michael the Archangel.
John once came to stay here at the beginning of Lent and,
as was his invariable custom, told his companions to find
some poor person who was either seriously infirm or in dire
want, so that he might live with them during their stay and
benefit from their alms.

In a village not far distant lived a dumb youth known to the
bishop; for he had often visited him to receive alms and had
never been able to utter a single word. In addition, he had so
many scabs and scales on his head that no hair ever grew on
the crown, but only a few wisps stood up in a ragged circle
round it. So the bishop ordered this youth to be fetched, and
a little hut to be made for him in the enclosure round the house
where he could live and receive his daily allowance. When
one week of Lent was past, on the following Sunday John told
the poor lad to come to him, and when he had entered he
ordered him to put out his tongue and show it him; then he
took him by the chin, and making the sign of the holy cross
on his tongue, told him to retract it and speak. 'Pronounce
some word,' he said: 'say *yea*,' which is the English word of
agreement and assent, *i.e.* 'Yes'. The lad's tongue was loosed,
and at once he did what he was told. The bishop then proceeded to the names of letters: 'Say A.' And he said 'A'. 'Now
say B,' he said, which the youth did. And when he had
repeated the names of each of the letters after the bishop, the
latter added syllables and words for him to repeat after him.
When he had uttered every word accordingly, the bishop set
him to repeat longer sentences, and he did so. All those who
were present say that all that day and the next night, as long
as he could keep awake, the youth never stopped saying something and expressing his own inner thoughts and wishes to
others, which he had never been able to do previously. He was
like the cripple healed by the Apostles Peter and John, who
stood up, leaped, and walked, entering the temple with them,
walking, and leaping, and praising God, rejoicing in the use of
his feet, of which he had been so long deprived. The bishop

was delighted at his cure, and directed the physician to undertake the cure of the youth's scabby head.

The physician did as he was asked, and with the assistance
of the bishop's blessing and prayers his skin healed, and a
vigorous growth of hair appeared. So the youth obtained a
clear complexion, readiness of speech, and a beautiful head of
hair, whereas he had formerly been deformed, destitute, and
dumb. In his joy at this recovery, he declined an offer from
the bishop of a permanent place in his household, preferring
to return to his own home.

CHAPTER 3 : *Bishop John heals a sick girl by his prayers*

BERTHUN described another miracle done by the bishop.
When the most reverend Wilfrid became Bishop of
Hexham after his long exile, and John became Bishop of York
on the death of the holy and humble Bosa, he came one day
to a convent of nuns at a place called Wetadun,[1] ruled at the
time by the Abbess Heriburg. 'When we had arrived and
been welcomed with general rejoicing, the abbess informed
us that one of the nuns, her own daughter, was very seriously
ill. She told us that the nun had recently been bled in the arm
and that, while she was being treated, she was suddenly seized
by a violent pain which rapidly increased, so that the wounded
arm grew worse and became so swollen that it could hardly
be encircled with two hands. In consequence, the nun was
lying in bed in terrible pain and seemed likely to die. The
abbess therefore begged the bishop to visit her and give her his
blessing, being sure that she would improve if the bishop
blessed or touched her. He enquired when the girl had been
bled, and when he learned that it had been on the fourth day
of the moon, he said: "You have acted most foolishly and
unwisely to carry out blood-letting on the fourth day of the
moon. I remember that Archbishop Theodore, of blessed

1. Watton, near Beverley.

memory, said that it was very dangerous to bleed at a time
when the light of the moon and the pull of the tide is increasing. And what can I do for the girl if she is going to die?" But
the abbess pressed him most earnestly on behalf of her daughter, who was very dear to her, and whom she intended to
appoint abbess in her own place, and at length she prevailed
on him to visit the sick girl. So he went in, taking me with him
to see the girl who, as I have said, lay helpless and in great pain,
with her arm swollen to such a size that she could not bend her
elbow. The bishop stood and said a prayer over her, and
having given her his blessing, went out. Some while later, as
we were sitting at table, someone came in and asked me to
come outside, saying: "Coenburg" – for that was the girl's
name – "wishes you to come back to her room at once." I did
so, and when I entered, I found her looking cheerful and
apparently in sound health. And when I sat down by her, she
said: "Would you like me to ask for a drink?" "Certainly,"
I replied, "I shall be delighted if you will." When a cup had
been brought and we had both drunk, she began to tell me
what had happened. "As soon as the bishop had blessed me and
gone away, I began to feel better; and although I have not yet
recovered my full strength, the pain has entirely left my arm
where it was most intense, and all my body. It was as though the
bishop took it away with him entirely when he left, although
the swelling on my arm seems to remain." As we were leaving
the convent, the disappearance of the pain in her limbs was
promptly followed by a subsidence of the swelling, and the
girl, saved from pain and death, gave thanks to our Lord and
Saviour with all the other servants of God in the place.'

CHAPTER 4: *The Bishop cures a thane's wife with holy water*

ABBOT BERTHUN also told the story of another miracle
not unlike the previous one performed by the bishop. He
said: 'Not far from our monastery, about two miles distant,

stood the country house of a thane named Puch, whose wife had been suffering from an acute complaint for forty days, and for three weeks it had been impossible to move her from the room where she lay. It happened at the time that the man of God had been invited there by the thane to dedicate a church; and when he had done this, the thane asked him to dine in his house. The bishop declined, saying that he must return to the monastery, which was close by. But the thane pressed him even more earnestly, promising to give alms to the poor if only the bishop would consent to come into his house to break his fast. I supported the thane's request, and also promised to give alms to the poor if he would go in to have a meal in the thane's house and give his blessing. After much difficulty, we persuaded him, and went in for some food. Meanwhile, at the hands of one of the brethren who had come with us, the bishop had sent the sick woman some of the holy water that he had blessed for the dedication of the church, telling him to give her some of it to drink and to apply some as a lotion to the place where the worst pain lay. When this had been done, the woman immediately got up cured. Then finding herself not only relieved of her long illness but restored to her former strength, she brought a cup to the bishop and us and, having performed this duty, continued to serve us with drink until the close of the meal. In this she followed the example of Saint Peter's wife's mother, who after being troubled by a burning fever was restored to health and activity at the touch of the Lord's hand and immediately arose and ministered to them.'

CHAPTER 5: *The Bishop's prayers recall the servant of a thane from death's door*

ON another occasion, the bishop was invited to consecrate the church of a thane named Addi. When he had completed the ceremony, the thane requested him to visit one of

his serving-lads who was so seriously ill that he had completely
lost the use of all his limbs and now seemed about to die:
indeed, a coffin had already been prepared to receive his
corpse. The thane pressed him with tears, earnestly begging
him to go in and pray for the boy, saying that his life was of
great concern to him. He was sure that, if only the bishop
were willing to lay his hand on him and bless him, he would
recover immediately. So the bishop went in and found the
boy at death's door, with the coffin in which he was to be
buried lying beside him. All present were in tears. After saying
a prayer and giving the boy his blessing, the bishop went out
with the stock formula of encouragement: 'Hurry up and get
well.' Later, while the company were sitting at table, the boy
sent to his master saying he was thirsty and asking if he might
have a cup of wine. Delighted that he could drink, the thane
sent him a cup of wine blessed by the bishop, and as soon as he
had drunk it he got up, threw off his disease, and put on his
clothes. Then he left his room and came in to greet the bishop,
saying that he would be glad to join them in eating and
drinking. They were delighted at his recovery, and told him
to sit down to dine with them; so he sat down and made merry
as one of the company. He lived for many years afterwards,
and retained the good health that had been restored to him.
Abbot Berthun says that he was not present when this miracle
took place, but that he had an account of it from those who
were.

CHAPTER 6: *By his prayers and blessing, Bishop John saves
from death one of his clergy who had been bruised in a fall*

I CANNOT leave unmentioned a miracle that God's servant
Heribald relates as having been performed for his benefit
by Bishop John. At the time he was one of the bishop's clergy,
but is now abbot of a monastery near the mouth of the river
Tyne. 'Living with him, and knowing his way of life very

intimately,' he says, 'I knew it to be wholly worthy of a bishop, so far as it is permissible for a man to judge. But I also proved by the experience of many others, and more especially by my own, how great his merit was in the eyes of Him who sees the heart; for by his prayer and blessing, as I shall tell, he brought me back from death's door and restored me to life. In my early youth I lived among his clergy, occupied in learning to read and sing; but my heart had not yet entirely abandoned youthful follies. As we were travelling with him one day, we happened to come to a level open road, well suited for galloping our horses. The young men with him, mainly layfolk, began to ask the bishop's permission to gallop and try out their horses against each other. At first he refused their request, saying that it was an unprofitable occupation; but at length he gave in to their unanimous wish, saying: "Do so if you wish; but Heribald is not to take part in the race." I begged him persistently to let me race with the rest, for I had confidence in an excellent horse he had given me; but I could not obtain his consent.

'When they had galloped to and fro several times, and came back spurring their horses in a race while the bishop and I watched, my hot-headed wilfulness got the better of me, and I could not restrain myself. Despite his prohibition, I joined in the sport and began to race with the others at full speed. As I did so, I heard the bishop behind me say in a sorrowful voice: "Oh, how you grieve me by riding like that!" But, although I heard him, I went on against his orders. Shortly afterwards, as my spirited horse took off in a powerful jump across a hollow in the path, I fell, and at once lost all feeling and power of movement as though I were dying; for at the spot lay a stone, level with the ground, lightly covered by turf, the only stone to be found in the whole of that level plain. And it happened by chance, or rather by the disposition of divine providence as a punishment for my disobedience, that I struck my head, and the hand which I had put under my head as I fell, on this stone. As a consequence, my thumb was

broken and my skull cracked, and, as I said, I lay as though
dead. As I was unable to move, they stretched an awning over
me for protection; and from an hour after midday until
evening I lay motionless as a corpse. Then I revived slightly,
and my companions carried me home, where I lay speechless
all night, vomiting blood as a result of some internal injury.
The bishop was greatly distressed about my accident and
possible death, because he was especially fond of me; and he
did not remain with his clergy that night as was his usual
custom, but spent all night in vigil and prayer, as I understand,
asking God of His mercy to restore me to health. Early next
morning he came and said a prayer over me, calling me by
name, and waking me out of what seemed to be a heavy sleep.
"Do you know who it is speaking to you?" he asked. Opening my eyes, I replied: "I do. You are my beloved bishop."
"Can you live?" he asked. "I can do so with the help of your
prayers, God willing," I replied.

'Having laid his hand on my head and blessed me, he went
back to his prayers. On his return after a short while, he found
me sitting up and well enough to talk. Then, inspired by God
– as was soon evident – he asked me if I knew for certain
whether I had been baptized. I answered that I was sure
beyond a doubt that I had been washed in the waters of salvation for the forgiveness of sins; and I told him the name of
the priest who had baptized me. But he said: "If you were
baptized by that priest, you were not validly baptized. For I
know him. When he was ordained priest, he was so slow-
witted that he could not learn how to catechize and baptize. For
this reason, I ordered him to cease presuming to exercise this
ministry, because he was too ignorant to carry it out properly."
He then proceeded to catechize me on the spot; and when he
happened to breathe on my face, I immediately began to feel
better. He called the surgeon, and told him to close and ban-
dage up the crack in my skull. After receiving his blessing, I
was so much better next day that I mounted my horse and
journeyed on with him to another town. I was soon com-

pletely recovered, and was then cleansed in the lifegiving waters of Baptism.'

John remained in his bishopric for thirty-three years, and then entered the kingdom of heaven. He was buried in Saint Peter's porch in his own monastery of In-Derawuda in the year of our Lord 721. When his advanced years prevented him from administering his bishopric, he consecrated his priest Wilfrid to the See of York, and retired to his monastery to end his days in a manner pleasing to God.

CHAPTER 7: *Cadwalla, King of the West Saxons, goes to Rome for Baptism: his successor Ini also makes a pilgrimage of devotion to the shrine of the Apostles* [A.D. 688]

I N the third year of King Aldfrid's reign, Cadwalla, King of the West Saxons, who had governed his people most ably for two years, abdicated from his throne for the sake of our Lord and his eternal kingdom and travelled to Rome. For, having learned that the road to heaven lies open to mankind only through baptism, he wished to obtain the particular privilege of receiving the cleansing of baptism at the shrine of the blessed Apostles. At the same time, he hoped to die shortly after his baptism, and pass from this world to everlasting happiness. By God's grace, both of these hopes were realized. Arriving in Rome during the pontificate of Sergius, he was baptized on Holy Saturday before Easter in the year of our Lord 689, and he fell ill and while still wearing his white robes* departed this life on the twentieth of April and joined the company of the blessed in heaven. At the time of his baptism, the aforesaid Pope had given him the name of Peter, in order that he might be linked by name to the most blessed Prince of the Apostles, to whose most sacred body the king's devotion had brought him from the ends of the earth. He was buried in the Apostle's church, and the Pope directed that an epitaph be inscribed on his tomb to preserve the memory of

his devotion for ever and inspire all who read or heard of it to
religious fervour. This inscription was as follows:

> High rank and wealth, offspring, and mighty realms,
> Triumphs and spoils, great nobles, cities, halls,
> Won by his forbears' prowess and his own –
> All these great Cadwal left for love of God.
> This royal pilgrim then sought Peter's Chair
> To slake his thirst at Peter's vital spring,
> And in his splendid, glowing light to bathe
> From whom life-giving radiance ever streams.
> Eager to win the prize of life renewed,
> Converted, he converts his barbarous ways
> And then his name itself to Peter's own
> At father Sergius' word, that at the font
> Christ's grace may wash him from all taint of sin
> And bring him clothed in white to heaven's gate.
> Great was his faith; Christ's mercy greater still
> Whose secret purpose mortals may not know.
> Safely he came from Britain's utmost shores,
> Through many peoples, over land and sea,
> Bearing his mystic gifts, to visit Rome
> And in the shrine of Peter lay them down.
> Now, robed in white, he moves among Christ's sheep:
> His body lies entombed, his soul on high.
> Wise king, his earthly sceptre to resign,
> And win from Christ in heaven His promised crown.

Cadwalla, also known as Peter, King of the Saxons, was buried here
on the twelfth day before the Kalends of May, the second indiction.
He lived about thirty years, during the reign of the most pious
Emperor Justinian Augustus, in the fourth year of his Consulship,
and in the second year of the pontificate of our apostolic lord Pope
Sergius.

On Cadwalla's departure for Rome, he was succeeded as
king by Ini, who was of the blood royal. Having ruled the
nation for thirty-seven years, Ini also abdicated and handed
over the government to younger men. He then set out to
visit the shrines of the blessed Apostles during the pontificate

of Gregory [II], wishing to spend some of the time of his earthly pilgrimage in the vicinity of the holy places, hoping thereby to merit a warmer welcome from the saints in heaven. At this period, many English people vied with one another in following this custom, both noble and simple, layfolk and clergy, men and women alike.

CHAPTER 8: *On the death of Theodore, Bertwald becomes archbishop* [A.D. 690]: *among bishops consecrated by him is Tobias, Bishop of Rochester, a man of great learning*

IN the year after Cadwalla's death in Rome, that is, the year of our Lord 690, Archbishop Theodore, of blessed memory, died old and full of years at the age of eighty-eight. He had long previously told his friends that he would die at this age, which had been foretold to him in a dream. He had held the archbishopric for twenty-two years, and was buried in the church of Saint Peter, where all the bodies of the Archbishops of Canterbury are buried. It may be said of him, as of all his colleagues in the same dignity, that '*their bodies are buried in peace, but their name liveth for evermore.*' To summarize briefly, the churches of the English made greater progress during his pontificate than they had ever done before. His epitaph publicly and clearly describes his character, life, age, and death to all who visit his tomb. This consists of thirty-four heroic verses, the first of which run:

> Here rests the holy Primate in his tomb –
> Great Theodore, a Greek by race and name.
> A prince of pontiffs, and a blest high priest
> Who taught to all his flock the light of truth.

And the last verses are:

> The nineteenth of September was the day
> That saw his spirit burst its earthly bonds,
> Rising in rapture to a newer life
> In sweet communion with the saints on high.

Theodore's successor in the archbishopric was Bertwald, Abbot of the monastery of Reculver, which stands on the north bank at the mouth of the river Yenlade. Although he can hardly be compared with his predecessor, he was learned in the Scriptures and well versed in ecclesiastical and monastic affairs. He was elected bishop on the first of July in the year of our Lord 692, when Wictred and Swaebhard were kings of Kent: but he was consecrated the following year on Sunday June the twenty-ninth by Godwin, Metropolitan of Gaul, and occupied his see on the thirty-first of August. Bertwald consecrated many bishops, including Tobias, a man of wide learning and a scholar of Latin, Greek, and Saxon, who became Bishop of Rochester on the death of Gebmund.

CHAPTER 9: *Egbert, a holy man, plans to travel to Germany and preach, but is prevented. Subsequently Wictbert goes, but meeting with no success, returns to his native Ireland*

AT this time, the venerable servant of Christ, Bishop Egbert, a man whose name deserves high honour, was living a life of exile in Ireland, as I have already mentioned, in order to attain his heavenly home. He planned to bring blessings to more people by undertaking the apostolic work of preaching the word of God to some of the nations who had not heard it. He had learned that there were many such nations in Germany, of whose stock came the Angles or Saxons now settled in Britain, who are for this reason still miscalled 'Garmans' by their neighbours the Britons. These nations include the Frisians, Rugians, Danes, Huns, Old Saxons, and Boructuars besides many other races in that region who still observe pagan rites. So this warrior of Christ planned to sail around Britain and attempt to snatch some of them from Satan and bring them to Christ. If this proved impossible, he proposed to travel to Rome, to visit and venerate the shrines of the blessed Apostles and martyrs of Christ.

From the execution of either of these projects, however, he was stayed by heavenly portents and manifestations. He had already chosen the boldest of his companions, whose distinguished lives and learning rendered them well fitted to preach the Gospel, and all preparations for the voyage were complete. Then early one morning he received a visit from one of the brethren, who had formerly been a disciple and assistant in Britain to God's beloved priest Boisil, when, as already related, he was Prior of the monastery of Melrose under Abbot Eata. This brother told him of a vision which he had seen that night: 'After the morning hymns,' he said, 'I had lain down on my pallet and fallen into a light sleep, when my old master and most loving teacher Boisil appeared to me, and asked whether I recognized him. "Of course I do," I said: "you are Boisil." He then said: "I have come to bring a message from our Lord and Saviour to Egbert, which you must deliver to him. Tell him that he is not to go on the journey that he has in mind; for it is God's will that he should go and instruct the monks of Columba."' Now Columba was the first teacher of the Christian Faith to the Picts living north of the mountains, and founder of the monastery on the Isle of Iona, which long remained venerated by the people of the Picts and Scots. For this reason, Columba is now known by some people as Columbkill, a name compounded from 'Columba' and 'cell'. When Egbert had heard about this vision, he ordered the brother who had related it not to tell anyone else, in case the vision were a delusion; but silently turning it over in his own mind, Egbert feared that it was true. But he did not abandon his preparations for his voyage to evangelize the heathen.

After a few days, this brother came to him once more, saying that Boisil had again appeared to him in a vision after Matins, saying: 'Why did you convey the message that I gave you for Egbert in such a careless and offhand fashion? Now go and tell him that, whether he wishes it or not, he is to visit the monks of Columba, because their ploughs do not run straight*

and it is his duty to recall them to the right way.' Hearing
this, Egbert again enjoined the brother not to disclose the
vision to anyone. But although he was now convinced of the
vision's reality, he none the less attempted to carry out his
projected voyage with the brethren. Then, when they had
stored the ship with everything necessary for the voyage and
had waited some days for a favourable wind, a storm of such
violence arose one night that the ship was left lying on her
beam ends among the breakers, and part of her stores was
lost. However, everything that belonged to Egbert and his
companions was salvaged. Then, like the prophet Jonah,
Egbert said: 'For my sake this great tempest is upon you.' So he
abandoned his plan, and resigned himself to staying at home.

But among Egbert's companions was one called Wictbert,
well known for his contempt for worldly things and for his
knowledge of doctrine, who had lived the life of a hermit in
great perfection for many years as an exile in Ireland. Wictbert
took ship and arrived in Frisia, where he preached the word of
life constantly for two years to the people and their king
Radbod; but his great efforts produced no results among his
barbaric hearers. He then returned to his beloved land of exile
and began to give himself to our Lord in his accustomed silence. And since he had been unable to help foreigners towards
the Faith, he sought to be of more help to his own people by
setting them a holy example.

CHAPTER 10: *Wilbrord preaches in Frisia and converts many
to Christ: his companions the Hewalds suffer martyrdom*
[A.D. 692]

So the man of God, Egbert, realized that he was not permitted to go and preach to the heathen, and that he was
retained to be of some other service to Holy Church, as he
had been forewarned by the vision. But, although he knew
that Wictbert had enjoyed no success when he visited those

parts, he still attempted to send other holy and zealous men for the work of preaching, among whom the outstanding figure by his priestly rank and his merit was one named Wilbrord.* When he and his twelve companions arrived, they made a detour to visit Pippin, Duke of the Franks, by whom they were graciously received. Since Pippin had recently conquered Nearer Frisia and driven out King Radbod, he dispatched them to preach there, supporting them with his imperial authority so that no one should interfere with their preaching, and granting many favours to those who wished to embrace the Faith. Consequently, aided by God's grace, they converted many folk in a short while from idolatry to belief in Christ.

Two other priests of English race, who had long lived as exiles in Ireland for the sake of the eternal kingdom, followed their lead and went to the province of the Old Saxons in order to try and win them for Christ by their teaching. They shared the same name and the same zeal, but with the distinction that, since their hair was of different colour, one was known as Hewald the Black, and the other as Hewald the White. Both men were devout and religious, but Hewald the Black was more learned in the holy scriptures. On entering the province, they were given hospitality by a certain reeve, whom they asked to conduct them to his lord, as they had a message to his advantage which they were bound to communicate to him. For these Old Saxons have no king, but several lords who are set over the nation. Whenever war is imminent, these cast lots impartially, and the one on whom the lot falls is followed and obeyed by all for the duration of the war; but as soon as the war ends, the lords revert to equality of status. So the reeve received and kept them with him for some days, promising to send them as they had asked to the lord to whom he was subject.

Now the Hewalds devoted themselves to psalms and prayers, and daily offered the sacrifice of the saving Victim to God, having with them sacred vessels and a consecrated table for use as an altar. And when the barbarous people realized that they belonged to a different religion, they began to distrust them, fearing that if they went to their lord and spoke to him, they might turn him from his gods and convert him to the new practice of the Christian Faith, so that the whole province would gradually be compelled to change its old religion for new. So they suddenly seized them and put them to death: Hewald the White was killed outright with a sword, and Hewald the Black was put to lingering torture and torn agonizingly limb from limb. Then they flung the murdered men into the Rhine. When the lord whom they had wished to see heard of this, he was extremely angry that strangers desiring to see him had not been allowed to do so; and he sent and slew all the villagers and burned down their village. These priests and servants of Christ suffered on the third of October.

Their martyrdom was not unmarked by heavenly signs; for when their bodies were thrown into the Rhine by the heathen, as I have described, they were carried upstream against the current for nearly forty miles to the place where their companions were. And a great ray of light reaching high into the sky shone all night above the spot where the bodies had arrived, and was also seen by the heathen who had murdered them. Moreover one of the two appeared by night in a vision to one of their companions, a distinguished man of noble family named Tilmon, a soldier turned monk, and told him that their bodies would be found at the spot where he saw the light shining from heaven to earth. This happened as he said: their bodies were found and buried with the honour due to martyrs, and the day of their death, or of the finding of their bodies, is observed in those parts with fitting respect. When Pippin, the most illustrious Duke of the Franks, later heard of these events, he directed that the bodies be brought to him, and buried them with great splendour in the church of the city of Cologne on the Rhine. It is said that a spring bubbled up at the scene of the martyrdom, which affords a plentiful supply of water to this day.

ON their first arrival in Frisia, as soon as Wilbrord learned that the prince had granted him permission to preach, he hurried to Rome, where Pope Sergius then ruled the apostolic see, in order to obtain his approval and blessing on the evangelistic work he wished to undertake. He also hoped to obtain from him relics of the blessed Apostles and martyrs of Christ, so that when he had destroyed the idols and built churches among the people to whom he preached, he might have the relics of the saints ready to put in them. And when he had deposited them, he intended to dedicate these places fittingly in honour of each of the saints whose relics they were. He also wished to learn and obtain many other things required for carrying out so formidable a task. And having obtained all that he wanted, he returned to preach.

At this time the brethren who were engaged in the ministry of the word in Frisia elected one of their number named Swidbert, who was modest in his ways and humble-hearted, to be consecrated their bishop. And they sent him to Britain, where, at their request, he was consecrated by the most reverend Bishop Wilfrid, who happened to be driven out of his own country at the time and was living in exile among the Mercians. For there was no bishop in Kent at this juncture, Theodore having died and Bertwald his successor, who had crossed the sea to be consecrated, having not yet returned to his episcopal see.

When he had been made bishop, Swidbert returned from Britain and shortly afterwards went to the Boructuars, many of whom he guided into the way of truth by his teaching. But after a short while, the Boructuars were defeated by the Old Saxons, and those who had accepted the word of God were scattered. The bishop himself went with certain others to Pippin, who at the request of his wife Plectrude, gave them a place of residence on an island in the Rhine, which in their language is called 'On the shore'.[1] Here he established a monastery, which is still occupied by his successors, and after leading a most austere life for some while, he ended his days there.

When those who had come over had taught in Frisia for a number of years, Pippin with their unanimous consent dispatched the venerable Wilbrord to Rome, where Sergius was still Pope, with the request that he might be consecrated Archbishop of the Frisian nation. His request was carried out in the year of our Lord 696, and Wilbrord was consecrated in the church of the holy martyr Cecilia on her feast day, when the Pope gave him the name of Clement. He was sent back to his bishopric without delay, fourteen days after his arrival in the city.

Pippin assigned him a place for his see in his own famous castle, which is known in the ancient language of that people as Wiltaburg, that is, the Town of the Wilts; but it is known in the Gallic tongue as Utrecht. Having built a church here, the most reverend prelate preached the word of God far and wide, recalling many from their errors and establishing several churches and a number of monasteries in those parts. And not long afterwards he appointed a number of bishops, choosing them from among the brethren who had come with him or after him to preach. Some of these have now fallen asleep in the Lord, but Wilbrord himself, surnamed Clement, is still living, and is much revered for his great age. He has been thirty-six years a bishop, and after the countless spiritual battles he has fought, longs with all his heart for the prize of a heavenly reward.

1. Now Kaiserswerth.

ABOUT this time, a noteworthy miracle, like those of olden days, occurred in Britain. For, in order to arouse the living from spiritual death, a man already dead returned to bodily life and related many notable things that he had seen, some of which I have thought it valuable to mention here in brief. There was a head of a family living in a place in the country of the Northumbrians known as Cunningham, who led a devout life with all his household. He fell ill and grew steadily worse until the crisis came, and in the early hours of one night he died. But at daybreak he returned to life and suddenly sat up to the great consternation of those weeping around the body, who ran away; only his wife, who loved him more dearly, remained with him, though trembling and fearful. The man reassured her and said: 'Do not be frightened; for I have truly risen from the grasp of death, and I am allowed to live among men again. But henceforward I must not live as I used to, and must adopt a very different way of life.' Then he rose and went off to the village church, where he continued in prayer until daybreak. He then divided all his property into three parts, one of which he allotted to his wife, another to his sons, and the third he retained and distributed at once to the poor. Not long afterwards, he abandoned all worldly responsibilities and entered the monastery of Melrose, which is almost completely surrounded by a bend in the river Tweed. There he was given the tonsure and entered a separate part of the house allotted him by the abbot, where he entered upon a life of such physical and spiritual penance to the day of his death that, even if he had kept silence, his life would have witnessed that he had seen many dreadful and many desirable things that remained hidden from others.

This was the account he used to give of his experience: 'A

handsome man in a shining robe was my guide, and we
walked in silence in what appeared to be a north-easterly
direction. As we travelled onwards, we came to a very broad
and deep valley of infinite length. The side to our left was
dreadful with burning flames, while the opposite side was
equally horrible with raging hail and bitter snow blowing and
driving in all directions. Both sides were filled with men's
souls, which seemed to be hurled from one side to the other
by the fury of the tempest. For when the wretches could no
longer endure the blast of the terrible heat, they leaped into
the heart of the terrible cold; and finding no refuge there,
they leaped back again to be burned in the middle of the un-
quenchable flames. A countless host of deformed spirits were
tormented far and wide in this wretched condition without
any interval of respite as far as the eye could see, and I began
to think that perhaps this was Hell, of whose intolerable torments I had often heard tell. But, as if in response to my
thoughts, the guide who preceded me said: "Do not think
this; for this is not Hell as you imagine."

'When he had led me gradually to the further end, much
alarmed by the terrible scene, I saw the place suddenly begin
to grow dim, and darkness concealed everything. As we
entered it, this darkness gradually grew so dense that I could
see nothing except it and the outline and robes of my guide.
And as we went on "through the nocturnal, solitary gloom",[1]
frequent masses of dusky flame suddenly appeared before us,
rising as though from a great pit and falling back into it
again. When my guide had brought me to this place, he
suddenly disappeared and left me alone in the midst of the
darkness before this horrible scene. Meanwhile these masses
of flame continued ceaselessly leaping up and falling back
again into the depths of the chasm, and I saw that, as the
tongues of flame rose, they were filled with the souls of men
which, like sparks flying up with the smoke, were sometimes
flung high in the air, and at others dropped back into the

1. Virgil: *Aeneid* VI, 268.

depths as the vapours of the fire died down. Furthermore, an indescribable stench welled up with these vapours, and filled the whole of this gloomy place.

'When I had stood there a long time terrified, not knowing what to do, where to turn, or what would happen to me, I suddenly heard behind me the sound of a most hideous and desperate lamentation, accompanied by harsh laughter, as though a rough mob were mocking captured enemies. As the noise increased and drew nearer, I saw a throng of wicked spirits dragging with them five human souls howling and lamenting into the depths of the darkness while the devils laughed and exulted. I saw among them one man tonsured like a clerk, a layman, and a woman. The wicked spirits dragged them down into the centre of the burning chasm, and as they descended deeper, I could no longer distinguish the weeping of the men from the laughter of the devils, but heard only a confused noise in my ears. Meanwhile, some of the dark spirits emerged from the fiery depths and rushed to surround me, harassing me with their glowing eyes and foul flames issuing from their mouths and nostrils. They threatened to seize me with the glowing tongs that they brandished in their hands, but although they frightened me, they did not dare to touch me. While I was thus beset about by enemies and black darkness and looked everywhere for some means of help to save me, there appeared behind me on the road by which I had come what seemed to be a bright star shining in the gloom, which grew in size and came swiftly towards me. As it approached, all the evil spirits who had tried to drag me away with their tongs, scattered and took to flight.

'The newcomer whose approach put them to flight was my former guide, who took a road to the right and began to lead me towards the south-east. He soon brought me out of darkness into an atmosphere of clear light, and as he led me forwards in bright light, I saw before us a tremendous wall which seemed to be of infinite length and height in all directions. As I could see no gate, window, or entrance in it, I began to wonder why we went up to the wall. But when we reached it, all at once – I know not by what means – we were on top of it. Within lay a very broad and pleasant meadow, so filled with the scent of spring flowers that its wonderful fragrance quickly dispelled all the stench of the gloomy furnace that had overcome me. Such was the light flooding all this place that it seemed greater than the brightness of daylight or of the sun's rays at noon. In this meadow were innumerable companies of men in white robes, and many parties of happy people were sitting together. And as my guide led me through these crowds of happy citizens, I began to wonder whether this was the Kingdom of Heaven, of which I had heard so often. But in response to my thought he said: "No, this is not the Kingdom of Heaven as you imagine."

'When we had passed through these abodes of blessed spirits and progressed further, I saw ahead of us a much more lovely light than before, and heard in it a sweet sound of people singing, while a scent of such surpassing fragrance emanated from the place that the earlier scent that I had thought so wonderful now seemed quite trifling. And even the wonderful light that had flooded the flowery meadow seemed thin and dim when compared with that now visible. As I was hoping that we should enter this delightful place, my guide suddenly halted and, without stopping, retraced his steps and led me back along the road by which we had come.

'When we returned to the happy dwellings of the souls robed in white, he asked me: "Do you know what all these things are that you have seen?" "No", I replied. Then he said: "The valley that you saw, with its horrible burning flames and icy cold, is the place where souls are tried and punished who have delayed to confess and amend their wicked ways, and who at last had recourse to penitence at the hour of death, and so depart this life. Because they confessed and were penitent, although only at death, they will all be admitted into the Kingdom of Heaven on the Day of Judgement. But many are helped by the prayers, alms, and fasting of the living, and especially by the offering of Masses, and are therefore set free before the Day of Judgement. The fiery, noisome pit that you saw is the mouth of Hell, and whosoever falls into it will never be delivered throughout eternity. This flowery place, where you see these fair young people so happy and resplendent, is where souls are received who die having done good, but are not so perfect as to merit immediate entry into the Kingdom of Heaven. But at the Day of Judgement they shall all see Christ and enter upon the joys of His heavenly Kingdom. And whoever are perfect in word, deed, and thought, enter the Kingdom of Heaven as soon as they leave the body. The Kingdom is situated near the place where you heard the sound of sweet singing, with the sweet fragrance and glorious light. You must now return to your body and live among men once more; but, if you will weigh your actions with greater care and study to keep your words and ways virtuous and simple, then when you die you too will win a home among these happy spirits that you see. For, when I left you for a while, I did so in order to discover what your future would be." When he told me this, I was most reluctant to return to my body; for I was entranced by the pleasantness and beauty of the place I could see and the company that I saw there. But I did not dare to question my guide, and meanwhile, I know not how, I suddenly found myself alive among men once more.'

This man of God would not discuss these and other things that he had seen with any apathetic or careless-living people, but only with those who were haunted by fear of punishment or gladdened by the hope of eternal joys, and were willing to take his words to heart and grow in holiness. But in the vicinity of his cell lived a monk named Haemgils, an eminent priest who adorned his office with good deeds: he is still living, and leads the life of a hermit in Ireland, supporting his latter years on a diet of bread and cold water. He often used to visit this man, and by repeated questioning learned from him what sort of things he had seen when freed from the body; and it is from his account that I have come to know these details that

I have briefly described. He also related his visions to King Aldfrid, a man of wide learning, who listened so readily and attentively to him that, at his request, he was admitted to the above monastery and received the monastic tonsure. And whenever the king visited those parts, he frequently went to listen to him. At the time of these events, the ruler of the monastery was the religious and humble abbot and priest Ethelwald, who at present most worthily occupies the episcopal see of the church of Lindisfarne.

This man was given a more secluded dwelling in the monastery, so that he could devote himself more freely to the service of his Maker in unbroken prayer. And since this place stands on the bank of a river, he often used to enter it for severe bodily penance, and plunge repeatedly beneath the water while he recited psalms and prayers for as long as he could endure it, standing motionless with the water up to his loins and sometimes to his neck. When he returned to shore, he never removed his dripping, chilly garments, but let them warm and dry on his body. And in winter, when the half-broken cakes of ice were swirling around him which he had broken to make a place to stand and dip himself in the water, those who saw him used to say: 'Brother Drycthelm (for that was his name), it is wonderful how you can manage to bear such bitter cold.' To which he, being a man of simple disposition and self-restraint, would reply simply: 'I have known it colder.' And when they said: 'It is extraordinary that you are willing to practise such severe discipline', he used to answer: 'I have seen greater suffering.' So until the day of his summons from this life he tamed his aged body by daily fasting, inspired by an insatiable longing for the blessings of heaven, and by his words and life he helped many people to salvation.

QUITE the reverse happened in the case of a man living in the province of the Mercians, whose visions and words – although not his way of life – benefited many others, but not himself. For in the reign of Coenred, Ethelred's successor, there was a layman who held a military command, and pleased the king as greatly by his public diligence as he displeased him by the carelessness of his private life. The king repeatedly warned him to confess and amend, and to abandon his wicked ways before a sudden death deprived him of any time for repentance and amendment. But, although frequently warned, he rejected his salutary advice, and promised that he would do penance at some future date. Meanwhile he fell ill and, taking to his bed, began to suffer severe pains. The king who was fond of him, visited him and urged him even then to repent of his sins before he died. But he answered that he did not wish to confess his sins at this time, but would do so when he recovered from his illness; for he did not wish his friends to accuse him of doing in fear of death what he had refused to do when he was well. He thought that he had spoken bravely, but it soon became clear that he had been deceived by the Devil's tricks.

As his illness grew more serious, the king again came to visit and reason with him; but the man at once cried out in a miserable voice; 'What do you want now? Why have you come here? There is nothing that you can do to help or save me now.' The king answered: 'Do not talk like that. Stop acting like a madman.' 'I am not mad,' he replied, 'but I have the knowledge of my wickedness set clearly before my eyes.' 'What do you mean by that?' the king asked. 'A short time ago,' the man said, 'two very handsome youths entered this house and sat down beside me, one at my head and the other at my feet. One of them produced a tiny but very beautiful book and gave it to me to read. When I looked at it, I found all the good deeds that I had ever done recorded; but they were few and trifling. Then they took back the book, but said nothing to me. Suddenly there arrived a horde of wicked spirits with horrible faces, who surrounded the house and occupied the greater part of it. Then one, who from the blackness of his dusky face and his exalted position seemed to be their chief, produced a horrible-looking book of enormous size and almost unbearable weight, which he ordered one of his satellites to bring me to read. When I read it, I found all my crimes clearly recorded there in black letters, not only sins of act and word, but even of the least thought. And he said to the glorious white-robed men who were sitting beside me: "Why are you sitting here? You know very well that this man belongs to us." They replied: "You are right. Take him, and enrol him in your company of the damned." With these words, they immediately vanished, and two wicked spirits rose and struck me with the tridents in their hands, one on the head and the other on the foot. These blows are now penetrating the inmost parts of my body with awful agony, and when they meet, I shall die. The devils will be waiting to snatch me away, and I shall be dragged down through the gates of Hell.'

So spoke the wretched man in his despair, and died shortly afterwards. So he is now vainly undergoing everlasting torments because he refused to undergo penance for a short while to win the grace of pardon. In his case it is clear – as Pope Gregory writes of certain people – that he did not see these things for his own benefit, since they did not help him, but for the benefit of others. For, when people learned of his death, they would fear to delay their penance while they still had time, lest the intervention of sudden death might cause them to perish unrepentant. When this man saw good and evil spirits offering him different records, this was done by divine providence in order that we should remember that our actions and thoughts are not scattered by the wind, but are all preserved to be examined by the Supreme Judge, and will be

shown to us at the last either by our friends the angels or by
our enemies. And whereas the white-robed angels first produced a white record, and the devils a black, the former tiny
and the latter enormous, let it be noted that in his early years
he did some good deeds which he completely obscured by his
evil-doing as a grown man. In contrast, if in his manhood he
had taken care to correct the errors of his childhood and cancel
them in God's eyes by well-doing, he might have been assigned to the company of those mentioned in the psalm:
'*Blessed are they whose transgression is forgiven, and whose sin is
covered.*' I have thought that this story should be told in a
straightforward way, as I heard it from the venerable Bishop
Pecthelm, to further the salvation of those who may read or
hear it.

CHAPTER 14: *Another man about to die sees the place of
punishment reserved for him in Hell*

I MYSELF know a brother – Ah, how I wish I had never
known him! – whose name I could mention were it desirable, who lived in a noble monastery but lived an ignoble life.
He was often taken to task by the brethren and authorities of
the house and warned to adopt a more disciplined life; and
although he refused to listen to them, they bore with him
patiently because they had need of his manual labour; for he
was a skilled worker in metal. But he was much addicted to
drunkenness and the other pleasures of a loose life, and used
to remain in his workshop day and night rather than enter the
church to sing and pray and to listen to the word of life with
the brethren. So it happened to him according to the proverb
that 'he that will not go through the church door in contrition willingly must needs be thrust through Hell door in
damnation unwillingly'. Falling ill, he summoned the brethren to his death-bed and, groaning like one already damned,
began to describe to them how he saw Hell open, and Satan

in the depths of the abyss, with Caiaphas and others who had
slain our Lord condemned like him to the avenging flames.
'Close to them, alas,' he cried, 'I see a place of eternal doom
prepared for my wretched self!' As the brethren listened, they
began earnestly to urge him to repent while he remained in
the body, but he answered in despair: 'There is no time left
for me to amend my ways. I have already seen my judgement
pronounced.'

With these words, he died without receiving the saving
Viaticum, and his body was buried in the remotest part of the
monastery, nor did anyone dare to say masses or sing psalms
for him, or even to pray for him. Oh, by how vast a distance
has God divided the light from the darkness! When the
blessed Proto-martyr Stephen was about to die for the truth,
he *saw the heavens opened, the glory of God revealed, and Jesus
standing on the right hand of God.* And in order that he might die
the happier, he fixed his mental gaze before death on the place
where he hoped to be after death. In contrast the metal worker,
a man of dark thoughts and deeds, saw Hell open as death
drew near, and saw the damnation of the Devil and his
followers. The unhappy man even saw his own place of
punishment among them, so that he might despair of salvation
and die in greater misery, but also that through his own perdition he might bequeath a means of salvation to the living
who learned of his fate. This happened recently in the
Province of the Bernicians, and was talked of far and wide,
rousing many people to do penance for their sins without
delay. And may the reading of this account have the same
effect.

At this period, by the grace of God, the majority of the Scots in Ireland, together with some of the Britons in Britain, conformed to the logical and canonical time of keeping Easter. Adamnan,* priest and abbot of the monks who lived on the Isle of Iona, was sent by his nation on a mission to Aldfrid, King of the English, and remained in his province for some while, where he observed the rites of the Church canonically performed. He was earnestly advised by many who were more learned than himself not to presume to act contrary to the universal customs of the Church, whether in the keeping of Easter or in any other observances, seeing that his following was very small and situated in a remote corner of the world. As a result he changed his opinions, and readily adopted what he saw and heard in the churches of the English in place of the customs of his own people. For he was a wise and worthy man, excellently grounded in knowledge of the Scriptures.

On his return home, he tried to lead his own people in Iona and those who were under the jurisdiction of that monastery into the correct ways that he had himself learned and wholeheartedly accepted; but in this he failed. Then he sailed over to preach in Ireland, and by his simple teaching showed its people the proper time of Easter. He corrected their ancient error and restored nearly all who were not under the jurisdiction of Iona to Catholic unity, teaching them to observe Easter at the proper time. Having observed the canonical Easter in Ireland, he returned to his own island, where he vigorously pressed his own monastery to conform to the Catholic observance of Easter, but had no success in his attempts. Before the close of the next year he departed this life. For God in his goodness decreed that so great a champion of peace and unity should be received into everlasting life before the time of Easter returned once more, and before he should be obliged to enter upon more serious controversy with those who refused to follow him in the truth.

Adamnan also wrote a book about the Holy Places, which is most valuable to many readers. The man who dictated the information to him was Arculf, a bishop from Gaul who had visited Jerusalem to see the Holy Places. Having toured all the Promised Land, Arculf had travelled to Damascus, Constantinople, Alexandria, and many islands; but as he was returning home, his ship was driven by a violent storm on the western coast of Britain. After many adventures, he visited Christ's servant Adamnan, who, finding him learned in the Scriptures and well acquainted with the Holy Places, was glad to welcome him and even more glad to listen to him. As a result, he rapidly committed to writing everything of interest that Arculf said that he had seen at the Holy Places. And by this means, as I have said, he compiled a work of great value to many people, especially those who live at a great distance from the places where the patriarchs and Apostles lived, and whose only source of information about them lies in books. Adamnan presented this book to King Aldfrid, and through his generosity it was circulated for lesser folk to read. The writer himself was sent back to his own land richer by many gifts. And I think it will be valuable to readers of this history if I make some extracts from this book, and include them in this history.

CHAPTER 16: *Descriptions from this book of the sites of our Lord's Birth, Passion, and Resurrection*

ADAMNAN wrote about our Lord's birthplace as follows: 'Bethlehem, the city of David, is situated on a narrow ridge almost entirely enclosed by valleys. It is a thousand paces in length from east to west, and has a low wall without towers built around the circumference of the plateau. At the eastern corner is a kind of natural grotto, the outer part of which is said to have been the place of our Lord's birth while the inner part is known as our Lord's manger. The interior of this grotto is entirely faced with precious marble over the exact spot where our Lord is said to have been born, and above it stands the lofty church of Saint Mary.'

On the site of Christ's Passion and Resurrection, he writes as follows:

'For those entering the city of Jerusalem from the northern side, the lay-out of the streets makes the Church of Constantine, known as the Martyrdom, the first of the Holy Places to be visited. This was erected by the Emperor Constantine in a magnificent regal style, for this is the place where his mother Helena discovered the Cross of our Lord. To the west, the Church of Golgotha comes into view, where can be seen the rock on which once stood the Cross, with the Body of our Lord nailed to it: it now supports an enormous silver cross, over which hangs a great bronze wheel bearing lamps. Beneath the site of our Lord's Cross a crypt has been hewn out of the rock, and the Holy Sacrifice is offered for the honoured dead on an altar here, while their bodies are left for the time outside in the street. To the west of this stands the Church of the *Anastasis*, which is the church of our Lord's Resurrection, circular in shape, surrounded by three walls, and supported on twelve columns. Between the walls are two broad passages, where three altars stand at three places against the central wall, to the north, south, and west. There are eight doors or entrances through the three walls, four facing east and four facing west. In the centre is the circular Tomb of our Lord, cut out of the rock, and a man standing inside it can touch the roof with his hand. The entrance faces eastward, and against it stands the great stone, which still bears the marks of iron tools. The exterior is completely covered with marble to the top of the roof, which is adorned with gold and bears a great golden cross. The Sepulchre of our Lord is cut out of the north side of the Tomb; it is seven feet in length, and raised three palms' breadth above the pavement. The entrance is on the south side, where twelve lamps burn day and night, four inside the sepulchre itself, and eight above it on the right-hand side. The stone that once formed the door of the Tomb has now been broken, but the smaller portion stands as a small square altar in front of the Tomb, while the larger portion forms another altar at the eastern end of the same Church, and is draped with linen cloths. The colour of the Tomb and Sepulchre is a mingled white and red.'

CHAPTER 17: *The site of our Lord's Ascension, and the tombs of the patriarchs*

ON the site of our Lord's Ascension, Adamnan writes: 'The Mount of Olives is of the same height as Mount Sion, but is broader and longer. It is sparsely wooded, except for olives and vines, but grows wheat and barley for the soil is thin and suitable only for grass and flowers. On the very top of the hill, where our Lord ascended into heaven, stands a lofty circular Church, with three roofed-in porches on the outside. The interior of the building could not be roofed and vaulted because of the upward flight of our Lord's body; but it has an altar on the east side, protected by a narrow canopy. In the centre of the Church, where our Lord ascended, can be seen His last footprints, exposed to the sky above. And although the earth is daily removed by the faithful, it remains undiminished, and still retains these marks resembling footprints. Round these lies a bronze wheel, as high as a man's neck, with great lamps hanging above it on a pulley and burning day and night. On the west side of the Church are eight windows and as many lamps hanging opposite them on cords. These cast their rays through the glass as far as Jerusalem, and their light is said to evoke a feeling of ardour and penitence in the hearts of all who see it. Each year on the day of our Lord's Ascension, at the end of Mass, a powerful rush of wind descends from above and throws to the ground all who are in the Church.'

On the situation of Hebron, and the tombs of the patriarchs, Adamnan writes:

'Hebron, once a city and the capital of David's kingdom, now only shows what it was by its ruins. In a valley one furlong to the east of it is a double cave, where the tombs of the patriarchs are enclosed in a square wall with their heads to the north. Each tomb is covered by a single stone slab, cut like those in a church: those of the three patriarchs are white, while that of Adam is of humbler and inferior workmanship, and lies not far from the others at the northern extremity of the wall. There are also three smaller and plainer monuments to three women. The hill of Mamre rises a thousand paces away from these monuments to the north, and is covered with grass and flowers. There is a level plateau at the summit, to the north of which stands Abraham's Oak – a trunk twice the height of a man, enclosed in a church.'

I have thought it useful to include these extracts from the works of the above author for the benefit of those who read this history, and have retained the sense of his words but summarized them in a shorter form. Should anyone wish to know more about his book, they may either study it in the original form or read the abridgement containing short extracts which I have recently compiled.

CHAPTER 18: *The South Saxons receive as their bishops Eadbert and Ealla, and the West Saxons Daniel and Aldhelm. The writings of Aldhelm* [*c.* A.D. 705]

IN the year of our Lord 705, Aldfrid, King of the Northumbrians, died after a reign of nearly twenty years, and was succeeded on the throne by his son Osred, a boy of about eight years of age, who reigned eleven years. At the commencement of his reign, Bishop Haeddi of the West Saxons departed

to the life of heaven. He was a good, just man, who carried
out his duties as bishop guided by an inborn love of goodness
rather than by anything learned from books. The most reverend Bishop Pecthelm – of whom more will be said in due
course – who was a fellow-monk or deacon for a long time
with Haeddi's successor Aldhelm, relates how many miracles
of healing occurred through Haeddi's holiness at the place
where he died. He says that the people of that province used
to carry away earth from it to mix in water for the sick, and
that many sick men and beasts who drank or were sprinkled
with it were restored to health. In consequence, there was a
considerable pit created there by the continual removal of the
hallowed soil.

At his death, the bishopric of the province was divided into
two dioceses, one of which was assigned to Daniel,* who
rules it to this day, and the other to Aldhelm,* who administered it with great energy for four years. Both bishops were
well acquainted with church matters and learned in the study
of the Scriptures. While Aldhelm was still a priest, and abbot
of the monastery known as Maelduib's Town,¹ he was
directed by a synod of his own people to write a notable
treatise against the errors of the Britons in observing Easter
at the wrong time and doing other things contrary to the
orthodoxy and unity of the Church. By means of this book
he persuaded many of those Britons who were subject to the
West Saxons to conform to the Catholic observance of our
Lord's Resurrection. He also wrote an excellent book *On
Virginity*, which he composed in a double form in hexameter
verse and prose on the model of Sedulius. He also wrote other
books; for he was a man of wide learning, with a polished
style and, as I have said, extremely well-read both in biblical
and general literature. At his death, Forthere, who is also a
man of great learning in the scriptures, was appointed to the
bishopric in his place and is still living today.

During their episcopates, it was decided by synodical decree

1. Malmesbury, Wiltshire.

that the province of the South Saxons, which had hitherto belonged to the diocese of Winchester under Bishop Daniel, should have an episcopal see and bishop of its own. Eadbert, who was Abbot of Selsey, a monastery founded by Bishop Wilfrid of blessed memory, was consecrated its first bishop, and at his death Eolla succeeded him in the office. After some years he also departed this life, and the bishopric has fallen into abeyance to this day.

CHAPTER 19: *Coenred, King of the Mercians, and Offa, King of the East Saxons, end their days in Rome as monks. The life and death of Bishop Wilfrid* [A.D. 709]

IN the fourth year of Osred's reign, Coenred, who had ruled the kingdom of Mercia with great renown for some while, resigned his kingly sceptre for a yet more noble kingdom. During the pontificate of Constantine, he went to Rome, received the tonsure, and became a monk at the shrine of the Apostles, passing the remainder of his days in prayer, fasting, and acts of mercy. He was succeeded on the throne by Ceolred, son of Ethelred who had ruled the kingdom before Coenred. With Coenred went Offa, son of Sighere the abovementioned king of the East Saxons, a very handsome and lovable young man who the entire nation greatly hoped would inherit and uphold the sceptre of the kingdom. But, fired by an equal ardour, he left his wife, lands, family, and country for the sake of Christ and his Gospel, hoping *to receive an hundred-fold in this life, and in the world to come life everlasting.* So, when they had arrived at the holy places in Rome, he received the tonsure, entered upon the monastic life, and at last attained the long-desired vision of the blessed Apostles in heaven.

During the same year in which these two left Britain, the renowned Bishop Wilfrid ended his days in the region of Oundle, after forty-five years as a bishop. The coffin containing his body was carried to his own monastery at Ripon and buried in the church of the blessed Apostle Peter with the honours due to so eminent a prelate. I will now turn back and recall briefly some of the events of his life.* As a boy, he was of a good disposition and behaviour for his age, always bearing himself modestly and thoughtfully, so that he was deservedly loved, admired, and welcomed by his elders as one of themselves. When he reached the age of fourteen, he chose monastic life rather than secular, and when he informed his father – for his mother was dead – he readily agreed to his heavenly desires and aspirations, and encouraged him to persevere in this laudable decision. He therefore went to the Isle of Lindisfarne and offered himself for the service of the monks, diligently setting himself to learn and practise all that conduces to monastic purity and devotion. Having a quick mind, he very soon learned the psalms and certain other books, before he received the tonsure, but not before he had become remarkable for monkish attributes more important than the tonsure, for humility and obedience, which naturally endeared him to the older monks as well as to his contemporaries. When he had served God in that monastery for some years, being a thoughtful youth, he gradually came to realize that the way of life taught by the Scots was far from perfect; so he decided to visit Rome and see what ecclesiastical and monastic customs were in use at the apostolic see. When he acquainted the brethren with his wish, they commended his proposal and encouraged him to carry out whatever he had in mind. Without further delay, he went to Queen Eanfled, who knew him and at whose request he had been accepted into the monastery, and told her of his desire to visit the shrines of the blessed Apostles. The youth's plan pleased the queen, who sent him to King Earconbert of Kent, her uncle's son, with the request that he would send him honourably to Rome. At this time Honorius, one of the disciples of blessed Pope Gregory and a man of great experience in church matters, was occupying the archbishopric with great

distinction. And while he was waiting there, Wilfrid, being
an active-minded young man, diligently set himself to study
everything that he saw. Another young man then arrived
named Biscop, known as Benedict, whom I have already
mentioned: he came of noble English family, and also wished
to travel to Rome. So the king gave Wilfrid to Benedict as his
companion, with instructions to accompany him to Rome.
On their arrival at Lugdunum,[1] Wilfrid was detained there
by Dalfin,[2] bishop of the city; but Benedict continued on his
journey to Rome without staying. For the bishop took great
pleasure in the young man's wise conversation, graceful
appearance, and enthusiasm for action, as well as in his
balanced and mature opinions. He therefore made ample
provision for all the needs of Wilfrid and his companions for
as long as they stayed with him, and offered to entrust to him,
if he were willing, the administration of a considerable area
of Gaul, to give him his young niece as wife, and make him
his own adopted son. Wilfrid thanked him for the kindness
that he had been pleased to show a stranger, but told him that
he had set his heart on a different way of life, which was the
reason why he had left his own country and set out on the
journey to Rome.

Hearing this, the bishop sent him on to Rome, providing
him with a guide and generously supplying everything that
the needs of the journey demanded. And he earnestly pressed
him to remember to come that way on his return journey to
his own country. When Wilfrid arrived in Rome, he devoted
himself daily to constant prayer and study of church matters,
as he had intended, and won the friendship of the most holy
and learned Archdeacon Boniface, who was also a Papal
Counsellor. Under his guidance he mastered each of the Gospels in turn and the correct method of calculating Easter, while
through this tutor he came to understand many other things
relating to church order which he had no means of learning

1. Lyons.
2. Actually Archbishop Annemund, brother of Dalfin Count of Lyons.

in his own country; and having spent some months engrossed in profitable study, he returned to Dalfin in Gaul. He remained with him three years, received the tonsure at his hands, and so won his affection that the bishop considered making him his heir. But the bishop's cruel death intervened to prevent this, and Wilfrid was destined rather to become a bishop of his own people the English. For Queen Baldhild sent soldiers with orders to kill the bishop, and Wilfrid as his clerk accompanied him to the place of execution, wishing to die with him, although the bishop strongly opposed this. But when the executioners learned that he was a foreigner and an Englishman, they spared him and refused to put him to death with his bishop.

On his return to Britain, Wilfrid was admitted to the friendship of King Alchfrid, who had learned to love and follow the Catholic laws of the Church. When he found Wilfrid to be a Catholic, the king gave him ten hides of land at a place called Stanford, and not long afterwards, a monastery with thirty hides at Ripon. This place had been formerly granted to monks who followed the Scots custom in order to build a monastery there. But since, when offered the alternative, they had preferred to abandon the place rather than adopt the Catholic Easter and other canonical rites in accordance with the usage of the Roman and apostolic Church, the king gave it to one whom he knew to be trained in better doctrines and customs.

At this time, under instructions from the king, Wilfrid was ordained priest at this monastery by the above-mentioned Agilbert, Bishop of the Gewissae, because the king wished to retain a man of such great learning and devotion as a priest and counsellor for his own special companionship. Shortly after the exposure and removal of the Scottish sect that I mentioned, and with the approval and advice of his father Oswy, the king sent Wilfrid to Gaul, asking that he be consecrated as his bishop, Wilfrid being at the time about thirty years of age. And when Agilbert, then Bishop of Paris, and eleven other bishops had gathered to make him a bishop, they carried out the rite of his consecration with great splendour. But since Wilfrid remained overseas for some while, a holy man named Chad was consecrated Bishop of York at the orders of King Oswy, as I have already described. Chad, having ruled the church very ably for three years, resigned the see and retired to his monastery of Lastingham, and Wilfrid then became bishop of the whole province of the Northumbrians.

Subsequently, as I have already told, Wilfrid was expelled from his bishopric during the reign of Egfrid, and other bishops were consecrated in his place. Intending to travel to Rome and plead his case before the apostolic Pope, he therefore took ship, but a strong westerly wind drove him to Frisia, where he was honourably received by the barbarous people and their king Aldgils. He preached Christ among them, teaching the word of truth to many thousands and cleansing them from the guilt of their sins in the font of our Saviour. He was the first to attempt the work of their evangelization, which was later completed so zealously by the most reverend Christian Bishop Wilbrord. Having spent the winter happily there with God's new people, Wilfrid set out once more for Rome. There his case was heard before Pope Agatho and several bishops, who were unanimous in acquitting him of the charges laid against him and declared him worthy of his bishopric.

At this time Pope Agatho summoned a hundred and twenty-five bishops to a Synod in Rome in order to combat those who were teaching that there was only one will and action* in our Lord and Saviour. He ordered Wilfrid to be summoned to take his place among the bishops, and to state his own belief and that of the province or island whence he had come. And when both he and his nation were shown to be Catholic in their belief, it was thought fitting to include this among the other findings of the synod in the following form: 'Wilfrid, beloved of God, Bishop of the city of York, having brought his case before the apostolic see, has been acquitted

by its authority from all charges against him, both definite
and indefinite. Appointed to take his seat in consultation with
one hundred and twenty-five bishops in synod, he affirmed
the true and Catholic Faith on behalf of all the northern part
of Britain, Ireland, and the islands inhabited by the English,
Britons, Scots, and Picts, ratifying this by his own signature.'

After this, Wilfrid returned to Britain and converted the
province of the South Saxons from their idolatrous rites to
the Faith of Christ. He also sent preachers to the Isle of Wight,
and during the second year of King Aldfrid, Egfrid's successor,
he was restored to his own see and bishopric at the king's
invitation. But five years later he was again accused and expelled from his diocese by the king and several bishops. He
travelled to Rome, and was given opportunity to defend himself in the presence of his accusers before the apostolic Pope
John [VI] and several bishops. It was unanimously decided
that his accusers had brought partially false charges against
him; and the Pope wrote to the English kings Ethelred and
Aldfrid that he had been unjustly condemned and that they
should restore him to his bishopric.

His acquittal was greatly forwarded by the reading of the
transactions of the Synod held by Pope Agatho of blessed
memory during Wilfrid's former visit to the city, when he
had sat at the council with the other bishops, as I have already
described. For when, as need required and at the direction of
the apostolic Pope, the transactions of this Synod were read
for some days in the presence of the nobility and many of the
people, they came to the passage where it is written: 'Wilfrid,
beloved of God and Bishop of the city of York, having
brought his case before the apostolic see, has by its authority
been acquitted from all charges etc.,' as already recorded.
When this was read, those who listened were surprised; and
when the reader finished, they began to ask one another,
'Who was this Bishop Wilfrid?' Then Boniface, Counsellor
to the apostolic Pope, and many others who had met him
there in Pope Agatho's time, explained that he was the same

bishop who had been accused by his own people and had recently come to Rome to be tried by the apostolic see. 'He came here long ago under a similar accusation,' they said, 'and the dispute between the two parties was quickly heard and decided. Pope Agatho of blessed memory showed that he had been unjustly expelled from his bishopric, and had so high a regard for Wilfrid that he ordered him to sit in the council of bishops which he had summoned, as a man of blameless faith and honest mind.' Hearing this, the Pope and all the assembly declared that a man of such authority, who had been a bishop for nearly forty years, should certainly not be condemned, but should be cleared of all the charges laid against him and return home with honour.

As Wilfrid was crossing Gaul on his return to Britain, he was suddenly overtaken by an illness, which grew so serious that he was unable to ride and had to be carried by his attendants in a litter. He was brought to Maeldum,[1] a city of Gaul, where he lay four days and nights as though dead, and only his faint breathing showed that he was still alive. He remained like this for four days without food or drink, speech or hearing, but at daybreak on the fifth day he sat up as though waking from a deep sleep. When he opened his eyes and saw around him a crowd of brethren singing psalms and weeping, he sighed and asked for the priest Acca, who came in at once when summoned and, seeing Wilfrid better and able to speak, fell on his knees and thanked God with all the brethren present. And when they had sat down, and began with some hesitation to talk of the judgements of heaven, the bishop told the others to leave them for an hour, and said to the priest Acca:

'I have seen a momentous vision, which I want you to keep secret until I know God's will for me. There stood beside me a noble being in white robes, who told me that he was Michael the Archangel. "I am come to recall you from death," he said, "for our Lord has granted you life at the prayers of your

1. Meaux.

311

brethren and the intercession of His blessed Mother the ever-virgin Mary. So I now pronounce that you shall be healed of this sickness: but be prepared, for I shall return to visit you after four years. When you return to your own country, you shall recover the greater portion of the possessions that were taken from you and end your life in perfect peace."' And to the delight of all, who gave thanks to God, the bishop recovered, resumed his journey, and arrived in Britain.

When they had studied the letters that Wilfrid had brought from the apostolic Pope, Archbishop Bertwald and Ethelred very readily supported him. The latter, formerly king but now an abbot, sent for Coenred, whom he had appointed king in his own place, and asked him to be a friend to Wilfrid, to which he agreed. Aldfrid, King of the Northumbrians, still refused to receive him; but he died shortly afterwards, and was succeeded by his son Osred. A synod was soon held near the river Nidd, and after some argument between the parties, it was generally agreed that Wilfrid should be restored to the bishopric of his own church. And so for four years, until the day of his death, he lived his life in peace. He died in his monastery in the region of Oundle during the rule of Abbot Cuthbald and was carried by the brethren to his first monastery at Ripon, where he was buried in the church of the blessed Apostle Peter close to the altar on the south side, as already recorded, and the following epitaph was inscribed above him:

> Here Wilfrid, mighty prelate, lies at peace
> Who, spurred by love of God, this temple raised,
> And hallowed it in Peter's noble name,
> To whom our Master Christ bequeathed the keys.
> Fair gold and purple vestments he bestowed,
> A noble cross of richly shining ore
> He placed aloft as sign of victory won.
> The Gospels four in golden letters writ
> At his command and in due order bound
> Were fitly cased in covers of red gold.
> Easter's mistimed observance he set right

> In due conformity with canon law
> Fixed by the Fathers, and to all his folk
> Banishing doubt, made manifest the truth.
> Here he established many flocks of monks
> And as a watchful shepherd bade them keep
> The Rule established by the saints of old.
> In his long life he weathered many storms,
> Discords at home and perils overseas.
> He ruled as bishop five and forty years,
> And passed rejoicing to God's heavenly realm.
> Grant us, O Jesus, his true flock to be,
> And tread with him the road that leads to Thee.

CHAPTER 20: *Albinus succeeds the devout Abbot Hadrian, and Acca succeeds to Wilfrid's bishopric* [A.D. 709]

I N the year following the death of the above Father Wilfrid, that is, the fifth year of King Osred, the most reverend father, Abbot Hadrian, fellow-worker in the word of God with Archbishop Theodore of blessed memory, died and was buried in the church of the blessed Mother of God in his own monastery. This was the forty-first year after his dispatch by Pope Vitalian with Theodore, and the thirty-ninth after his arrival in Britain. Among other testimonies to his learning and that of Archbishop Theodore is the fact that his disciple Albinus, who succeeded him as abbot of his monastery, was so well grounded in the study of the Scriptures that he had no small grasp of Greek, while he understood Latin as thoroughly as his native English tongue.

Wilfrid's successor as Bishop of the church of Hexham was his priest Acca, a man of great energy and noble in the sight of God and man. He greatly beautified and enlarged the structure of his church, which was dedicated in honour of blessed Andrew the Apostle. He devoted much care, as he still does, to obtaining relics of the blessed Apostles and martyrs of Christ from various places, and builds altars for their veneration, placed for this purpose in recesses within the walls of his church. He has also collected accounts of their sufferings and other books on religious subjects, to form a very complete and excellent library. And he has been diligent in providing sacred vessels, lights, and similar articles necessary for the furnishing of God's house. He also invited a famous singer named Maban, who had been trained in vocal music by the successors of blessed Pope Gregory's disciples in Kent, to come and instruct him and his clergy. He retained his services for twelve years, to teach them whatever church music they did not know, and also to restore to their original form any familiar chants that had become imperfect through lapse of time or neglect; for the bishop himself was a singer of great experience. He was also most learned in the holy Scriptures, orthodox in his profession of the Catholic Faith, and well acquainted with the rules of church administration. And in all these activities he remains unflagging until the time comes for him to receive the reward of his piety and devotion. For he was reared and trained from boyhood among the clergy of the most holy Bosa, God's beloved Bishop of York; he later came to Bishop Wilfrid in the hope of improving himself, and remained under him continuously until the latter's death, travelling to Rome with him, and there learning many valuable things about the organization of Holy Church which he had no means of learning in his own country.

CHAPTER 21: *Abbot Ceolfrid sends church architects to the King of the Picts, and with them a letter about the Catholic Easter and tonsure* [c. A.D. 710]

AT this time, Nechtan, King of the Picts, living in the northern parts of Britain, convinced after assiduous study of Church writings, renounced the error hitherto maintained by his nation about the observance of Easter and adopted the Catholic time of keeping our Lord's Resurrection with all his

people. In order to do this more smoothly and with greater
authority, the king asked help from the English people, whom
he knew to have based their practice long previously on the
pattern of the holy, Roman, apostolic Church. So he sent
messengers to the venerable Ceolfrid, Abbot of the monastery
of the blessed Apostles Peter and Paul, which he ruled most
illustriously as successor of the above-mentioned Benedict.
This monastery stands at the mouth of the river Wear, and
also close to the river Tyne at a place called In-Gyrwum.[1] The
king requested Ceolfrid to write him a letter of guidance that
would help him to refute those who presumed to keep Easter
at the wrong time; and although he was relatively well informed on these matters himself, he also required information
about the form and reason for the tonsure that clergy should
wear. In addition, he asked that architects be sent him in order
to build a stone church for his people in the Roman style,
promising that he would dedicate it in honour of the blessed
Prince of the Apostles and that he and his people would follow
the customs of the holy apostolic Roman Church, as far as
they could learn them in view of their remoteness from the
Roman people and from Roman speech. The most reverend
Abbot Ceolfrid complied with his devout wishes and requests,
sending him the architects he asked for, together with the
following letter.[2]

'To the most excellent and illustrious lord, King Nechtan,
from Abbot Ceolfrid – Greetings in our Lord.

'In response to your devout enquiries as a God-fearing
king, I am most willing and ready to attempt to explain the
Catholic observance of Easter in accordance with the rulings
of the apostolic see; for we know that whenever Holy Church
sets itself to learn, teach, or maintain the truth concerning our
Lord, this truth is revealed to it from heaven. As a secular

1. Wearmouth and Jarrow are here treated as constituting a single
monastery.
2. There can be little doubt that Ceolfrid's letter was composed by his
monk Bede.

writer very truly said,[1] the world would be in the happiest possible state if kings were philosophers or philosophers were kings. And if a man of the world could make a true estimate of this world's philosophy and judge rightly about the state of this world, how much more is it to be desired and sincerely prayed for by the citizens of our heavenly home, who are pilgrims in this world, that the greater any man's position in this world, the more he should exert himself to obey the commands of the Supreme Judge, and by his example and authority induce those committed to his charge to follow him in observing them!

'There are three rules in holy scripture that determine the time of keeping Easter, and which no human authority may change. Two of these are decreed by God in the Law of Moses, and the third is added in the Gospel as a consequence of the Passion and Resurrection of our Lord. For the Law directed that the Passover should be kept in the first month of the year, and in the third week of that month, that is, between the fifteenth and twenty-first days of the month. To this, the apostolic ordinance in the Gospels adds that we are to wait for the Lord's Day in this third week and begin to observe Eastertide on that day. Whoever keeps this three-fold rule correctly will never make a mistake in fixing the Feast of Easter. But if you wish to hear more clear and detailed information about this, it is written in Exodus, where the people of Israel, before their deliverance from Egypt, are directed to keep the first Passover, that "*The Lord said to Moses and Aaron: This month shall be unto you the beginning of months; it shall be the first month of the year to you. Speak ye unto all the congregation of Israel, saying, In the tenth day of this month they shall take to them every man a lamb, according to the house of their fathers.*" And a little later, "*And ye shall keep it up until the fourteenth day of the same month: and the whole assembly of the congregation of Israel shall kill it in the evening.*" These words make it very clear that, in the paschal observance, the fourteenth day is

1. Plato, in *The Republic*.

mentioned not because it was the day on which the Passover is commanded to be kept, but because the lamb is commanded to be killed on the evening of the fourteenth day, that is, at the fifteenth rising of the moon (which marks the beginning of the third week): and because it was on the night of the fifteenth moon that the Egyptians were smitten, and Israel redeemed out of its long slavery. "*Seven days shall ye eat unleavened bread,*" it is said. In these words, all the third week of the first month is directed to be solemnly observed. But lest we should think that those seven days were to be reckoned from the fourteenth to the twentieth day, it is added: "*On the first day ye shall put away leaven out of your houses; for whosoever eateth leavened bread from the first day until the seventh day, that soul shall be cut off from Israel*" and so on, until he says: "*For in this selfsame day I will bring your army out of the land of Egypt.*"

'So the day on which God was to bring out their army from Egypt is called the first day. It is clear, however, that they were not brought up out of Egypt on the fourteenth day, on the evening of which the lamb was killed and which is properly known as the *Pascha* or *Phase*, that is, the Passover, but on the fifteenth day, as is quite plainly recorded in the Book of *Numbers*; "*So they departed from Rameses in the first month, on the fifteenth day of the month; on the morrow after the Passover the children of Israel went out with an high hand.*" So the seven days of unleavened bread, on the first of which the Lord's people were led up out of Egypt, are to be reckoned from the beginning of the third week, as I have said: that is, from the fifteenth day of the month to the twenty-first day of the same month inclusive. But the fourteenth day is noted down separately from this number under the title of the Passover, as is clearly defined in the ensuing passage of *Exodus*, where it is said: "*For in this selfsame day I will bring your army out of the land of Egypt,*" and immediately adds: "*Therefore shall ye observe this day in your generations by an ordinance for ever. In the first month, on the fourteenth day of the month at even, ye*

317

shall eat unleavened bread, until the one and twentieth day of the
month at even. Seven days there shall be no leaven found in your
houses." Who can fail to see that, if the fourteenth day is included, there are not seven but eight days from the fourteenth
to the twenty-first days? But if, as careful study of the scriptures reveals the truth, we reckon from the evening of the
fourteenth day to the evening of the twenty-first, we shall at
once see that this fourteenth day gives its evening to the beginning of the Paschal feast, so that the entire sacred solemnity
comprises no more than seven days and nights. Accordingly
our definition is shown to be correct, in which we stated that
the Paschal period should be celebrated during the first month
of the year and in its third week. For it is in fact the third week,
because it begins on the evening of the fourteenth day, and
closes on the evening of the twenty-first.

'After the sacrifice of Christ our Passover, the Lord's Day
(which the ancients called the first day after the Sabbath) was
made holy for us by the joy of his resurrection: and the tradition of the Apostles established this day for the Easter feast,
in such a way that the lawful Paschal period should be neither
forestalled nor cut short. Rather it is laid down that, according
to the Law, the first month of the year and its fourteenth day
and the evening of that day should be awaited. And if by
chance this day fell on the Sabbath, *They shall take to them
every man a lamb according to the house of their fathers* and sacrifice
it in the evening – that is to say, all churches throughout the
world, who constitute the one Catholic church, should prepare bread and wine as a sacrament of the Body and Blood of
the spotless Lamb who *taketh away the sins of the world*. And
after suitable prayers, in the solemn celebration of Easter, they
should offer these to the Lord in the hope of their future redemption. For that is the very night on which the people of
Israel were snatched out of Egypt by the blood of the Lamb,
and the very night on which all God's people was freed from
eternal death by Christ's resurrection. And when the Lord's
Day dawns on the morrow, they should celebrate the first

day of the Easter feast. For that is the very day on which the glory of the Lord's resurrection was joyfully revealed to his disciples, and is also the first day of unleavened bread, of which it is clearly written in Leviticus: "*In the fourteenth day of the first month at even is the Passover; and on the fifteenth day is the feast of unleavened bread unto the Lord; seven days ye must eat unleavened bread. The first day shall be the most renowned and holy.*"

'Therefore if it could be brought about that a Sunday should always fall on the fifteenth day of the first month, that is, on the fifteenth appearance of the moon, we should be able always to celebrate our Easter at the very same time as the ancient people of God, as we do by the very same faith, although by a different kind of sacrament. But because the days of the week do not keep pace with the phases of the moon, the apostolic tradition (preached by the blessed Peter at Rome and confirmed by the evangelist Mark and his interpreter at Alexandria) decreed that, when the first month came round and the evening of its fourteenth day, they should wait further for a Sunday, from the fifteenth to the twenty-first day of that month. And on whatever of those days Sunday should occur, Easter should be celebrated on that day, because this falls within the seven days of unleavened bread. So it comes about that our Easter never diverges in either direction from the third week of the first month, but either occupies the whole of it, that is, all the Law's seven days of unleavened bread, or at any rate occupies some of these days. For even if only one of them is included, that is, the seventh day (which scripture commends so highly, saying "*the seventh day shall be more renowned and holy; ye shall do no servile work therein*"), no one can accuse us of not keeping correctly the Easter Day, which we have received from the Gospel, in the third week of the first month as the Law decrees.

'The reasons for the Catholic practice are therefore evident: equally evident is the irrational error of those who presume without real necessity to anticipate or to overrun the periods

prescribed in the Law. Those who consider that the day of
our Lord's Resurrection should be kept between the fourteenth day of the month and the twentieth day of the moon
anticipate without any reasonable necessity the time prescribed in the Law; for when they begin to keep the vigil of
the holy night from the evening of the thirteenth day, it is
evident that they regard that day as the beginning of their
Easter, and they cannot show any authority for this in the
decrees of the Law. And when they refuse to keep the Lord's
Easter on the twenty-first day of the month, they clearly
exclude from their observance a day which the Law often
recommends as suitable for greater festivity than the other
days. Consequently, they disarrange the proper order, sometimes even placing Easter entirely in the second week and
never keeping it on the seventh day of the third week.

Those who consider that Easter should be celebrated between
the sixteenth day of the said month and the twenty-second,
no less incorrectly, deviate from the correct course on the
other side and, as though avoiding shipwreck on Scylla, are
sucked down and drowned in the whirlpool of Charybdis.
For when they teach that Easter is to begin at moonrise on the
sixteenth day of the first month, that is, from the evening of
the fifteenth day, it follows that they entirely exclude from
their solemnity the fourteenth day of the month, which the
Law particularly recommends. Consequently, they barely
include the evening of the fifteenth day – the day on which
God's people were redeemed from slavery in Egypt, on which
our Lord redeemed the world from the darkness of sin by His
own Blood, and on which He was buried, bestowing on us
the hope of blessedness and peace after death. When they
place the Lord's day of Easter on the twenty-second day of
the month, these people *receive in themselves the recompense of
their error* and openly violate the legitimate limits of Easter,
beginning it on the evening of the day on which the Law had
directed that it should be finished and completed. They also
appoint as the first day of Easter a day of which no mention

is made in the Law, that is, the first day of the fourth week.

'Both these factions are sometimes mistaken not only in defining and calculating the age of the moon, but even in discovering the first month. However, this controversy is too lengthy to be dealt with fully in this letter. I will say only that the first and last months of the lunar year can always be accurately determined by reference to the vernal equinox. According to the views of all the eastern nations, and in particular of the Egyptians, who are especially skilled in such calculation, the vernal equinox occurs on the twenty-first of March, as we can prove by horological observation. Therefore, whatever moon is at the full (that is, in its fourteenth or fifteenth day) before the equinox, this rightly belongs to the last month of the preceding year and consequently is not suitable for keeping Easter. But the full moon falling either on or after the equinox itself certainly belongs to the first month; on it the ancients used to keep the Passover, and on it, when the Lord's day comes, we should keep Easter. There is a very convincing reason why this should be so, because it is written in *Genesis*: "*God made two lights, the greater light to rule the day, and the lesser light to rule the night;*" or, as it appears in another version: "*the greater light to usher in the day, and the lesser light to usher in the night.*" Therefore, as the vernal equinox was first determined by the rising of the sun on its emergence from the midpoint of the east and later, while the sun was setting at evening, the moon, being then full, followed from the midpoint of the east, so every year the same first month of the moon must be observed in the same order, so that the full moon must not fall before the equinox, but either on the day of the equinox itself, as it was in the beginning, or else after it. And if the full moon falls so much as one day before the time of equinox, the above reason shows that it may not be assigned to the first month of the new year, but to the last of the preceding year, and is therefore not eligible for the observance of the Easter Festival.

'If it pleases you to know also the symbolic reason in this matter, we are directed to keep Easter in the first month of the year, which is also known as the Month of New Fruit, because we should celebrate the mysteries of our Lord's Resurrection and our own deliverance with our minds refreshed to love of heavenly things. We are bidden to keep it in the third week of the month, because Christ, who had been promised before the Law and under the Law, came with Grace in the third age of the world to be sacrificed as our Passover; because he also rose from the dead on the third day after the offering of His Passion, and wished this to be known as the Lord's Day and kept annually as the Easter feast; and because we only observe this rite truly, that is, His passing out of this world to the Father, if we are careful to do so with Him in faith, hope, and love. We are commanded to keep the full moon of the Paschal month after the equinox, so that first the sun may make day longer than night and then the moon may show the whole of her light face to the world, because first *"the Sun of Righteousness with healing in His wings"*, that is the Lord Jesus, overcame all the darkness of death by the triumph of His Resurrection and then, having ascended into heaven, sent down the Spirit from on high and so filled His Church, which is often symbolically described as the moon, with the light of inward grace. This was the plan of our salvation which the prophet had in mind when he said: *"The sun was exalted, and the moon stood still in her habitation."*

'Whoever argues, therefore, that the Paschal full moon can occur before the equinox, disagrees in the observance of our highest mysteries with the teaching of the scriptures, and allies himself with those who believe that they can be saved without the assistance of Christ's grace. Such people presume to assert that they could have attained to perfect goodness even if the true Light had not overcome this world's darkness by His Death and Resurrection. So after the rising of the equinoctial sun, and after the ensuing full moon of the first month, that is, after the close of the fourteenth day of that month – all of which we have received as necessary observances under the Law – we still wait until the Lord's Day in the third week as the Gospel directs. Then at length we keep our proper Feast of Easter, to show that we do not, like the ancients, celebrate the breaking of the Egyptian yoke of slavery, but that we venerate with faith and devotion the Redemption of the whole world, which was foreshadowed in the liberation of God's ancient people and completed at Christ's Resurrection. In this way we show that we rejoice in the most certain hope of our own resurrection, which we believe will take place on the Lord's Day.

'This calculation of Easter which I have explained to you depends on a cycle of nineteen years, which began to be observed by the Church long ago in the time of the Apostles, especially in Rome and Egypt, as I mentioned earlier. But through the industry of Eusebius, who took his surname from the blessed martyr Pamphylus, it was reduced to a clearer system, so that whereas notification was formerly sent each year to all the churches by the Patriarch of Alexandria, thenceforward it could be easily understood by everyone, because the fourteenth day of the moon fell in a regular sequence. Theophilus, Patriarch of Alexandria, drew up an Easter table for the ensuing hundred years for the benefit of the Emperor Theodosius; similarly, his successor Cyril drew up a table for ninety-five years in five cycles of nineteen years. After him, Dionysius Exiguus added others in the same way, which extend down to our own day. This table will soon expire; but today there are so many people able to calculate that even in our own Church in Britain there are many who understand the ancient rules of the Egyptians, and can readily compute the cycles of these paschal times for an indefinite number of years, even for five hundred and thirty-two years ahead if they so desire. After this period, all that concerns the sequences of sun and moon, month and week, recurs in the same order as before. But I do not propose to send you these cycles of times to come, because you only asked to be informed

about the reasons for the time of Easter and said that you were
provided with Catholic Easter tables.

'Having written about Easter as you requested, albeit
cursorily and briefly, I also urge you to make sure that the
tonsure, about which you also asked me to write, is worn in
accordance with Christian ecclesiastical practice. We know
that the Apostles were not all tonsured in the same manner
and, although the Catholic Church is united in one faith,
hope, and love in God, it has not adopted one unvarying
form of tonsure throughout the whole world. On a wider
view, looking back to the earlier days of the patriarchs, we
find that Job, the pattern of patience, shaved his head in time
of trouble, which shows that in times of prosperity he allowed
his hair to grow. But Joseph, remarkable for his practice and
teaching of chastity, humility, piety, and other virtues, shaved
his head when about to be freed from slavery, which shows
that, while he was living in prison as a slave, he did not cut his
hair. But notice how each of these men of God, while differing
in their outward appearance, are alike in cherishing grace and
virtue in their inmost hearts. So we may frankly admit that a
variety in tonsure does no harm to those who have a pure faith
in God and sincere charity towards their neighbour, especially
since we do not read that there was ever any controversy
among the catholic fathers about differences of tonsure such
as there has been about diversity in Easter observance or in
matters of doctrine. Nevertheless, of all the tonsures to be
found either in the Church or among the races of mankind, I
consider none more worthy of being imitated and adopted
than that worn on the head of the disciple to whose confession
our Lord replied: "*Thou art Peter, and upon this rock I will build
my church, and the gates of hell shall not prevail against it: and I
will give unto thee the keys of the kingdom of heaven.*" Nor do I
consider any to be more abhorrent and detestable to all the
faithful than that worn by the man to whom, when he wished
to purchase the gift of the Holy Spirit, Peter said: "*Thy money
perish with thee, because thou hast thought that the gift of God may*

be purchased with money. Thou hast neither part nor lot in this matter."[1] But we are not shaven in the form of a crown solely because Peter was shorn in this way, but because Peter was shorn in this way in memory of our Lord's Passion. Therefore we who desire to be saved by Christ's Passion like Peter wear this sign of the Passion on the crown of the head, which is the highest part of the body. For, as the whole Church came into being through the Death of Him who gave it life, so each member of it bears the sign of the Holy Cross on his forehead, so that this emblem may afford constant protection against the assaults of wicked spirits and serve as a continual reminder that he must crucify the flesh with all its vices and evil desires. Similarly, those who have taken monastic vows or are in Holy Orders should bind themselves to stricter self-discipline for our Lord's sake, and wear their heads tonsured in the form of the crown of thorns which Christ wore on His head in His Passion, so that He might bear the thorns and briars of our sins and thus bear them away from us. In this way their own appearance will be a reminder to them to be willing and ready to suffer ridicule and disgrace for His sake, and a sign that they are always hoping to receive "*the crown of everlasting life which the Lord hath promised to those that love Him*", and in order to win this crown regard both adversity and prosperity as of equal insignificance. As for the tonsure that Simon the magician is said to have worn, I ask what faithful Christian will not instantly detest it, like magic itself, with the scorn it deserves. On the forehead it has indeed a superficial resemblance to a crown; but when you look at the neck, you will find the apparent crown cut short, so that you may fairly regard this fashion as characteristic of simoniacs and not of Christians. For in this life deluded people thought such men worthy of a lasting crown of glory; but in the life to come they are not only deprived of all hope of a crown but condemned to eternal punishment.

'Do not think that I have spoken in this way about those

1. *Acts* viii, 20–21.

who wear this tonsure as though they are damned even if they maintain Catholic unity in belief and practice. On the contrary, I am sure that many of them were holy men and pleasing to God. Among them is Adamnan, a renowned priest and abbot of the Columbans, who when he was sent on an embassy from his nation to King Aldfrid and chose to visit our monastery, displayed remarkable wisdom, humility, and devotion in his ways and conversation. I said to him in the course of discussion: "Holy brother, you believe that you are on the right road to receive the crown of life that knows no term. Why then, I beseech you, do you wear on your head the image of a crown which, in a fashion that belies your faith, is terminated? And if you seek the society of blessed Peter, why do you imitate the tonsure of the man whom Peter cursed? Why do you not do everything in this life to show that you love to imitate him with whom you desire to live in blessedness for ever?" He replied: "My dear brother, rest assured that, although I wear Simon's tonsure after the custom of my country, I wholeheartedly abominate and reject all simoniacal wickedness. So far as my frailty permits, I wish to follow in the footsteps of the most blessed Prince of the Apostles." I then said: "I am sure that this is so. Nevertheless, you should give some indication of your inward esteem for whatever derives from the Apostle Peter by displaying openly whatever you know to be his. For I think that your wisdom clearly appreciates that it would be better for you, who are vowed to God, to alter your outward appearance from any resemblance to a man whom you wholeheartedly detest, and whose hideous face you would loathe to see. On the other hand, since you wish to follow the example and teachings of Peter, it would be fitting for you to conform to the outward appearance of him whom you desire to have as your advocate in the presence of God."

'Such, then, were my words to Adamnan, who showed how greatly he had profited by seeing the observances of our Church; for after he had returned to Scotland, he won over large numbers to the Catholic observance of Easter by his preaching. But although he was their lawfully constituted head, he was unable to persuade the monks of Iona to adopt a better rule of life. Had his authority been sufficiently great, he would surely have taken care to correct the tonsure also.

'I now beg Your Majesty in your wisdom, together with the nation over which the King of kings and Lord of lords has placed you, to set yourself to follow all that fosters the unity of the Catholic and Apostolic Church. In so doing, when the might of your earthly kingdom has passed away, the most blessed Prince of the Apostles will gladly open the gate of the heavenly kingdom to you and yours and admit you to the company of God's elect.

'Most dearly beloved son in Christ, may the grace of God the everlasting King keep you in safety to reign many years, and preserve us all in peace.'

When this letter had been read in the presence of King Nechtan and many of his more learned men, and carefully translated into their own tongue by those who could understand it, he is said to have been so grateful for its guidance that he rose among his assembled chieftains and fell on his knees, thanking God that he had been accounted worthy to receive such a gift from England. 'I already knew that this was the true observance of Easter; but I now understand the reasons for it so clearly that my previous knowledge of it now seems to me to have been very slight. I therefore publicly proclaim in the presence of you all that I intend to observe this time of Easter with all my people for ever. And I decree that all the clergy of my kingdom shall adopt the tonsure of which we have now heard the full explanation.' The king at once enforced his statement with his royal authority. The nineteen-year cycles were immediately sent out under a public order to all the provinces of the Picts to be copied, learned, and adopted, and the erroneous eighty-four year cycles were universally abolished. All the ministers of the altar and monks adopted the circular tonsure, and the reformed nation was

glad to be placed under the direction of Peter, the most blessed
Prince of the Apostles, and secure under his protection.

CHAPTER 22: *The monks of Iona and the monasteries under
its jurisdiction begin to adopt the canonical Easter at the
preaching of Egbert* [A.D. 716]

NOT long afterwards, the monks of the Scottish nation
who lived in the Isle of Iona, together with the monasteries under their jurisdiction, were led by God's providence
to adopt the Canonical rite of Easter and style of tonsure. For
in the year 716, during which King Osred was killed and
Coenred succeeded to the government of the Northumbrian
kingdom, Egbert the beloved of God – a father and bishop to
be mentioned with high respect, of whom I have already
spoken more than once – came to them from Ireland and was
welcomed with honour and great joy. Being a most persuasive
teacher who most faithfully practised all that he taught, he was
given a ready hearing by everyone, and by his constant devout
exhortations he weaned them from the obsolete traditions of
their ancestors, to whom the Apostle's description is applic-
able: '*they had a zeal of God, but not according to knowledge.*' As I
have said, he taught them to observe our chief solemnity in
the Catholic and Apostolic manner, wearing the symbol of an
unbroken crown. This seemed to happen by a wonderful
dispensation of God's grace, in order that the nation which
had willingly and ungrudgingly laboured to communicate its
own knowledge of God to the English nation might later,
through the same English nation, arrive at a perfect way of
life which they had not hitherto possessed. In contrast the
Britons, who had refused to share their own knowledge of
the Christian Faith with the English, continue even now,
when the English nation believes rightly, and is fully instructed in the doctrines of the Catholic Faith, to be obdurate and
crippled by their errors, going about with their heads im-

properly tonsured, and keeping Christ's solemnity without fellowship with the Christian Church.

Through Egbert's teaching, the monks of Iona under Abbot Duunchad adopted Catholic ways of life about eighty years after they had sent Aidan to preach to the English nation.★ God's servant Egbert remained thirteen years on the island, where he restored the gracious light of unity and peace to the Church and consecrated the island anew to Christ. In the year of our Lord 729, during which our Lord's Easter was kept on the twenty-fourth of April, Egbert celebrated the solemnity of the Mass in honour of our Lord's Resurrection and departed to him the same day. So he began his enjoyment of the greatest of all festivals with the brethren whom he had won to the grace of unity, and ended it with our Lord, the Apostles, and all the citizens of heaven, where he now enjoys it for ever. And by a wonderful dispensation of divine providence, the venerable Egbert passed from this world to the Father not only on Easter Day, but when Easter was being kept on a day when it had never been kept before in those parts. So the brethren had the joy of a sure and Catholic knowledge of the time of Easter, and rejoiced in the protection of their father departed to our Lord, by whom they had been converted. Egbert himself showed great joy that he had been permitted to live until he saw his disciples accept and keep with him the Easter day that they had previously always rejected. So the most reverend father was assured of their conversion. *He rejoiced to see the Lord's Day: he saw it, and was glad.*

CHAPTER 23: *The present state of the English nation and the rest of Britain* [A.D. 725–31]

IN the year of our Lord 725, which was the seventh year of King Osric of Northumbria the successor of Coenred, Wictred son of King Egbert of Kent died on the twenty-third of April, leaving the kingdom that he had ruled for thirty-four and a half years to be inherited by his sons Ethelbert, Eadbert, and Alric. In the following year Bishop Tobias of Rochester died. He was a very learned man, as I said earlier, and had been a disciple of Archbishop Theodore and Abbot Hadrian of blessed memory. Consequently, in addition to his knowledge of ecclesiastical and general literature, he understood the Greek and Latin languages so thoroughly that they were as familiar to him as his own native tongue. He was buried in the porch of Saint Peter the Apostle, which he had built within the church of Saint Andrew for his own burial place. He was succeeded as bishop by Aldwulf, who was consecrated by Archbishop Bertwald.

In the year of our Lord 729, two comets appeared around the sun, striking terror into all who saw them. One comet rose early and preceded the sun, while the other followed the setting sun at evening, seeming to portend awful calamity to east and west alike. Or else, since one comet was the precursor of day and the other of night, they indicated that mankind was menaced by evils at both times. They appeared in the month of January, and remained visible for about a fortnight, pointing their fiery torches northward as though to set the welkin aflame. At this time, a swarm of Saracens* ravaged Gaul with horrible slaughter; but after a brief interval in that country they paid the penalty of their wickedness. During this year the man of God Egbert departed to our Lord on Easter Day as I have mentioned, and immediately after Easter, on the ninth of May, King Osric of Northumbria departed this life after a reign of eleven years, having appointed Ceolwulf, brother of his predecessor Coenred, to follow him. Both the outset and course of Ceolwulf's reign were filled by so many grave disturbances that it is quite impossible to know what to write about them or what the outcome will be.

On the ninth of January in the year of our Lord 731, Archbishop Bertwald died of old age, having held the see for thirty-seven years, six months, and fourteen days. In the

same year Tatwin, from the province of Mercia, who had
been a priest in the monastery of Bredon, was made archbishop in his place. He was consecrated in the city of Canterbury on Sunday the tenth of June by the venerable Bishops
Daniel of Winchester, Ingwald of London, Aldwin of Lichfield, and Aldwulf of Rochester. Tatwin was a man distinguished for his religion and wisdom, and extremely learned
in holy Scripture.

At the present day* Tatwin and Aldwulf preside over the
churches of Kent; Ingwald is Bishop of the East Saxons;
Aldbert and Hadulac are Bishops of the East Angles; Daniel
and Forthere are Bishops of the West Saxons; and Aldwin is
Bishop of the Mercians. Walchstod is Bishop of the folk who
live in the west, beyond the river Severn; Wilfrid is Bishop
of the Hwiccas; Cynibert is Bishop of the province of Lindsey. The bishopric of the Isle of Wight belongs to Daniel,
Bishop of Winchester. The province of the South Saxons
has now been without a bishop for some years, and seeks
the offices of a bishop from the prelate of the West Saxons.
All these provinces, together with the others south of the
river Humber and their kings, are subject to Ethelbald, King
of the Mercians.

In the province of the Northumbrians, ruled by Ceolwulf,
four bishops hold office: Wilfrid in the church of York, Ethelwald at Lindisfarne, Acca at Hexham, and Pecthelm in the
see known as The White House,* where the number of
believers has so increased that it has recently become an
episcopal see with Pecthelm as its first bishop.

At the present time, the Picts have a treaty of peace with
the English, and are glad to be united in Catholic peace and
truth to the universal Church. The Scots who are living in
Britain are content with their own territories, and do not
contemplate any raids or stratagems against the English. The
Britons for the most part have a national hatred for the
English, and uphold their own bad customs against the true
Easter of the Catholic Church; however, they are opposed

by the power of God and man alike, and are powerless to obtain what they want. For, although in part they are independent, they have been brought in part under subjection to the English.

As such peace and prosperity prevail in these days, many of the Northumbrians, both noble and simple, together with their children, have laid aside their weapons, preferring to receive the tonsure and take monastic vows rather than study the arts of war. What the result of this will be the future will show.*

This, then, is the present state of all Britain, about two hundred and eighty-five years after the coming of the English to Britain, but seven hundred and thirty-one years since our Lord's Incarnation. May the world rejoice under his eternal rule, and Britain glory in his Faith! *Let the multitude of isles be glad thereof, and give thanks at the remembrance of his holiness!*

CHAPTER 24: *A chronological summary of the whole book, and a personal note on the author*

As an aid to memory, I have thought it helpful to make a concise summary of events already dealt with at greater length.

In the sixtieth year before the Incarnation of our Lord, Gaius Julius Caesar was the first of the Romans to make war on Britain and was victorious, but was unable to hold the kingdom.

In the year of our Lord 46, Claudius was the second of the Romans to come to Britain and received the surrender of the greater part of the island. He also added the Isles of Orkney to the Roman Empire.

In the year of our Lord 167, Eleutherus became Bishop of Rome, and ruled the Church most gloriously for fifteen years. Lucius, a king of Britain, sent him a letter asking to be made a Christian, and obtained his request.

In the year of our Lord 189, Severus became Emperor and reigned seventeen years. He fortified Britain with an earthwork stretching from sea to sea.

In the year 381, Maximus became Emperor while in Britain. He crossed into Gaul and killed Gratian.

In the year 409, Rome was taken by the Goths, and thenceforward Roman rule came to an end in Britain.

In the year 430, Pope Celestine sent Palladius to be the first bishop to the Christian Scots.

In the year 449, Marcian became co-Emperor with Valentinian. He reigned seven years, during which time the English came to Britain at the invitation of the Britons.

In the year 538, an eclipse of the sun occurred on the sixteenth of February, lasting from Prime to Terce.

In the year 540, an eclipse of the sun occurred on the twentieth of June, and the stars appeared for nearly half an hour after the hour of Terce.

In the year 547, Ida began his reign, which lasted for twelve years. From him the royal family of the Northumbrians derives its origin.

In the year 565, the priest Columba came into Britain from the land of the Scots to teach the Picts, and built a monastery on the Isle of Iona.

In the year 596, Pope Gregory sent Augustine and his monks to Britain to preach the word of God to the English people.

In the year 597, these teachers arrived in Britain. This was about one hundred and fifty years after the coming of the English to Britain.

In the year 601, Pope Gregory sent the *pallium* to Britain for Augustine, who had already been made a bishop. He also sent several ministers of the word, including Paulinus.

In the year 603, the Battle of Degsastan was fought.

In the year 604, the East Saxons under King Sabert received the Faith of Christ through Archbishop Mellitus.

In the year 605, Pope Gregory died.

In the year 606, King Ethelbert of Kent died.

In the year 625, Archbishop Justus consecrated Paulinus as Bishop of the Northumbrians.

In the year 626, Eanfled, daughter of King Edwin, was baptized on Whit Saturday with twelve others.

In the year 627, King Edwin and his people were baptized on Easter Day.

In the year 633, King Edwin was killed, and Paulinus retired to Kent.

In the year 640, King Eadbald of Kent died.

In the year 642, King Oswald was killed.

In the year 644, Paulinus, first Bishop of York and later Bishop of Rochester, departed to our Lord.

In the year 651, King Oswin was killed, and Bishop Aidan died.

In the year 653, the Middle Angles under Peada their prince accepted the mysteries of the Faith.

In the year 655, Penda was slain, and the Mercians became Christians.

In the year 664 an eclipse occurred. King Earconbert of Kent died, and Bishop Colman returned to his own land with the Scots. A plague came. Chad and Wilfrid were consecrated Bishops of the Northumbrians.

In the year 668, Theodore was consecrated bishop.

In the year 670, King Oswy of the Northumbrians died.

In the year 673, King Egbert of Kent died. A synod was held at Hertford in the presence of King Egfrid under the presidency of Archbishop Theodore. It was valuable, and enacted ten canons.

In the year 675, Wulfhere, King of the Mercians, died after a reign of seventeen years, and left the throne to his brother Ethelred.

In the year 676, Ethelred ravaged Kent.

In the year 678, a comet appeared. Bishop Wilfrid was expelled from his see by King Egfrid: Bosa, Eata, and Eadhaed were consecrated bishops in his place.

In the year 679, Elfwin was killed.

In the year 680, a synod was held in the plain of Hatfield under the presidency of Archbishop Theodore to affirm the Catholic Faith: John, an abbot from Rome, attended. Abbess Hilda died at Streanaeshalch.

In the year 685, Egfrid, King of the Northumbrians, was killed. King Hlothere of Kent died.

In the year 688, Cadwalla, King of the West Saxons, left Britain for Rome.

In the year 690, Archbishop Theodore died.

In the year 697, Queen Osthryd was killed by her own people, the Mercian chieftains.

In the year 698, Bertred, the royal commander of the Northumbrians, was killed by the Picts.

In the year 704, Ethelred became a monk after ruling the Mercians for thirty years, and resigned the kingdom to Coenred.

In the year 705, King Aldfrid of the Northumbrians died.

In the year 709, Coenred, King of the Mercians, after a reign of five years, went to Rome.

In the year 711, the ealdorman Bertfrid fought against the Picts.

In the year 716, Osred, King of the Northumbrians, was killed, and Ceolred, King of the Mercians, died. The man of God Egbert converted the monks of Iona to the Catholic Easter and the canonical tonsure.

In the year 725, King Wictred of Kent died.

In the year 729, comets appeared: the holy Egbert departed this life: Osric died.

In the year 731, Archbishop Bertwald died. In the same year, the fifteenth of the reign of King Ethelbald of the Mercians, Tatwin was consecrated ninth Archbishop of Canterbury.

*

WITH God's help, I, Bede, the servant of Christ and priest of the monastery of the blessed apostles Peter and Paul at Wearmouth and Jarrow, have assembled these facts about the history of the Church in Britain, and of the Church of the English in particular, so far as I have been able to ascertain them from ancient writings, from the traditions of our forebears, and from my own personal knowledge.

I was born on the lands of this monastery, and on reaching seven years of age, I was entrusted by my family first to the most reverend Abbot Benedict and later to Abbot Ceolfrid for my education. I have spent all the remainder of my life in this monastery and devoted myself entirely to the study of the Scriptures. And while I have observed the regular discipline and sung the choir offices daily in church, my chief delight has always been in study, teaching, and writing.

I was ordained deacon in my nineteenth year, and priest in my thirtieth, receiving both these orders at the hands of the most reverend Bishop John at the direction of Abbot Ceolfrid. From the time of my receiving the priesthood until my fifty-ninth year, I have worked, both for my own benefit and that of my brethren, to compile short extracts from the works of the venerable Fathers on Holy Scripture and to comment on their meaning and interpretation. These books are as follows:

The Beginning of Genesis, up to the birth of Isaac and Ishmael's rejection: four Books.

The Tabernacle: its vessels and priestly vestments: three Books.

The First Part of Samuel, up to the death of Saul: three Books.

On the Building of the Temple: an allegorical interpretation like the others: two Books.

Thirty Questions on the Books of Kings.

On the Proverbs of Solomon: three Books.

On the Song of Songs: seven Books.

On Isaiah, Daniel, The Twelve Prophets, and part of Jeremiah, with chapter headings taken from blessed Jerome's Treatise.

On Ezra and Nehemiah: three Books.

On the Song of Habakkuk: one Book.

On the Book of the blessed father Tobias: an allegorical interpretation on Christ and the Church: one Book.

Chapters of Readings on the Pentateuch of Moses, Joshua, and Judges.

On the Books of Kings and Chronicles.

On the Book of the blessed father Job.

On Proverbs, Ecclesiastes, and the Song of Songs.

On the Prophets Isaiah, Ezra, and Nehemiah.

On the Gospel of Mark: four Books.

On the Gospel of Luke: six Books.

Homilies on the Gospel: two Books.

On the Apostle: in which I have carefully transcribed in order whatever I have found on the subject in the works of Saint Augustine.

On the Acts of the Apostles: two Books.

On the Seven Catholic Epistles: one Book on each.

On the Apocalypse of Saint John: three Books.

Also, *Chapters of Readings* from all the New Testament except the Gospel.

Also, a book of *Letters* to various persons, including one on the six ages of the world; on the dwellings of the children of Israel; on Isaiah's saying, '*And they shall be shut up in the prison, and after many days shall they be visited*': on the reason for the bissextile year; and on Anatolius' explanation of the equinox.

Also, *The Histories of the Saints*. I have translated Paulinus' metrical work on the *Life and Sufferings of the confessor Saint Felix* into prose. And I have corrected, to the best of my ability, the sense of a book on *The Life and Sufferings of Saint Anastasius*, which had been badly translated from the Greek, and worse amended by some unskilful person. I have also written the *Life* of our father, the holy monk and Bishop Cuthbert, first in heroic verse and later in prose.

I have written in two books *The History of the Abbots Bene-*

dict, *Ceolfrid*, and *Hwaetbert*, rulers of this monastery in which I delight to serve the Divine Goodness.

The Church History of our island and people: in five Books.

A Martyrology of the feast-days of the holy martyrs: in which I have carefully tried to record everything I could learn not only of the date, but also by what kind of combat and under what judge they overcame the world.

A Book of Hymns in various metres or rhythms.

A Book of Epigrams in heroic or elegiac verse.

On the Nature of Things, and *On Times:* a book on each, and one larger book *On Times*.

A Book on *Orthography*, arranged in alphabetical order.

A Book on *The Art of Poetry*, with a small work appended *On Tropes and Figures*; that is, the figures and manners of speech found in holy scripture.

*

I PRAY YOU, noble Jesu, that as You have graciously granted me joyfully to imbibe the words of Your knowledge, so You will also of Your bounty grant me to come at length to Yourself, the Fount of all wisdom,
and to dwell in Your presence
for ever.

NOTES

P. 33 King Ceolwulf, a man of considerable learning, resigned his throne in A.D. 737 and became a monk at Lindisfarne.

P. 33 Bede's authorities. Albinus succeeded Hadrian as Abbot of the monastery of S. Peter and S. Paul, Canterbury, *circa* A.D. 709. He died *c*. A.D. 732.

Nothelm appears to have visited Rome to examine the papal archives during the pontificate of Gregory II (A.D. 715–731). As this pope had been librarian of the Roman Church before his elevation, he would have been well qualified to direct Nothelm's researches. Nothelm became Archbishop of Canterbury in A.D. 735, and died *c*. A.D. 736.

P. 37 In his early chapters, Bede quotes from earlier authorities such as Orosius and Pliny. His statements here are not based on his own observations.

P. 38 The Scots. When Bede refers to the Scots, it should be remembered that he is speaking of the people of Ireland (Hibernia). These emigrated in large numbers to the northern parts of Britain between the second and fifth centuries.

P. 42 Claudius' purpose in annexing the Orkneys was to counter attacks on the island of Britain from the north. In the ninth century, they were to become an important base of operations for the Scandinavian invaders.

P. 48 In brief, the Arian heresy denied the reality of the divine nature in Christ. It takes its name from Arius, its propagator, whose false teachings were condemned by the Church at the Council of Nicaea in A.D. 325.

P. 49 Pelagianism, 'the British heresy', denied the reality of original sin, and affirmed that man could attain perfection by his own efforts, unaided by the grace of God. This misconception is still strong today!

P. 53 Bede makes no mention of the mission of S. Patrick, who was also sent by Pope Celestine. The origins of Christianity in Ireland remain very uncertain.

P. 68 Indictions were cycles of fifteen years. Bede says elsewhere of this system: 'If you wish to find the indiction, take the year of our Lord, add three, and divide by fifteen: the remainder gives you the indiction of the current year.'

P. 69 The Anglo-Saxon 'hide' was originally the amount of land necessary to support one family. As the quality of land varied from place to place, the term was elastic, and there was no uniform measurement for the hide throughout England.

P. 72 Gregory refers to clergy in minor orders. Marriage was forbidden to those in major orders: i.e. subdeacon, deacon, and priest, although celibacy does not seem to have been enforced in the earlier centuries; e.g., S. Patrick was son of a deacon.

P. 76 The *pallium*. An ornament granted by the Pope to archbishops as a mark of dignity and authority. It can be seen in the arms of the See of Canterbury, and takes the form of a circular white stole worn on the shoulders, with a pendant front and back, marked with four crosses. It is made of lamb's wool woven in the convent of S. Agnes at Rome. It was originally an Imperial mark of favour and adopted by the popes, who made it an essential mark of authority, without which no archbishop could exercise jurisdiction.

P. 86 Relics of the saints are sealed into the altar of a church during the ceremony of its consecration. Bede tells how many bishops were indefatigable collectors of relics for this purpose.

P. 90 Gregory is referring to the current expectation that the end of the world would come in the year A.D. 1000 (see *Revelation* xx, 2–7).

P. 91 Christ Church, Canterbury, predecessor of the present Cathedral. The Anglo-Saxon Chronicle records that it was consecrated on June 9, the feast of S. Primus and S. Felician, probably in the year A.D. 603.

P. 101 It is often forgotten that the Christian Church was firmly established in Britain several centuries before the mission of Augustine, and its bishops naturally looked askance at the newcomer's claim to supreme authority. The origins of the Celtic Church are veiled in the mists of antiquity, and offer a fascinating field for valuable research. Glastonbury claimed to have been founded by Joseph of Arimathaea, and the Celtic saints and bishops had certainly evangelized large areas of Britain by an earlier date than is generally realized. But, as Augustine foretold, their refusal to attempt the conversion of the Saxon invaders resulted in the ultimate decay of Celtic influence and customs.

P. 102 The Paschal question long remained a matter of dispute between the Roman and Celtic Churches, and was finally settled for Northumbria in favour of the former at the Council of Whitby in A.D. 664. Bede often speaks with deep disapproval of Celtic obstinacy. While no fundamental doctrinal issues were at stake, these differences caused considerable confusion. Bede mentions (III. 25) how King Oswy of Northumbria was celebrating Easter in accordance with the Celtic customs, while his queen was still fasting and observing Palm Sunday.

P. 108 The Anglo-Saxon Chronicle retrospectively calls these seven kings 'Bretwalda'.

P. 112 The Four Crowned Martyrs – *Quatuor Coronati* – were Severus, Severianus, Victorianus, and Carpophorus. Their church on the Caelian Hill, Rome, is mentioned as early as the time of Gregory I.

P. 126 The question of the national religion was evidently debated upon in the Witenagemot. Coifi's entirely materialistic reasons for a change of religion show that mass conversions were seldom sincere or lasting. This was borne out by the widespread apostasy which followed Edwin's death.

P. 128 All native buildings in Britain at this period were of timber or wattle. Building in stone was a craft learned mainly through Roman influence, and in many cases masons and architects were brought over from Gaul, as in the case of Benedict Biscop's church at Wearmouth.

P. 132 The *Tufa* was a standard of Roman origin, and took the form of a winged globe mounted on a spear. It was perhaps adopted as the personal standard of the Bretwalda or High-King of Britain.

P. 136 Most of the Scottish Church leaders to whom this letter was addressed can be identified: Tomianus (Tomene) was Abbot and Bishop of Armagh; Columbanus (Colman), Abbot and Bishop of Clonard; Cromanus (Cronan), Abbot of Nendrum; Dimnaus (Dima), probably Bishop of Connor; Baithanus

341

(Baeithin), Bishop of Tibohine; Cromanus (Cronan), Abbot of Movilla; Ernianus (S. Ernan), Abbot of Tory Island; Laistranus (Laisren), Abbot of Leighlin or (alternatively) of Holywood; Scellanus (Sillan), Bishop of Devenish; Segenus (Seghine), Abbot of Iona; Saranus (Saran Ua Critain).

P. 138 Cadwalla, otherwise Cadwallon, was King of Gwynedd, the leader of the Welsh in the struggle against the Angles, and Edwin's most dangerous antagonist.

P. 145 The Scots monastery on the island of Hii (Iona) was founded by S. Columba, and became a centre of intense spiritual activity, from which the Celtic missionaries carried the light of the Gospel far and wide in Britain. It was often known as *I Columb-kill*, i.e. the island of Columb's Cell.

P. 146 S. Ninian, a native of North Wales, was a redoubtable opponent of his fellow-countryman the heretic Pelagius. He was a great scholar and traveller, and corresponded with S. Martin of Tours, to whom he dedicated his church after the latter's death *c*. A.D. 400. According to Ailred, Martin sent him masons from Gaul to build his stone church at Whithorn in Galloway (*Candida Casa*). His diocese seems to have extended from the neighbourhood of Glasgow to the borders of Westmorland.

P. 146 The amazing life and labours of S. Columba were recorded sixty years after his death by Adamnan, Abbot of Iona from A.D. 657 to 669. Columba is said to have died on June 7, A.D. 597, the year of S. Augustine's landing in Kent.

P. 147 The Celtic Church was organized on a tribal and monastic basis rather than diocesan. The abbot of a monastery exercised ecclesiastical jurisdiction over the *provincia*, while the bishop, who was a member of the monastic community, exercised his episcopal functions at the behest of the abbot. The abbot himself – like S. Columba – was not of necessity a bishop, and did not exercise episcopal functions such as ordination. Bede, as a supporter of the Roman diocesan system, disapproved of the Celtic custom.

P. 151 Haeddi was bishop from A.D. 676 to 703 (or 705). The original cathedral at Winchester was built by Coenwalh, and was consecrated in A.D. 648.

P. 153 Faremoûtier-en-Brie, founded by S. Fara, a disciple of S. Columban, in A.D. 617.

Notes

P. 153 Those already established included Canterbury, Lindisfarne, Bury St Edmunds, Melrose, and Malmesbury.

P. 154 This was a double monastery of monks and nuns, each living in their own enclosure. The arrangement was later adopted in Britain in such houses at Ely and Whitby, but fell into disuse after the Danish invasions.

P. 161 In A.D. 875 the monks, fearing the Danes, abandoned Lindisfarne, and took away with them the body of S. Cuthbert and the head of King Oswald. After a series of temporary resting-places, these were eventually deposited at Durham.

P. 162 Acca, who became Bishop of Hexham in A.D. 709, was a close friend of Bede, and several of the latter's books are dedicated to him.

P. 170 This has sometimes been claimed as the origin of the University of Cambridge, but the school was probably at Dunwich. The schools at Canterbury were probably founded by S. Augustine, and were the predecessors of those established by Theodore.

P. 170 Bury St Edmunds.

P. 172 Burgh Castle, near Yarmouth.

P. 175 Lagny, on the Marne.

P. 176 The Gyrwas' province included parts of Northants, Hunts, Lincoln, and Cambridge. The Book of Ely says: 'The Gyrwas are all the southern Angles living in the great fen in which lies the Isle of Ely.'

P. 177 At-Wall: probably Walton or Walbottle, near Newcastle.

P. 177 The see was first established at Repton. S. Chad later moved it to Lichfield, where it remains to this day.

P. 179 Ythancaestir was probably Othona, a Roman military settlement in Essex (now St Peter's on the Wall).

P. 184 Whitby was a double foundation for monks and nuns, ruled by an abbess. The princess became co-abbess with her mother Queen Eanfled, who probably retired here soon after Oswy's death. Aelffled was a friend of S. Cuthbert. Wilfrid owed much to her support in his troubles, and Eddi describes her as 'a very wise woman, the best of comforters and counsellors in the whole province'.

P. 192 S. Aldhelm employs the same argument with King Gerontius of Cornwall. 'If the keys of the kingdom of Heaven were entrusted to Peter, how can anyone who disregards the law of the church hope to enter the gates of paradise?'

P. 193 The case for the Roman style of tonsure is presented in Ceolfrid's letter to King Nechtan (Bede, V. 21). The claim that it originated with S. Peter is, of course, unhistorical. It seems to have been adopted as a sign of monastic profession in the early centuries, and in the fifth century it became also the mark of all clerics. The Roman clergy shaved the crown, and left a circle of hair around the head above the temples, in memory of our Lord's crown of thorns. The Celtic clergy shaved the front of the head, and allowed the hair to grow at the back. Their Roman opponents denounced this as the tonsure of Simon Magus.

P. 196 Egbert became Abbot of Iona in A.D. 716. See Bede. V. 22.

P. 197 Clothair III, King of Neustria.

P. 197 These bishops were probably Cornish. This fact is of interest, as it indicates the beginning of cooperation between the Celtic and English bishops. Hitherto their relations had been distant and strained by the mutual hostility between the two races, and by the refusal of the British bishops to submit to the claims and customs of the Roman Church.

P. 204 Not far from S. Benedict's Abbey of Monte Cassino.

P. 206 This statement is incorrect. Prior to Wilfrid's consecration, there had been five bishops of English birth whose orthodoxy was unquestioned – Ithamar, Thomas, Boniface, Deusdedit, and Damian.

P. 207 On his reconsecration, Chad was translated to Mercia. The grounds of Theodore's doubt on the validity of Chad's consecration appear to have been (1) That he had been consecrated to a see that was not vacant. (2) That two British bishops not in communion with Rome had taken part in his consecration.

P. 212 In A.D. 1148, the relics of S. Chad were translated to Lichfield.

P. 213 Mayo. Alcuin later wrote to these monks as 'exiles for love of Christ's Name' and said: 'The great light of your leaning has spread far and wide throughout the land . . . let your light shine among that barbarous nation like a star in the western skies.' It is noteworthy that, whereas the Irish had formerly taught the English, the roles now seem to be reversed. Up to

Notes

a late date, Mayo was known as *Magheo na Saxan* – Mayo of the Saxons.

P. 213 This refers to the abandonment of Celtic customs, and the adoption of Roman.

P. 217 Aecci was appointed to the original See of Dunwich *c.* A.D. 673; Bedwin to the See of Elmham in Norfolk.

P. 219 The morning Offices of Matins and Lauds were sung before dawn.

P. 225 St Paul's, London.

P. 227 That is, those Picts north of the Forth who were tributary to the kingdom of Northumbria. In 685 they repudiated their allegiance, and Bishop Trumwin had to abandon his see at Abercorn and retire to Whitby.

P. 227 The eastern part of Hampshire: the name is preserved in Meonstoke.

P. 234 The heresy of Eutyches was Monophysite, i.e. a denial of the coexistence of two perfect natures, divine and human, in our Lord. This heresy, together with Monotheletism, was finally condemned by the sixth General Council at Constantinople, A.D. 680–81. To prepare for this Council, Pope Agatho called a synod in Rome in A.D. 680, to which Archbishop Theodore was invited. In his absence, Wilfrid, already in Rome on his personal affairs, vouched for the orthodoxy of the northern provinces.

P. 235 The first Lateran Council, A.D. 649.

P. 238 S. Etheldreda (Audrey). Her life is included in Thomas of Ely's *Historia Eliensis*. Her feast day is Oct. 17.

P. 239 Sexburga had received the veil from Archbishop Theodore in Sheppey, where she founded a large convent of nuns.

P. 240 Grantchester, near Cambridge, was a Roman settlement, and this sarcophagus was doubtless of Roman origin.

P. 243 Blood-feuds could be averted by the payment of compensation (*wergeld*) by the offending party to the family of the deceased. The sum payable was based on a recognized scale, and depended on the status of the dead man, whether royal, noble, free, or slave.

P. 244 A similar story is told in the *Life of S. Cadoc*.

P. 253 The Holy Sacrament was evidently reserved for the use of the sick in the Infirmary of the monastery.

Notes

P. 257 The Battle of Nechtansmere (Dunnichen Moss, Forfar), A.D. 685.

P. 271 Later known as S. John of Beverley. He ordained Bede deacon and priest.

P. 279 Among other rites at Baptism, which was normally administered at Easter and Whitsun, the newly baptized was given a white robe, which symbolized his purification. This was worn until the Sunday after Easter, known as *Dominica in albis depositis* – i.e. the Sunday when the white robe is laid aside.

P. 283 Meaning that they had turned aside from the true faith.

P. 285 Wilbrord was born in Northumbria *c.* A.D. 657. His father became a hermit near the mouth of the Humber, and entrusted the child to the monks of Ripon. In A.D. 677, Wilbrord crossed to Ireland, and remained with Egbert and Wigbert for twelve years. In A.D. 690, he landed at the mouth of the Rhine, and travelled to Utrecht, where he found all the Frisians heathen. After an arduous and successful apostolate, he died and was buried at Echternach in A.D. 738.

P. 299 Adamnan was ninth Abbot of Iona, which he ruled A.D. 679–704. He wrote the famous *Life of S. Columba*.

P. 304 Bede mentions Daniel in his Preface as the source of his information about the growth of the Church in Wessex, Sussex, and the Isle of Wight.

P. 304 S. Aldhelm, a learned writer and an energetic missionary, was connected with the royal family of Wessex. He became a monk at Malmesbury, a bishop in A.D. 705, and died in A.D. 709. He is said to have been a talented harpist, and to have composed sacred songs to interest and instruct the simple people, which King Alfred considered the best extant English poetry.

P. 306 Bede had plenty of material to draw upon for the life of Wilfrid. Aedde (Eddi), one of Wilfrid's cantors, had already written his life, while Bede himself had personal acquaintance with Wilfrid, and had doubtless learned much from him. Bede evidently has the warmest admiration for Wilfrid's zeal and courage, but less for the autocratic and uncompromising spirit that involved him in so many quarrels.

P. 309 In preparation for the sixth General Council which took place at Constantinople from Nov. A.D. 680 to Sept. 681, Pope Agatho summoned the leaders of the Western Church to a synod in Rome in March A.D. 680. Archbishop Theodore did not attend, but held a council at Hatfield, which re-affirmed the loyalty of the English Church to the Catholic Faith. Meanwhile Wilfrid, who was already in Rome to appeal for the Pope's support against his expulsion from his bishopric, was invited to sit at the synod and to vouch for the orthodoxy of the English Church.

P. 329 Aidan's mission probably began in A.D. 635, so the Iona monks adopted Catholic practices about A.D. 716.

P. 330 The Saracens or Moors overran Spain between A.D. 710 and 713, and crossed the Pyrenees to plunder the rich provinces of France. In 732 they suffered a severe defeat at the hands of Charles Martel at the battle of Tours, and were thus pre-vented from establishing a grasp on France such as they had on Spain. In his theological works, Bede regards the Saracens as the type of all enemies of the Christian Faith – 'sons of Ishmael, whose hand is against every man'.

P. 331 When Bede completed his history in A.D. 731, there were seventeen Saxon sees: In the Kingdom of Kent; Canterbury and Rochester. In Northumbria: York, Lindisfarne, Hex-ham, and Whithorn. In Mercia: Lichfield, Worcester, Here-ford, Dorchester, Lindsey. In the East Saxon Kingdom: London. In East Anglia: Dunwich and Elmham. In Wessex: Winchester and Sherborne. In Sussex: Selsey.

P. 331 The White House, or *Candida Casa*, was at Whithorn in Galloway. Pecthelm, who had been one of Aldhelm's monks, became the first bishop under a Saxon Dynasty. But, as Bede himself mentions (III. 4), the see had been founded by S. Ninian. Tribal wars and the Saxon invasions, however, probably caused several interruptions in the succession of bishops between Ninian and Pecthelm.

P. 332 Bede had become alarmed at the large numbers of men and women entering monasteries for unworthy or improper reasons (see IV. 25). In a letter to his friend Bishop Egbert, he calls attention to the fact that some did so in order to evade their proper obligations to the community, and not to live a life of religion. He suggests that any houses where this abuse was countenanced should be suppressed as 'useless to God and man', and their endowments diverted to increase the inadequate number of bishoprics.

1. KENT

Wictgils
├── Hengist ── Horsa
│   Oisc
│   Octa
│   Irminric
│   Ethelbert I
│   Eadbald
│   Earconbert
│   ├── Egbert ── Hlothere
│   │   ├── Edric ── Wictred
│   │   ├── Eadbert ── Ethelbert II ── Alric

GENEALOGIES OF ENGLISH KINGS

2. EAST SAXONS

Sledda = Ricula (sister of Ethelbert I of Kent)
├── Sabert ── Sexbald
│   ├── Sexred ── Saeward
│   │   ├── Sigbert I ── Sebbi
│   │   │   ├── Sighere
│   │   │   ├── Sighard ── Swefred
│   │   │   │   └── Offa
│   Sigbald
│   ├── Sigbert II ── Swidhelm

3. EAST ANGLES

Wuffa

Tytila

X = (wife) = Redwald   Eni

Sigbert   Earpwald   Raegenhere   Anna   Ethelhere   Ethelwald

Egric (kinsman of Sigbert)   Aldwulf

4. MERCIANS

Penda

Wulfhere   Ethelred

Coenred   Ceolred   Ethelbald

5. NORTHUMBRIANS

(Kings of Deira)   (Kings of Bernicia)

Yffi   Ida

Elfric   Aelle   Ethelric

Osric   Coenburg = Edwin = Ethelberga   Acha = Ethelfrid

Oswin   Osfrid   Edfrid   Eanfled = Oswy = X   Eanfrid   Oswald

Yffi   Alchfrid   Egfrid   Elfwin   Aldfrid   Ethelwald

Osric   Osred

Note that Edwin's first wife Coenburg was daughter of a Mercian king Cearl, whose connexion with the preceding genealogy is not clear; his second wife Ethelberga was daughter of Ethelbert I of Kent.

6. WEST SAXONS

The genealogy of these kings, mainly derived from sources other than Bede, is too complicated to justify its inclusion here.

INDEX

The following abbreviations are used: ab. abbot; archb. archbishop; b. bishop; br. brother; d. daughter; E. East; k. king; M. Middle; N. North; n. note; q. queen; S. South; s. son; W. West.

Index

Angles, East, 34–5, 56, 171–2; bishops of, 131, 176, 217; kings of, 107, 130, 152, 170–71, 183, 246

Angles, English, 56; church (churches) of, 73–5, 106, 234, 237, 281, 310, 336; language of, 38, 66, 145, 150, 250–51, 272, 282, 313; origin of, 56

Angles, Middle, 56, 176–7, 184, 212, 226, 248

Anglesey [Wales], 108, 114

Angulus [Angeln in Schleswig, N.W. Germany], 56

Anna, k. of E. Angles, 152, 154, 171–2, 180, 183, 238

Annemund, archb. of Lyons, 307n.

apathy of our times, 148

Aquileia, Italy, 49

Arculf, b. of (?) Périgueux, 300

Arius, heresy of, 48, 235

Arles [Bouches-du-Rhône, France], 67, 71, 76, 84, 205

Armorica [Brittany], 38, 65

Arwald, k. of Wight, 233

Asterius, called b. of Genoa (recte archb. of Milan), 151

Attila, k. of Huns, 54

Augustine, b. of Canterbury, 66–92, 98, 100–105, 261, 333

Augustine, b. of Hippo, 49, 337

Augustine's Oak (?), 101

Augustus, Emperor, 41

Auxerre [Yonne, France], 58

Badon Hill (?), 58

Baduthegn, lay brother of Lindisfarne, 267–8

Badwin, b. among E. Angles, 217

Baeithin, Irish b., 136, 341

Baldhild, q. of W. Franks, 308

Bamburgh [Northumberland], 150, 161, 167

Bangor [Flint], 102–3

baptism, 62, 71, 76–7, 102, 109, 128–30, 145, 182, 227, 229, 278–9

Bardney [Lincs.], 158, 161

Barking, Essex, 218–23

Barwe [? Barrow, Lincs.], 208, 217

Bassus, Northumbrian thane, 139

baths, 38

Bebba, q. of Northumbrians, 150, 167

Bede, monk of Jarrow: experiences of, 39, 211, 336–8; informants of, 33–5, 132, 156, 161–2, 167, 169, 196, 211, 229, 238, 245, 256, 268, 270–71, 297; verses of, 242; writings of, 315n., 336–8

Begu, nun of Hackness, 249

Benedict Biscop, ab. of Wearmouth, 236, 307, 336–7

Bernicia (Northumberland etc.), 129, 141, 143, 146, 150, 164, 184, 226, 298

Bernwini, nephew of Wilfrid, 233

Bert, Northumbrian ealdorman, 257

Bertfrid, Northumbrian ealdorman, 335

Bertgils (Boniface), b. of E. Angles, 176, 217

Bertha, q. of Kent, 69, 108

Berthun, ab. of Beverley, 271–6

Berthun, S. Saxon ealdorman, 232

Bertred, Northumbrian ealdorman, 335

Bertwald, archb. of Canterbury, 105, 282, 287, 312, 330, 335

Bethlehem, Palestine, description of, 300–301

Betti, English priest, 177

Beverley (Derawuda), Yorks., 271, 279

Birinus, b. of W. Saxons, 151, 225

bishops: consecration of, 71, 75, 104, 114, 134, 153, 179, 197–8, 204, 207, 216, 227, 263, 282, 309; duties of, 72, 148, 165, 198, 208, 215–16, 229, 263, 287

Bisi, b. of E. Angles, 214, 217

Blaecca, reeve of Lincoln, 131

Boisil, prior of Melrose, 259, 262, 283

Boniface (Bertgils), b. of E. Angles, 176, 217

Boniface, papal counsellor, 307, 310

Boniface IV, Pope, 106–7

354

Index

355

Index

Index

Eadhaed, b. of Lindsey, 197, 226, 334

Eafa, Mercian thane, 185

ealdormen (commanders), 92, 145, 232, 335

Eanfled, d. of Edwin, 116, 139, 166, 184, 186, 258, 306, 334

Eanfrid, k. of Bernicia, 141-2, 156

Eanfrid, a ruler of Hwiccas, 227

Eappa, ab. of Selsey, 227, 230-31

Earconbert, k. of Kent, 153, 203, 239, 306, 334

Earcongota, d. of Earconbert, 153-5

Earconwald, b. of E. Saxons, 217-18, 224

Earconwald, chamberlain of Franks, 175

Earpwald, k. of E. Angles, 130-31, 170

Easter, date of, 101-2, 106, 136-7, 144-5, 147, 169-70, 186-93, 197, 200, 206, 215, 299, 304, 307-8, 312-29

Eata, b. of Lindisfarne and Hexham, 193-4, 226-7, 259-60, 263, 271, 283, 334

Ebba, abbess of Coldingham, 239, 255

Ebroin, Frankish mayor of the palace, 205

eclipses, 195, 203, 333-4

Eddi (Stephen), choirmaster, 206

Edgar, b. of Lindsey, 226

Edgils, monk of Coldingham, 256

Edith, nun of Barking, 220

Edric, k. of Kent, 258-9

education, 139-40, 170, 195, 206, 219, 236-7, 247, 307, 336

Edwin, k. of Northumbrians, 107, 114-34, 138-9, 141, 151, 156, 163, 166, 184, 246, 334

eels, 37, 228, 241

Egbert, k. of Kent, 198, 203, 205, 217, 258-9, 334

Egbert, of Iona, 147, 195-6, 211-12, 282-4, 328-30, 335

Egfrid, k. of Northumbrians, 183, 197, 214, 226-7, 229, 234, 236,

238-9, 243, 257-9, 262-3, 271, 309, 334-5

Egric, k. of E. Angles, 170-71

Elaphius, British chief, 64

Eleutherus, Pope, 42, 332

Elfric, br. of Aelle, 141

Elfwin, br. of Ethelred, 243, 335

Elmet [Yorks.], 130

Ely [Cambs.], 239-41

Emme, b. of Sens, 205

English: see Angles, English

Eni, father of Anna, 171

Eolla, b. of S. Saxons, 305

Ephesus [Asia Minor], council at (A.D. 431), 235

Ernianus, Irish priest, 136, 341

Esi, abbot, 35

Étaples (Pas-de-Calais, France), 205n.

Ethelbald, k. of Mercians, 331, 335

Ethelberga, d. of Anna, 154-5

Ethelberga, d. of Ethelbert I, 115, 120-22, 139

Ethelbert I, k. of Kent, 68-70, 89-91, 100, 104-5, 107-8, 115, 163, 333

Ethelbert II, k. of Kent, 330

Ethelburga, abbess of Barking, 218-22

Etheldreda, abbess of Ely, 209, 238-42, 245

Ethelfrid, k. of Northumbrians, 92-3, 103, 123-5, 141, 234

Ethelhere, k. of E. Angles, 183

Ethelhilda, abbess, 159

Ethelhun, br. of bishop Ethelwin, 195-6

Ethelhun, s. of Edwin, 129

Ethelred, k. of Mercians, 158, 226-7, 243, 248, 295, 305, 310, 312, 334-5

Ethelthryd, d. of Edwin, 129

Ethelwald, b. of Lindisfarne, 294, 331

Ethelwald, hermit of Farne, 270-71

Ethelwald, k. of Deira, 180, 183

Ethelwald, k. of E. Angles, 180

Ethelwalh, k. of S. Saxons, 227, 229, 232

357

Index

Herebert, hermit, 264–5

Hereric, nephew of Edwin, 246, 248

heresies, 48–9, 58–65, 96, 234–7, 309

Hereswith, sister of Hilda, 246

Heribald, ab. of Tynemouth, 276–9

Heriburg, abbess of Watton, 273–4

hermits, 167, 261–2, 264–5, 270–71, 284, 293

Hertford, 214, 334

Hewald the Black, 285–6

Hewald the White, 285–6

Hexham [Northumberland], 143, 226–7, 263, 271–3, 313

Hiddila, priest, 233

hides (family holdings), 69, 114, 146, 184–5, 187, 208, 227, 229, 233, 308

Hilarus, archpriest, 136

Hilda, abbess of Whitby, 184, 187, 245–52, 335

Hildilid, abbess of Barking, 222

Hlothere, k. of Kent, 217, 234, 245, 258, 335

Holy Places (in Palestine etc.), 300–303

Honorius, archb. of Canterbury, 131, 134–5, 139, 163, 176, 186, 306

Honorius, Emperor, 49–50, 53

Honorius I, Pope, 133–6, 139, 151

Horsa, br. of Hengist, 56

horse-racing, 277

Humber river, 56, 68, 104, 107, 131, 331

Huns, 54, 282

Hunwald, Northumbrian ealdorman, 164

Hwaetbert, ab. of Monkwearmouth and Jarrow, 338

Hwiccas, branch of W. Saxons, 101, 227, 248, 331

Hygbald, ab. of (?)Bardney, 211–12

Ibas, b. of Edessa, 235

Ida, k. of Northumbrians, 333

Idle river, tributary of Trent, 125

idols, 86, 89, 119, 128, 130, 153, 178, 201–2

Imma, Northumbrian thane, 243–5

Immin, Mercian thane, 185

Inchkeith [Fife, Scotland], 51

Ingwald, b. of London, 331

Ini, k. of W. Saxons, 232, 280–81

Inishboffin [Co. Mayo], 213

Iona, Isle of [near Mull, Argyllshire], 145–9, 168, 177, 213, 283, 299, 328–9, 333

Ireland, 39–40, 54, 152, 161–2, 171, 195, 213, 255, 282, 285, 293, 299, 328–9; ravaged by Northumbrians, 257. *See also* Scots

Irminric, father of Ethelbert, 108

Italy, 106, 139, 186, 188

Ithamar, b. of Rochester, 163, 176

James, deacon, 132, 139–40, 186, 206

Jarrow [Co. Durham], 167, 315, 336

Jaruman, b. of Mercians, 185, 201, 207

Jerusalem, description of, 300–303

jet, 38

John, ab. of St Martin's, Rome, 236–8, 335

John, archb. of Arles, 205

John, papal counsellor, 137

John, papal notary, 137

John IV, Pope, 136–7

John VI, Pope, 310

John of Beverley, b. of Hexham and York, 247, 271–9, 336

Julian, b. of Eclanum, 49

Julius, British martyr, 47

Justus, archb. of Canterbury, 85, 104, 106, 109–12, 134, 139, 334

Jutes, 56, 233

Kaelcacaestir [? Tadcaster, Yorks.], 246

Kaiserswerth, Germany, 288

Kent, 34, 56, 68, 139, 166, 186, 226, 258–9; kings of, 68, 108, 115, 153, 203, 217, 282, 324–30

Kilpatrick, Old (Peanfahal, Penneltun) [Dunbartonshire, Scotland], 52

Index

Index

Redbridge (Hreutford) [Hants.], 233

Redwald, k. of E. Angles, 107, 122–5, 130, 170

relics, sacred, 61, 85–7, 150, 162, 194, 200, 268, 313

Rendlesham [Suffolk], 180

retribution, divine, 47, 55, 103–4, 109, 254–7

Reuda, leader of Scots, 39

Rhine river, 50, 286–7

Ricbert, E. Angle, 131

Richborough, Kent, 37

Ricula, sister of Ethelbert, 104

Ripon [Yorks.], 187, 197, 227, 270, 306, 308, 312

roads, Roman, 50

Rochester [Kent], bishops of, 104, 111–12, 139, 163, 176, 207, 226, 282, 330

Romanus, b. of Rochester, 112, 139

Romanus, Kentish priest, 186–7

Rome, 40, 69, 94, 99–100, 140; *Pantheon* in, 107; visitors to, from Britain, 34, 106, 134, 198, 203, 214, 225, 227, 236, 247, 279–81, 288, 305–11, 314, 335

Ronan, Scot, 186

Rufinianus, sent to help Augustine, 85

Rugians, German tribe, 282

Sabert, k. of E. Saxons, 104, 109, 333

Saethryd, abbess of Brie, 154

St Albans (Verulamium) [Herts.], 47

Saracens, 330

Saranus, Irish cleric, 136, 342

Saxons, 44. *See also* Angles, English

Saxons, East, 34, 56; bishops of, 104, 179, 217, 222, 331; kings of, 104, 109, 178–80, 225, 305

Saxons, Old, 56, 282, 285, 287

Saxons, South, 34, 56, 176, 227–8, 230, 258, 310, 331; bishops of, 305; kings of, 107

Saxons, West, 34, 56, 101, 116, 197; bishops of, 151–3, 225, 304; kings

of, 107, 116, 151–2, 232, 279–80

Scellanus, b. of Devenish, 136, 342

Scots, 38, 51–4; in Ireland, 39–40, 53, 105–6, 136, 145, 193; in Britain, 39–40, 92–3, 108, 141, 144–5, 198, 258, 308, 331; land of [Ireland and part of Scotland], 184, 193, 213, 333; language of, 145–6, 150, 187, 213

Scriptures, study of, 90, 147–8, 152, 162, 182, 204, 206, 211, 247, 258–9, 265, 282, 285, 299–300, 304, 307, 313–14, 331, 336–7

Scythia [? Scandinavia], 38

Sebbi, k. of E. Saxons, 201, 217, 223–5

Sedulius, Caelius, 304

Segenus, ab. of Iona, 148

Segenus (? same as above), 136, 342

Selsey [Sussex], 229, 305

Sens [Yonne, France], 205

Sergius, Pope, 279–80, 287–8

Severianus, Pelagian bishop, 58

Severinus, Pope, 136–7

Severn, river, 331

Severus, b. of Trier, 64

Severus, Septimius, Emperor, 43, 50, 52, 333

Sexbald, E. Angle, 180

Sexburg, q. of Kent, abbess of Ely, 154, 239

Sexwulf, b. of Mercians, 217, 226

shellfish, dye from, 37

ships, 38, 40, 53, 55, 166, 284, 300, 309

Sigbert, k. of E. Angles, 131, 170–71

Sigbert the Good, k. of E. Saxons, 178–80

Sigbert the Small, k. of E. Saxons, 178

Sighard, k. of E. Saxons, 225

Sighere, k. of E. Saxons, 201, 217, 305

Sirmium [Mitrovica, Yugoslavia], 49

Slack [Yorks.]: *see* Campodunum

slaves, 229; English sold as, 99, 244–5

Solent, 234

362

Index

Spain, Spaniards, 37, 48
sparrow, soul compared to, 127
Stanford [? Stamford, Lincs.], 308
Stoneham (*Ad Lapidem*) [Hants.],
233
storms, 38, 40, 58–9, 139, 166, 211,
270–71, 284, 300
Streanaeshalch: *see* Whitby
Surrey, 218
Swaebhard, k. in Kent, 282
Swale river [Yorks.], 130
Swefred, k. of E. Saxons, 225
Swidbert, ab. of Dacre, 268
Swidbert, ab. of Kaiserswerth,
287–8
Swidhelm, k. of E. Saxons, 180,
201
synods, church councils, 106–7,
187–93, 214–17, 234–6, 262, 304,
309–10, 312
Syria, 42, 300

Tadcaster [Yorks.]: *see* Kaelcacae-
stir
Tarsus in Cilicia, 204
Tata (Ethelberga), 115
Tatfrid, b. elect of Hwiccas, 248
Tatwin, archb. of Canterbury, 331,
335
Thames, river, 41, 104, 179, 218
thanes (royal officials), 127, 132, 145,
209, 227, 243–5, 275–6
Thanet, Kent, 68–9
Theodbald, br. of Ethelfrid, 92–3
Theodore, b. of Mopsuestia, 235
Theodore of Tarsus, archb. of
Canterbury, 34, 105, 153, 186,
204–7, 214, 225, 227, 234–6, 243,
247–8, 262–3, 273, 281–2, 287,
313, 330, 334–5
Theodoret, b. of Cyrus, 235
Theodosius I, Emperor, 49, 323
Theodosius II, Emperor, 53
Theophilus, b. of Alexandria, 323
Thomas, b. of E. Angles, 176
Thruidred, ab. of Dacre, 269
Thrydwulf, ab. of Leeds, 130
Tilbury [Essex], 179
Tilmon, monk, 286

Tiowulfingacaestir (?), a town on
the Trent, 132
Titillus, notary, 216
Tobias, b. of Rochester, 282, 330
tombs, 105, 108, 181, 184, 211, 219,
222, 224–5, 239–40, 265–8,
279–81, 286, 301–2, 312, 330
Tomianus, b. of Armagh, 136, 341
Tondbert, prince of Gyrwas, 238
Tondhere, Northumbrian thane,
164
tonsure, mode of, 187, 193, 204,
324–6, 328
Tortgyth, nun of Barking, 220–22
Tours [Indre-et-Loire, France], 237
Trent river, 132, 185, 243
Trier [Germany], 64
Trinovantes, British tribe, 41
Troyes [Aube, France], 58
Trumbert, monk of Lastingham,
211
Trumhere, b. of Mercians, 177,
184–5, 201
Trumwine, b. of Picts, 227, 258,
262
Tuda, b. of Lindisfarne, 193, 195
tufa, standard called, 132
Tunbert, b. of Hexham, 227, 263
Tunna, abbot, 244
Tunnacaestir (?), 244
Tweed river, 259, 289
Tyne river, 272, 315
Tynemouth, 276
Tytila, father of Redwald, 130

Ultan, br. of Fursey, 175
Utrecht (Wiltaburg) [Netherlands],
288
Utta, ab. of Gateshead, 166–7,
177

Valentinian III, Emperor, 65
Vergilius, archb. of Arles, 84
Verulamium, Verlamacaestir: *see*
St Albans
Vespasian, Emperor, 42
Vienne [Isère, France], 50
vines, 37, 40
virginity, 155, 183, 238–42, 304

363

Index

MORE ABOUT PENGUINS

Penguin Book News, which appears every month, contains details of all the new books issued by Penguins as they are published. From time to time it is supplemented by *Penguins in Print*, which is a complete list of all books published by Penguins which are in print. (There are over three thousand of these.)

A specimen copy of *Penguin Book News* will be sent to you free on request, and you can become a subscriber for the price of the postage – 3s for a year's issues (including the complete lists). Just write to Dept EP, Penguin Books Ltd, Harmondsworth, Middlesex, enclosing a cheque or postal order, and your name will be added to the mailing list.

Some other Penguin Classics are described on the following pages.

Note: *Penguin Book News* and *Penguins in Print*
are not available in the U.S.A. or Canada

EUSEBIUS

THE HISTORY OF THE CHURCH

Translated by G. A. Williamson

Bishop Eusebius, intimate friend of the Emperor Constantine, wrote the only surviving account of the Church during its crucial first 300 years. His grand theme, the working of Providence through the Apostolic Succession, embraces the ordeals of 146 martyrs, the teachings of 47 heretics, and the proceedings leading up to Nicaea and the other great Councils. G. A. Williamson's translation puts clarity first. Tedious repetitions have gone, sentences and sections are kept short and clear, editorial headings signpost the reader. *The History of the Church* has always been a source of vital and fascinating information; in this translation it is also readable.

GEOFFREY OF MONMOUTH

THE HISTORY OF
THE KINGS OF BRITAIN

Translated by Lewis Thorpe

It is difficult to say whether Geoffrey of Monmouth in writing his famous *Historia Regum Britanniae*, relied more on the old chroniclers or on a gift for romantic invention. However, leaving aside its merits as history, his heroic epic of such half-legendary kings as Cymbeline, Arthur and Lear enjoyed great popularity and served to inspire Malory, Spenser and Shakespeare among other writers.

Geoffrey's taste for quaint historical episodes, real or imaginary, and his varied style, which skilfully echoes every mood from quiet description to impassioned oratory still lend living interest to this twelfth-century chronicle.

THE PENGUIN CLASSICS

The Most Recent Volumes

ROUSSEAU
The Social Contract *Translated by Maurice Cranston*

FROISSART
Chronicles *Translated by Geoffrey Brereton*

POEMS FROM THE SANSKRIT
Translated by John Brough

GOLDONI
Four Comedies *Translated by Frederick Davies*

EARLY CHRISTIAN WRITINGS
Translated by Maxwell Staniforth

DESCARTES
Discourse on Method and Other Writings
Translated by F. E. Sutcliffe

BALZAC
Cousin Pons *Translated by Herbert Hunt*

NIETZSCHE
Twilight of the Idols *and* The Anti-Christ
Translated by R. J. Hollingdale